The Devil and Oliver's Zipper

God's Blessings,
O. D. Church

By

O. D. Church

c.2

CHAPTER 1

I pulled up in the old red pickup mom gave me after dad died and parked in the mud in front of Betty's Café— "Mexican and American food." The faded sign out front, one hinge loose, swayed in the wind. Indoors the television set mounted high above the back counter was tuned to the news.

Involuntarily I clenched a fist when I heard about drug smugglers operating south of Tucson. How could I care about evidence we were losing the drug war sixteen hundred miles southwest of Gillette? I couldn't believe such news could still affect me, or that I still saw red and wanted vengeance above all.

I kept getting hooked on "P" girls: Pam, Penelope, Patsy. I was too young when Pam came into my life. Penelope didn't last long. Patsy, my one true love, dumped me for my brother, Arlo. I neither forgave nor forgot. Never again spoke to either.

Not even when she left him at the altar to run off with the drug dealer to Tucson. Arlo died a week later. Lot of guilt I feel about that.

For weeks after that I thought about heading to Arizona and hunting down Patsy, if only to see what had happened to her. Now I was packed and ready to take off, except I might detour, go round by Las Vegas first. Was I vacillating? You bet, because I can't see the motivation. Did I want to hook up with Patsy again? Ride up in my red pickup like a knight in shining armor to slay the drug-dealing dragon and rescue the damsel in distress? Catch him dealing, report him; kill him? Or did I just think I could save her from herself, in case by now she was an addict or deeply involved in smuggling drugs up from Mexico? I wasn't sure, so I was taking my time about getting down there.

With the commercial break on the television set over the counter, I shook myself, focused, and returned to reality. The aroma of piping hot Mexican food reached my nose. Mmm, Betty's cooking was good enough to make your mouth water and mine did.

Seated at the counter awaiting a beef burrito with green chili, and contemplating the grime of coal dust and oil wells embedded in my palms and fingers, I heard them first. Then I spotted them pulling up in the gravel and mud. Seventeen, count 'em, seventeen bikers in black leather. My Adam's apple jerked up and back down.

Betty was out of sight in the kitchen. The only other person in the drafty five-stool, six-table café was Tina, fourteen going on twenty, Betty's very pretty daughter. Or would be if she'd act her age. Tina wore a short tight skirt. Breasts pushed up, their round top half-moons peeped over the low-cut blouse.

Thirteen guys and four gals clomped in, laughing, calling back and forth, pulling out chairs. Tina grabbed menus, her eyes wide. She was a peach, ripe and ready for the plucking, a heifer eager to jump the fence after the bulls. As she sashayed through the crowd, her narrow hips swinging, I wondered how long before one of those big male hands reached out to pinch her on the back side.To think otherwise would be like trying to imagine a room full of famished ten-year-old boys sitting before a platter of mouth-watering chocolate-chip cookies hot from the oven with nobody grabbing one.

Unfolding my long legs I stood to slip behind the counter and into the kitchen. A small black radio over the gleaming chrome-trimmed stove tuned to a Spanish language station blared with guitars and Mexican music.

"Oooh, you startled me," Betty squealed. She was pouring green chili over my burrito. "My favorite customer. Hi, Oliver." A Clint Eastwood fan, she claimed I was his clone, a younger version.

I didn't know what one gangly Clint Eastwood look-alike could do about intimidating a bunch of black leather bikers, but I agreed. Unsmiling, shrugging, I left the kitchen.

Out in the small crowded dining room under a low ceiling, its plaster cracked and chips breaking off and dropping like rice, two of the women stared through the murky front window. Not much to see, mostly great heaps of melting snow and slush. The wind howled, rattling the windows. Across the gravel and mud parking lot and the narrow state highway running through Gillette, a long train lumbered by, carrying coal out of Wyoming. I knew about coal and petroleum, both popular export products in this state, for I'd worked as a coal miner with my dad and as a roughneck in the oil fields beside my brother. Both are dead now. Mom recently remarried.

Behind the counter I filled water glasses, set them on a tray, and went to distribute them among the diners. At the raucous laughter and crude remarks, I scowled, hoping my disapproval would be interpreted as a hands-off warning. Didn't impress anybody.

Ignoring the thin, straggly-haired blonde seated next to him, a bearded muscular hulk grabbed at Tina, hauling her down on his lap.

"Hey!" his blonde companion yelled.

Speechless, Tina gasped, jerked, and tried to pull free.

"Let's me and you party, whatcha say, girl."

The two women ceased staring out the window to giggle nervously.

I set down the tray of glasses and stepped forward. "Get your mitts off her," I growled.

"Yeah? And who's gonna make me?" he snarled back, clutching Tina tighter. "A skinny guy like you?"

Denim jacket concealing muscles and clenched fists hiding calluses, I could have been a bookish wimp. I didn't argue. Without another word I shot out my fist. Ignoring the chiseled jaw I went straight for the burly guy's red-veined bulbous nose. Crunch!

"Son of a gun!" he yelped, releasing Tina to let her slide off his lap to the floor. She crawled away, off to the corner where she crouched like a beat dog.

I whirled, kicked out with my cowboy boot, and caught another biker on the chin. Somebody started heaving a stack of heavy plates at me. When I ducked, two went sailing straight through the front window. I caught a third and tossed it back, rather like playing Frisbee. Then my personal hell opened and I dropped in. Without Eastwood's .45 Magnum, the one he used in the *Dirty Harry* movies, and with neither sidekick nor back-up team, I was sadly out-numbered.

People jumped up, pushing tables aside and knocking over chairs. The women squealed and clapped their hands; their men yelled and leaped at me. Big hands, knotted fists, sharp pointy-toed boots. Half the mob fell on me at once, striking out, pummelling. I'd be mush in minutes. Deftly rolling on the floor, I tried reaching the counter's shelter.

Bursting through the kitchen door and hefting a heavy iron skillet, Betty whacked one of my attackers over the head. In the corner Tina wailed. On hands and knees I pushed myself up, grabbed a chair, and broke it over the back of another biker. Pandemonium.

Out the door streamed the bikers to grab helmets off their Yamahas and leap aboard like cowboys onto horses in the old days of Butch Cassidy and the Sundance Kid. A true-life legend in this part of the country.

Trailing the crowd was their leader, clutching a soiled handkerchief to his bleeding nose. "You'll pay for this, buddy. Big time," he snarled, exiting.

Preoccupied with Tina, Betty gave no heed to my bruises and blood. She sat on the floor in the corner cuddling her daughter, rocking back and forth and crooning something in Spanish.

Dazed, I leaned against the counter wiping my face where I'd taken hits to jaw, cheeks, and eyes. One eye was half-closed, my face already swelling. Just then I heard a swoosh and through my one good eye spied a flash. And then a great ball of fire.

"Ohmigosh," I whispered hoarsely through bruised lips, unable to yell because of the smack I'd taken to the Adam's apple.

Both little ladies leaped to the window. "Oh, no!" Betty mumbled, aghast. "They torched your truck, Oliver."

They had, indeed, before taking off for South Dakota and points east on their cycles. Right then a siren wailed and the cops pulled up. Betty muttered that she'd called them before rushing in with the frying pan.

They were too late for me. Gone was my inheritance, dad's old red pickup. Gone was every possession and personal belonging, including the books mom had laid on me; plus every last cent except for a few dollars in my wallet. I was on my way out of town, out of the state, when I'd stopped by Betty's for an early lunch and to say good-bye.

Also destroyed was much of the interior of Betty's café; the chairs and tables and dining room trashed. Insurance would take care of that, if she had any. More importantly, I hoped she could salvage Tina's self-esteem. Yeah, mom says I take other people's problems to heart, especially the helpless, like ladies and girls.

CHAPTER 2

B ill, the first officer on the scene, a fullback on our high school team when I was quarterback, knew me well. His mom and mine were friends. Briefly, before getting down to business, he asked after my mom. Bill knew how I felt about her new husband. In my opinion Hernandez is one sorry dude.

Bill grinned. "Looks like somebody worked you over real good. That your dad's truck out front?" He knew it was. "Get yourself cleaned up. I'll take your statement later. After Betty's." The huge guy with the close-cropped, kinky hair had seniority here. He turned aside.

Another pickup, green, pulled up, followed by a bunch of gawkers, all before the fire truck with siren screaming roared in. In the unisex restroom I assessed the damage, dabbing my face with iodine from Betty's medicine cabinet and adding Band-Aids on cheek, nose, and neck. Talk about *sorry*, I was a sight.

"Where you headed, Oliver?" asked the old geezer from the green pickup. "I'm only going home to my ranch but I can give you a lift that far if you're headed south."

He could have been clairvoyant. South was Casper, Cheyenne, and Denver. I hadn't decided yet whether to go through Colorado or Utah on my way farther south; Utah, and I'd hit Las Vegas first before heading down Arizona way. Besides searching for Patsy and her drug dealer, I was looking to get warm. Put this bitter cold winter with the temporary January thaw behind me. I nodded and said thanks.

"Ain't you got a sheepskin, or a topcoat?"

I jerked my thumb over a shoulder at my dad's vehicle, now a pile of still smoldering junk. He caught on without my having to say a word.

"Got a windbreaker in the truck you can have. He turned his back, assuming I'd follow. I did. We headed down state highway number 59.

That ride got me only half-way to Wright, a village forty or so miles out of Gillette on the cold wind-swept high plains where not much grows— sage brush and scrub grass, no trees at all. Critters live here, though—sage hens, prairie chickens, antelope, rabbits, red fox, porcupine, coyote, ferret, snakes, and plenty of birds, bees, butterflies, blue cranes, and grasshoppers in summer.

Except for its people, Campbell County's riches lay mostly beneath the ground in coal and oil deposits. Standing out there on that deserted stretch of narrow highway with the wind blowing hard, I pulled up the collar of the windbreaker over my unlined denim jacket. Right about then I wished I'd been wearing a Russian fur hat with earflaps instead of my cowboy hat.

A car approached from up ahead. The old Ford slowed, the door opened on the passenger side, and out flew a bundle before the car picked up speed and passed me. Litterbugs, humph. Curious, I crossed the road to peer inside an unfastened black plastic bag. Huddled there and whimpering pitifully was a puppy. Tenderly I removed the pitiful little fellow and held him to my face."Bet you don't care what I look like, either."

After a few licks and a hug, the first from him, the second from me, I unzipped and tucked the small bundle of mistreated fur inside my windbreaker and zipped back up. "Just you and me out here in the cold, Hugo," I muttered, his new name coming unbidden to my lips. I couldn't help smiling. Two orphans, Hugo and me.

The next ride took me another twenty-some miles. Pam, my date to our high school prom, took pity on me; pretty Pam with her three kids and a cat. Meow said the cat, woof said Hugo. Ah, my new puppy was still alive. To the delight of the three children, ranging from, say, two to five, our critters got along just fine. So did Pam and I. I told her the puppy's name.

She smiled tenderly. "Don't you remember? That's my father's name."

At Reno Junction, a bar-slash-café at the turn-off to Wright, where Pam said they lived now, she suggested a beer and a chat over old times. "I'm buying," she said after taking a long hard gander at my appearance.

Heady aromas greeted us; steaks broiling and fries sizzling commingled with beer from tap and can. I wanted to say I could use some lunch. My stomach was growling after missing that delicious burrito Betty makes. Good thing, though. I would have barfed it with that kick to the belly.

Catching on, Pam led us to the café side where the kids insisted on pampering Hugo along with Kitty. "We never got around to naming her," Pam admitted, handing me her menu and changing subjects. "Where you headed?"

I briefly explained my predicament and why I was a bit battered. Then I said I needed to call my mom. She handed me her cellphone. "Use mine."

I knew mom would hear the news on television. I wanted her to hear it from me, first. "Yeah, I'm okay. Lost dad's truck, though."

Naturally she moaned and groaned and carried on, but I cut her off. Time was a-wastin' and I was in no mood for all this sympathy. "You lost your clothes, then," she said matter-of-factly, after settling down. "And your books." Before we broke the connection, me promising to call when I got wherever I was going, she said she'd be gathering things to ship me: tee shirts, books. "You can't be traveling to that foreign country without your Bible and Shakespeare."

Mom's an anomaly. Religious in the fundamental way, she's also into culture—classical music, the classics in literature. Or, maybe not. Could be she merely wanted to rub off the rough edges of her son's upbringing that came from my dad's people and from growing up in this working man's county.

I handed back the phone. Pam, too, knew my family. "How's your mom?" she asked politely, without mentioning Hernandez. Luis in dad's place made me want to barf. If dad was rough edges, mom's new husband was prickly pear. I didn't see why she couldn't have gone after somebody else, if she was so all-fired bent on getting another man in the house so soon after dad died.

Good thing Pam was perceptive, as I was in no mood to go into all that. Although I didn't believe it for a minute, I hoped Hernandez would do well by mom. He could be making a decent living in construction, but he must have believed his true calling was holding down the couch.

Pam droned on about married life and motherhood between sighs and winks and leers, suggesting the sex was good. Back in high school, she and I never got around to making out in the back seat of mom's car, though we came close. Too close. I grinned.

Since those innocent days I'd had a few other girlfriends, including Penny, but I only came close to marrying Patsy. That still hurt, Patsy dumping me for my brother. Caught by a runaway cable off a new oil well installation, Arlo died in a breath. No point now thinking ill of the dead. Patsy took off for

Tucson, while I still yearned. In the meantime I shied away from anything or anybody so much as hinting of commitment.

While I was woolgathering and the kids were getting restless, starting to tease Hugo and Kitty on the long booth bench between them, Pam excused herself for the ladies' room. I watched her leave the table and walk across the big room with the wooden tables and vinyl covered booths. She'd kept her figure, still had those cute legs and flat stomach. As my dad used to say, "A man usually looks before he leaps, Son. Or, he should."

Busy with entertaining the children by making goofy faces, I didn't notice Pam's return until she hovered over the table, grabbed the check, and pointed across the room to another booth. "See those two old ladies? They've agreed to give you a lift. After I vouched for you, Oliver. So behave yourself, ya hear," she said, her soft smile tempering the tone of her mommy voice.

Pam made the introductions, grinned at me, and said *"Aus wiederzehen."* The two women were traveling all the way to Salt Lake City, they said. That settled it. I wouldn't go straight to Tucson in search of Patsy, passing through Denver and Albuquerque. Instead, it was on to Las Vegas by way of Utah. I needed a job and a stake before hitting Arizona anyhow.

Soon Hugo and I were hunkering down in the back seat that we would share with the ladies' hand luggage. Belly full, the throbbing from my wounds leveling off to a dull ache, I hoped to catch a nap.

Dream on. In their high-pitched girlie voices the ladies chattered all the way southwest across the state, into and out of Casper and on to Rawlins and Rock Springs. Their questions nosy and personal, I tried providing brief and unrevealing replies, but it wasn't easy.

"So," said the white-haired passenger, "you're heading for Las Vegas. Better steer clear of those casinos. You'll lose all your money."

They were Mormons, they said, who'd never visited the Latter Day Saints headquarters. "Time we did," said white hair.

They didn't mind having Hugo along. When he wasn't prowling the floor and back seat he'd lean against me, whimpering, until I figured out he wanted back against the comforting warmth of my chest inside the zipper. In the warm car I traded denim jacket for the blue nylon windbreaker. When we stopped for gas or food I led him off to the side, to an alley or ditch to do his business.

In Salt Lake City the ladies insisted on escorting me to the south end of town, letting me off near Interstate 15 leading on through Utah and direct into Las Vegas. "Mind what we told you, Oliver. Be a good boy. We'll pray for you."

# # # # # #

Like any small-town boy, I gawked, meandering downtown and then hitting the Strip. *New York, New York* was something else. Never having visited the Big Apple, I was sure its highlights were well recreated here. Forget the roller coaster; been there, done that. Indoors I saw fake stars high overhead, windows suggesting apartments with a lamp on here, a window box full of flowers there. Wall Street's stock market façade appeared around the next corner, then a touch of Georgetown and Central Park, plus restaurants galore, shows, and of course the casino itself.

Enough of this, I needed to make a plan. I was outdoors by then, staring up at the Statue of Liberty, when something caught my eye—a kid running away. On the sidewalk sprawled a man, his bag of groceries spilling over the walk, oranges rolling into the gutter and tomatoes spilling out. He pointed and sputtered, "Stop, thief! Stop that kid!"

Reflexes taking over, I bent to snatch a couple of tomatoes off the walk to send them flying. My pitching arm still accurate, I smacked the kid in the back of the neck with one and, when he turned, Splat! Right in the face with the other. Couldn't have hurt, much, but he yowled, anyhow. Dropping the downed man's wallet, he rubbed his face with both hands.

A couple of big men walking by grabbed the kid. Held on tight, while I helped his victim up on his feet. While I gathered his groceries, the pair of guys with the kid between them approached. "Hey, you want we should call the cops?" demanded the fellow wearing Bermuda shorts. "You can press charges."

The man sporting a Hawaiian shirt handed over the billfold.

Looking bewildered and then amused, my guy said, "Naw, let him go. I got my money back."

I couldn't believe it, until he said, "I'll pray for you, son." One of those.

Looking sheepish, the kid blushed, nodded, pulled away from his captors and in the blink of an eye was off through the crowd.

# # # # # # #

And that's how I got a job with a preacher.

I'd wanted something different. Man, I guess.

When I called mom, she gloated. "Perfect job for you. It even suits your name, Oliver Temple. You've made my day. I spend all that money on your piano lessons and sending you to parochial school and you never do anything with either, until now. Me thinks it's providence. The hand of God."

Then she wanted me to describe Brother John. Not in colorful detail, but in general comparisons. "Think of my soaps, Oliver, or the old and great movie stars. Is your preacher man a Clark Gable, a John Wayne?"

That's another among her incomprehensible hobbies, hard to understand when compared to Shakespeare and the Scriptures. She's hooked on the TV soap operas. I tried to think. I didn't know enough about them, or the television stars who played those characters. Struggling, I came up with Gary Cooper. Brother John might not be a look-alike, but he was long and lean with craggy face and a smile that crinkled the skin around his mouth and eyes. Yeah, Cooper would have to do.

I told mom to take care of herself, but I didn't mention Hernandez. I figured he was busy playing couch potato.

First things first. After my new boss gave me walking around money, I checked in with a vet to get Hugo's shots for distemper, rabies, whatever else was recommended. The doctor said the puppy was in pretty good shape, no problem except perhaps emotional. "Emotional?"

"Dogs have feelings, too. Your Hugo was poorly treated. It will take time to build trust." I paid the vet and left, with my puppy tucked back inside my windbreaker and the zipper half zipped.

Playing the organ in a wedding chapel on the Strip was about as far from the coal mine and oil well as a body could get. I wondered why the reverend didn't use canned organ music. He wanted live, he said. When I'm not pumping out wedding music on the organ, I'll be his chauffeur, handyman, and *general factotum*, whatever that is.

Mom's bundle arrived shortly, with the Bible and a book of Shakespeare's plays on top. I laughed when I saw her next gift, the music book; a not so subtle hint that I should put in some practice with the classical music she loved. I flipped through the pages: Bach's *Air for the G String,* Schumann's *Traumerei,* Johann Pachelbel's *Canon in D,* that was used on the sound track of *Ordinary People.* The book closed with another of mom's favorites, a damn difficult thing that might not go over well on the organ at a wedding chapel on the

Strip: Bach's *Fugue in D Minor*. Oh well, mom's heart was in the right place even if her head got goofy, out of step with her friends and new husband.

Underneath the books was a pile of tee shirts, their slogans and inscriptions again shouting loudly from the Biblical and classical influence. She would have had them especially made.

Brother John, of course, got a kick out of my new acquisitions. When I offered him first choice of the tees, he chose *Jesus Wept*, *Love thy neighbor as thyself*, and *Thou shalt not kill*. We agreed the latter was an odd choice for mom to have had made up. Imagine walking around with such things emblazoned on one's chest. I was glad my new boss relieved me of those.

Together we read through the remainder, from Shakespeare's *King Richard the Third, King Henry the Sixth,* and from *Comedy of Errors*. Brother John wondered aloud at her choices. I merely shrugged.

First came *So wise so young, they say, do never live long*. Hah, was that subtle advice I should mind my Ps and Qs? Conversely, *God defend the right!* could mean that mom approved of my defending the defenseless, like little Tina and Brother John.

Two more tees, both of these slogans about fear: *Of all base passions, fear is most accurs'd*. Also, *Extreme fear can neither fight nor fly*. I couldn't comprehend mom's thinking when she made those selections. When was I ever afraid? I didn't run from the schoolyard bully. My heart may have raced, but I don't remember feeling fearful on the football field. Or out in the oil field. Or the coal mine. I shrugged, while Brother John arched an eyebrow.The two slogans I really didn't understand would one day come back to haunt us both, Brother John and me: *For we may pity, though not pardon thee* and *O Tiger's heart wrapp'd in a woman's hide.*

Neither one made any sense to me. Not then. But, oh man, someday.

CHAPTER 3

Forget that *reverend* business, said Brother John, the title my new boss preferred. Tall and slender with dark blue eyes beneath sculptured eyebrows, his face was craggy with chiseled nose and jaw. I figured we made a good match. The older man could have been my father. Mount his head and face atop a body like Gary Cooper's, and you got Brother Lucas John. A bit naïve for this time and place, but I found his sweet nature appealing.

The chapel was small, a hole in the wall; fixed up pretty, although I'm not a good judge of such things. Once a couple stepped over the threshold, they were greeted with the sound of canned organ music, the fragrance of fresh lilacs and roses, and the sight of pink and white curlicues along walls and ceiling. The focal point was a white latticed archway beneath which they spoke their vows.

The flashing pink and green neon on the front was an advertising gimmick. Brother John gritted his big white teeth when he said it. "You ever heard that old saying, *Build a better mousetrap, and the world will beat a path to your door?* No such thing these days. Got to market. Tell the people, show 'em you got a better mousetrap—in our case a wedding ceremony—and then maybe, just maybe, we can capture a tiny share of the wedding market."

He invariably said "we," never "I," as if to draw me in, convince me we're partners in this wedding game. Brother John said my background could be of good use. Nights on the community college branch campus I had taken a mixed array of courses. When I first dropped in to see how things worked, they shoved what they called a catalog at me. A *catalog,* in my opinion, is something you shop from. I shopped by enrolling in psychology, literature, accounting, and marketing. Yes, I said, I'd heard the mousetrap metaphor in my marketing class. He thought the accounting was good, too. I could keep the books.

Then I remembered that he might call the college to check on my transcript. I didn't want to admit the truth, but better not hold back. I grimaced. "Uh, I also took a couple of courses in religion."

Brother John smiled gently, as if reading my mind. "Good," he said.

Every day I told myself, "Tomorrow. Or next week." That's when I would leave Vegas and Brother John. Head for Tucson and launch my search for Patsy Parsons and the Truth. I wondered who would be easier to locate first, Patsy or that drug-dealing jerk she called a boyfriend, Malcolm Barr. She told me he went by Mal. Good names, both of them: Mal for malevolent; Barr, yeah, right, put Mal behind bars.

With no place to stay and no money when I arrived in town, Brother John set up a cot in the back room. Hugo was welcome, too, he said. Then he gave me an advance on what would, he apologized, be a small salary. Talk about trust and nurturing. No wonder I grabbed the job the moment it was proffered.

I often practiced at the organ. Hugo's bed was a box with a small scrap of old rug from the reverend's cache. Days, the puppy's home sat behind the organ; nights, next to my cot. By then I'd gotten used to the routine—couples coming in, the young girls excited and dewy eyed, the guys nervous and sweating, me sitting at the organ pumping out romance. Lucas John said it wasn't what he'd anticipated. He wanted to counsel these kids, warn them what to expect when the dew dried and the blush from the roses faded. Tell them to keep God in their marriage, the love alive with caring and nurturing.

Unless they came armed with their own wording for their wedding vows, Brother John had his preferred version, part of which came from Genesis 2:24: *A man shall leave his father and his mother, and shall cleave unto his wife; and they shall be one flesh.* That sounded good. The part I liked read something like this: *Whom God has joined together, let no man put asunder,* and especially the next part: *Do you vow to take this man, to love and cherish him, to keep yourself for him and away from all others, all the days of your life?*

I'd distanced myself about as far as a confirmed bachelor can get from the marriage ceremony. Yet those words got to me. I rather liked that bit about "keeping oneself <u>for</u> your mate and <u>from</u> all others." I wished Patsy had heard them before she bedded my brother. Might not have made any difference, but I liked to think so.

No point talking about the location of the chapel. Construction, as the old ladies who gave me a ride had predicted, was going on everywhere. Soon, Brother John said, they would be tearing down this property. He waved the eviction notice under my eyes. "One more wedding and then we close up shop, Oliver," Brother John said. I gulped, wondering what my next job would be like, when he continued. "Then we get shut of this place. Look for greener pastures." He favored cliches.

What did Lucas John mean by the "we" this time? Was I supposed to read his mind? Did he mean "we," as in together, or separately? Perhaps it was no more than habit, his natural way of speaking.

"Hope springs eternal," he sometimes said, the partial quote surfacing after failing to capture a young couple's attention long enough to deliver one of his mini-sermons. "Maybe next time."

"What is it you want to tell them, Sir?"

"One of these days somebody will be interested. Then you'll find out."

One of these days? What was he talking about? One more wedding, he'd said. Meaning God would send just the right couple to "us." Yeah, he had me doing it, too, talking in terms of a partnership.

Without even contemplating my possible refusal, Lucas John said, "Here's what we're gonna do, Oliver." He waved another sheet of paper beneath my nose. Then he pulled up a wooden folding chair next to the organ bench. "We've been invited down to Arizona. The pastor of a struggling church is in trouble and fancies we can help. How quick can you be ready to leave?"

Superficial question. He knew how few possessions I owned: Hugo, plus mom's tee shirts, a few changes of socks and underwear, a nice suit jacket with two interchangeable white shirts, and one tie for the ceremonies. He liked the "look, sound, and feel of church," he'd claimed, staking me right off the bat to the *Sunday-go-t'meetin' clothes*, as he called them.

Glumly, I thought it might be best to dump a dose of reality on him. "What you need me for?"

Jumping off the wobbly chair to send it reeling and folding in on itself, he shook a finger at me. "Oliver Temple, if you don't realize by now you're like a son to me, nothing I can say will convince you. Besides," he added, turning away, "I believe the Lord has called you to do His work."

If Brother John's first statement didn't turn me off, the second one well might. I rather enjoyed playing the organ, driving, handling the heavy work, doing the accounts, but *a son* to Lucas John? *A man called of God?* I don't think so. Still, at the moment I had no other options. "Uh, what do I do?"

"Same as you been doing. Drive the RV, for one. I hate driving, as you know. Play the organ and keep records. Heft loads."

Loads of what, I wondered; boxes of hymnbooks and Bibles? Set up and dismantle folding chairs? Design brochures and run around asking storekeepers to mount posters in their windows?

I knew Brother John liked evangelism best—preaching and praying at revivals, dropping in temporarily and departing quickly following mass conversions. Back in his younger days, he'd told me, the traveling tent revival meetings were popular. He didn't see why they couldn't be again.

"People need their spirits lifted, son."

I couldn't help but recall Steve Martin in *Leap of Faith*. Was that Brother John's goal? Amass a whole batch of equipment and a whole bunch of people as supporting cast? That would cost a bundle, meaning he'd have to generate a bundle and a half every week. I wanted no part of some great con game designed to bilk the gullible out of their hard-earned cash while faking healings.

I thought of all the opportunities in this city. You want con games? Try the casinos. Must be plenty of jobs I could qualify for, now that I'd cached most of my wages, bought clothes and all.

I must have been staring at him, looking dubious, because Brother John suddenly grinned and clapped me hard on the shoulder. "I s'pect I know what you're thinking, boy. You should know me better by now. I'm not thinking criminal schemes, I'm talking real genuine conversions. Saving souls."

Relieved, I settled back. Job hunting takes a lot of effort and I already had a job. It also takes a lot of get-up-and-go to make a change. Besides, I thought the old chap might really need me. So I agreed to go along with him. In the back of my mind, though, was something else. I had an ulterior motive in agreeing to accompany him to Arizona.

Perhaps like Pam, Patsy was happily married by now with a SUV full of kids and pets. But what if she weren't? She might be a drug addict herself. Could be dead. Either way, I needed to know, to put my mind at ease, my heart to rest; try to bury the guilt. I still couldn't believe I'd allowed that little slip of a girl to come between my brother and me. Why did I never speak to him again?

As usual I walked Hugo, fed him, patted him, or carried him around inside my windbreaker with the zipper pulled halfway up. Now I asked him what he thought. "Hey, Hugo," I said. "What do you think? Shall we go to Arizona?"

That evening after we closed I went out to get in some nightlife, maybe play some slot-machine poker. First, however, I bought a second tie. If I were to go into this religion business in a big way, I'd better get serious.

Before leaving a few days later I wired home a bundle of money for mom. I'd been saving, and I imagined she could use the extra funds. Hernandez could support her, if he only would. Anyhow, it was habit for me, looking after mom. Dad had gotten hurt in an accident out at the coal mine. Paralyzed, he could no longer work. Mom needed me for moral support and my paychecks for income. Dad's care before he died was a time-consuming burden but mom remained faithful to the end. When it came to nurturing, she'd set me a good example.

Before I hit the sack, I called mom to tell her the money was on its way and that I was leaving Las Vegas for Tucson and points south. That's when I heard the bad news: Hernandez' latest scheme. Another way to skin the cat and collect a bundle: sue my brother Arlo's employer, the oil company.

"I didn't tell you before you left, Oliver," she said, her voice soft in my ear, "because I didn't feel quite right about it. But Luis said a big oil company has deep pockets. They wouldn't miss a few hundred thousand. Perhaps a million. Think of that, Oliver! Luis and I could retire, go to Florida or Arizona with you. No more dishpan hands." She worked as a cook and dishwasher at Campbell County High School. Mom, Margaret Rose, is pretty. She could have been a younger version of Estelle Getty.

I said nothing. Correctly reading the disapproval in my silence, her tone switched from gentle sweetness to defensive firmness. "I know you don't like Luis, Oliver, but he could have been right, you know."

What was this *could have been?* Did she mean the lawsuit fell through or she'd backed out before signing any papers? "I don't trust Hernandez, Mom. Have you seen a lawyer? If it's not too late, drop this dumb idea. You know it's not right. I've worked in the oil field, too, you know. That cable shouldn't have come loose to snap around and kill Arlo. He should have been tending to business. If negligence was involved, it must have been his fault."

"Hear me out, Son," she said. Talking fast to keep me from interrupting, possibly, she continued. Yes, she'd signed the documents, but in retaliation the oil company attorneys demanded that Arlo's corpse be exhumed and an autopsy performed. "That's when they discovered the cocaine in your brother's body tissues. Arlo was on drugs when he died, Oliver."

I was shocked. To my knowledge, he'd never touched the stuff. I couldn't interpret her sigh—of disgust, or relief that there would be no lawsuit?

"I thought you should hear all this from me, Oliver, before somebody else spilled the beans." Of course she had backed off then, she admitted.

Hernandez' keen scheme, like so many that had gone before, went down the toilet. I worried about mom, wondering what he would come up with next.

Breaking the connection after assuring her of my love and continuing respect (for her, not her exasperating husband), I returned to the chapel to sit cross-legged beside Hugo's box. The puppy crawled out from inside the unzipped windbreaker to climb into my arms. He reached up to deliver a lick to my cheek.

Holding the brown and white puppy close, I switched back and forth, feeling anger, disgust, and then a deep sadness that permeated my very soul.

How was it possible my brother could have been into drugs?

Later, after a light and lonely supper of canned Del Monte Beef Stew, a great curiosity began to cover me like a blanket. The younger brother I knew was no junkie. Despite the size of the high school, one of the biggest and finest in the state, he never got in any trouble, hadn't got mixed up with toughs or joined a gang. Had Arlo made a drug connection through the oil company? Like I'd told mom, I was right there, working not in the same field but nearby. I couldn't begin to fathom how he'd got on drugs.

Settling down for the night on my cot, feet hanging off the end and arms crossed behind my head, the light dawned. Patsy Parsons! Of course. The love of my life first dumped me for Arlo. Like me, he fell hard, like the hammer on a securely operational oil well. He asked Patsy to marry him and she said yes. He gave her a five-thousand-dollar diamond because, he told mom, she deserved the very best. He borrowed the money from mom, who got it from me, for what I thought was another reason entirely, for I was no longer speaking to him.

With the wedding date set and the invitations mailed, Patsy took off for Arizona with Malcolm Barr, a known drug dealer. Question: instead of the passive, innocent bystander, had she already got hooked? And then pulled my love-smitten brother down to the depths of hell with her?

Made sense. I needed to find out. Now my casual desire to simply discover what had happened to her turned into a burning quest. I wouldn't say it was vengeance I sought. But it sure was a lot more than mere curiosity driving me. If, or rather <u>when</u>, I located Patsy Parsons in or near Tucson, I'd decide then what to do about her and Malcolm. I clenched my fists.

My first thought was Murder! For now, call it a hunt for The Truth.

The night before leaving, Brother John called out for pizza and I constructed a green salad from the small refrigerator. I worked at the sink next to my cot in the back room. Nothing smells so good as hot Mexican food, but fresh pizza pulled out of its insulated envelope has gotta come in second.

Moving day dawned under an overcast sky. The front door opened just as we were making ready to dismantle. (Brother John had sold his decorations, the organ, and the rest of the furniture to other wedding chapels) In walked the cutest couple you'd ever want to meet.

When I saw the bride, my jaw dropped. Funny how fast the mind works. At first glance I could have sworn it was Patsy. Not quite, but Megan could have been my former sweetheart's younger sister.

Megan, with a baby-doll face, rather like Drew Barrymore's, wasn't all that tall, but with those long legs, she gave that impression. She had long silky blond hair, squeaky clean, and a slender frame; a drop-dead figure. Everything was in all the right places, in just the right proportions. To die for. Reminder of what I'd lost, first to Arlo and then to Malcolm, brought a catch in my throat. Derek was no slouch, either. Tall, lean, muscular and handsome, he too was blond and slender. They could have been bookends. If they were as sweet as their smiles implied, this could be a marriage made in heaven.

My heart ached. Not for them; for myself, and what I'd lost.

Returning to the present and the young couple standing before us, involuntarily I sighed. Too bad theirs couldn't be a big wedding, back home with her parents footing the bill and her mom commandeering a full staff of caterers, photographers, florists, and *general factotum (factoti?)*. My heart went out to these impoverished innocents.

They were poor, they said. They couldn't afford much in the way of extras. "However," Megan said, in her soft honeyed voice as she planted herself on one of our rickety folding chairs. "Know what we'd really appreciate?" She stared with pleading blue eyes into Brother John's serious brown ones. "Some marriage counseling first."

Derek reached for her little hand to hold it between his two big ones. "Right," he said, equally serious and appealing. "If you could just spend a little time with us, we'd like to hear your views on what makes a good marriage."

Lucas couldn't believe it and neither could I. At last. The reverend glanced at me and I swear there was a tear in the corner of his left eye.

They got their wish. And so did Brother John. I excused myself for their private consultation; but, I admit it, I hovered just out of sight around the corner listening to every word. I won't go into his whole spiel right now but suffice it to say they got their money's worth. And then some. Because Brother John said that in honor of his last wedding chapel ceremony, the uniting of these two people so precious in God's eyes, the wedding was free.

And what a she-bang it was. I slipped out to buy fresh flowers, peach roses and lily of the valley, as a bridal bouquet with huge matching vases full of the same arrangements to flank the latticed altar. They needed two witnesses and they had nobody. Lucas said we could count me but he had to find somebody else. He went next door to enlist a store clerk, the most nicely dressed and coifed from an otherwise motley crew. Brother John then dragged out a pretty veil from his trunk. It looked so pristine I wondered if some bride, changing her mind, had left it behind.

I pulled out all the stops on the organ, too, finally getting to play (and sing!) everything I'd practiced. I asked if they had any preferences. Hesitantly Megan whispered, "*From this Moment*, by Shania Twain, and *The Prayer*, by Celine Dion and Andrea Bocelli." She knew the good ones, even their composers.

After clearing my throat and setting a glass of water near the organ, I gave the bride and groom the best imitation of a professional soloist I could muster. Mom would have been proud of me. Then I passed out music and invited everybody to sing a couple of Christian songs, *Household of Faith* and *Cherish the Treasure*. Brother John beamed as though he had written the music himself or raised me in his own image; one or the other. Then I closed with *Jesu, Joy of Man's Desiring*, a popular number generally used as a processional while ushering in the parents and all those others in the wedding party: candlelighters, flower girls, ring-bearer, bridesmaids and groomsmen; all those. Yeah, I'd had experience "doing" weddings.

Brother John, of course, employed the words of his favorite wedding ceremony, which he knew by heart. The small white Bible in his hands was no more than stage prop. The ladies cried. The men gulped. Even Hugo behaved.

Afterwards we served cake and punch, which I'd also picked up while out ordering flowers. I was beginning to understand what *general factotum* meant.

A few yaps from Hugo after the ceremony earned him a nice petting. Megan asked whether my puppy could eat cake. I smiled. "You can try." She did, holding out her hand to Hugo. Tentatively at first and then voraciously, he licked her hand clean. I couldn't believe he'd leave my zippered wind-breaker, now my discard and his *Linus blanket*, long enough to make friends, but he did.

Courteous, considerate, Megan asked why theirs was our last wedding. Brother John admitted the rented chapel would be torn down along with a block of stores to make way for another mammoth hotel and casino.

Derek puckered his brow. "Too bad, Sir. Your type of ministry is important." Then he asked what the reverend intended doing instead.

When Lucas said we were off to southern Arizona—south of Tucson, north of Tubac—their eyes lit up. Neither said why. It was obvious they couldn't wait to get out of there and launch their new life together.

We had no idea where Derek and Megan were from, or where they were headed. They couldn't afford a fancy honeymoon they said, but I doubted that mattered. They had each other. "For all time," said Brother John, enthusiastically shaking Derek's hand and bending to plant a gentle kiss on Megan's brow. In no time the festivities were over and we bade the Dolans, husband and wife, adieu and God Speed.

CHAPTER 4

With Lucas in the passenger seat studying an Arizona map and me behind the wheel, we took off. He said we would cross Hoover Dam on Lake Mead and connect with Arizona State Highway 93 into Kingman.

The trip was beautiful and scenic on that lonely narrow road through mountains and down among an abundance of different cacti. I expected to see barrel cactus and prickly pear. Lucas named the others, among them the fat cholla, the ocotillo with its fire-red blooms, and the towering saguaro, the latter listed among the protected. These things, some of which were centuries old and huge, amazed me. When I stopped to walk Hugo he discovered the Joshua tree by getting stuck with stickers to the leg he raised. He yapped as though personally insulted. With me right behind him, Hugo hurried back to the RV to hop in his box and poke his head inside my unzippered windbreaker.

Frankly, I was glad to get out of the full-time wedding business. Too poignant a reminder that Patsy had left Arlo practically standing at the altar. And leaving me before I could even get her to wear my engagement ring. We might have had a good life together if she hadn't dumped me for Arlo.

When I initiated my secret mission in or around Tucson, Brother John—if and when I confessed— might wonder why I hadn't checked on Patsy in Gillette. Truth is, I had tried to extract some news from her kinfolk, back when I was merely curious about her whereabouts and lackadaisical about searching for her. Few in number, those who remained were private, secretive, and elusive. They might have tagged me as a stalker, they were so determined to avoid me. Or Patsy with her drug-dealing lover could have been absorbed within those great masses collectively labeled as the underworld and her family knew it and wouldn't admit it.

Eventually I had forgotten about this fruitless quest. When I remembered, another tour of Patsy's kin revealed they had all disappeared. They could have been rabbits in a hat whose magician had waved over them his magic wand. Or they could have been gypsies, wandering off after dark in their caravans. In this case, actually, they lived in small, trashy trailers.

Now I was feeling guilty for another reason besides failing to speak to my brother before he'd died. If I were so determined to discover whether my long-lost love had been the cause of Arlo's death, why didn't I pursue the search for her with every fiber of my being? It must be dread that kept me vacillating and detouring. The truth could be too devastating to accept.

Certainly there were plenty of other things to occupy me. Many other *factotum* things to do with and for Lucas, I imagined, before I could make time to look for Patsy in Tucson. I had no idea how to even start.

While Lucas napped and Hugo occasionally poked his head out from beneath my old wind-breaker, I mused upon what if any adventures awaited our arrival at the "church in trouble." I hadn't thought to ask what kind. Budgetary, I supposed.

In the commodious rig, a four-bed recreational vehicle, we had packed all our worldly goods. Brother John kept his books and ministerial para-phernalia. Into the RV went dishes, pots and pans, linens, a television set and microwave oven, computer and printer. All these recent luxuries plus the price of the RV came from liquidating his chapel business, house and furniture. On the kitchen counter the microwave was screwed down tight for security while traveling, with the TV set mounted likewise on an overhead shelf. To view television we would sit on one side of the table or in either of the well-cushioned chairs up front. Both driver and passenger seats could swivel to face into the living area.

My room was in the rear along with the tiny, compact bathroom. I got the double bed, with a single bunk overhead. Lucas said he preferred sleeping up front in the over-the-cab bed. The computer station with equipment, the latter screwed into the desk, sat along the wall facing the cushioned booth with eating (and working) table. He liked staying up late, he said, creating sermons and accessing the Internet.

He could have added emailing his e-pals, friends from all over the world, a few he had married, others he had counseled. Or, as he put it, he'd "just happened to run into along life's fascinating journey."

Occasionally, as Lucas napped and I pondered my upcoming search for Patsy, I thought I heard noises coming from the back. I chalked it up to rear axle or tire problems, if not Hugo. More adventurous now, the puppy had set about exploring, trotting back and forth in the central aisle, skidding on the slippery tile with the RV's swaying. Every time he reached the rear, before returning Hugo yapped, a puppy version of a bark.

Something happening back there. We climbed into the mountains, with plans to stop in Wickenburg for lunch. Again I stared in the mirror, thinking to discover what was attracting Hugo's attention. I spotted them! Two blond heads peeking out from beneath a sheet on the back upper bunk.

"What th'hell!" I shouted, braking sharply and bringing Lucas awake.

"Hear, hear, Son. Watch your language."

"We've got stowaways, Brother John."

Nervous giggling emanated from the rear. Derek and Megan lifted the sheet to stare at us sheepishly.

Brother John demanded to know what they thought they were doing.

"W-we needed a r-ride," Megan stammered.

"To get us down to the Green Valley-Tubac area," Derek said.

"Where my brothers just opened a new restaurant."

"We have no money and didn't want to ask Mike and Matt to stake us."

"They've got jobs for us, though. So if we can get there, we'll be okay."

CHAPTER 5

B rother John naturally agreed to escort our two stowaways all the way to their destination. Dragging out their backpacks from behind the shower curtain where they had stashed them, the newlyweds changed to fresh tees and jeans. Now she looked even more like Patsy. The trio sat in the back of the RV happily chatting as Megan and Derek put lunch together. We ate ham and American cheese sandwiches and drank lemonade while traveling. We heard their history.

Megan Derry's father had left the family years earlier, his current whereabouts unknown. Matt and Mike were older than she, but only by a few years. With Matt's twenty-first birthday, the boys left Kansas for Arizona where they opened a restaurant. The minute Megan turned seventeen, their mom took off, too, for Europe on a budget tour. That was six months ago and the only news they had was a series of sparsely separated postcards. Mrs. Derry was carrying bedpans in a Swiss hospital. She was about to leave Geneva as sidekick to a racecar driver heading for Paris. She was waitressing on the French Riviera. At least the kids had each other now, plus Derek, the genuine orphan, for his parents were both dead and he was an only child.

In Phoenix I took Interstate 10 south to Tucson where I turned off on I-19 that runs a mere sixty-three miles straight into Mexico through the two Nogales; the first one state side, the second across the border. More cacti, which Brother John identified, including a whole hillside full of saguaro, ocatillo, organ pipe, agave, and the colorfully blooming rainbow, fish hook and hedge hog; plus palo verde and some kind of stunted trees. Lots of rattlesnakes, gila monsters, and scorpions we were told while stopping for gas in South Tucson, so walking in the desert wasn't advisable. Dry, arid land and warm air. I drove with my window down and my left arm, already tanned from the Las Vegas climate, propped along the window sill.

Mostly quiet, thinking his own thoughts, Lucas sat in the passenger seat. He too stared ahead and to left and right. Across the Santa Cruz River and in the near distance to the east rose a range of mountains climbing steadily heavenwards with the Coronado National Forest marching up and walking across the rim. To the west rose the Sierrita Mountains, with copper mining interrupting the foothills. This part of southern Arizona, we were told, was the land once reigned over by Cochise, chief of the Apaches.

Behind us Megan chattered, eliciting the occasional comment from Derek. Intermittently they hugged, kissed, and cuddled. Hugo, more daring these days, scampered from his box in the back up the aisle to join the humans. When he decided to settle, it was on the table, where he could press his wet nose against the window. He too wanted to see the sights.

I wondered where Patsy was. Did she make her home in South Tucson in one of those cracker-box houses we'd passed? Was she living an upscale life now, finding a home in a high-rise apartment building or the affluent suburbs? Or would I find her out in the sticks in another trashy trailer?

We passed through Green Valley, the highway running right down the middle like a ribbon, with the retirement community two long strips of spaghetti along each side and growing north and south. Stopping for snacks, we learned that the old folks couldn't build more than a few blocks east or west. Pecan orchards hemmed them in on the east, a copper mine on the west. This meant we could get a pretty good view of the whole length of town as we drove through it. Stucco and brick dwellings from small to gargantuan predominated, with swimming pools and golf courses galore. I longed to stop, rent clubs, and hit the links, as I hadn't played since the previous summer.

On south I drove, passing an old building set back from the highway with a huge longhorn cow's head out front and a sign telling us this was the Cow Palace—restaurant and tavern. The parking lot was full of vehicles, from old pickups to shiny new luxury model cars.

Standing to look over my shoulder, Megan got all excited. "My brother Mike said the Cow Palace is a popular place and a landmark. Won't be long."

Right. A few miles father along, on the left side, we spotted another structure, also old. This one sported a big plaster of paris cat at the entrance. A wooden sign on the roof proclaimed our destination—the Cat Castle. So this was Mike and Matt's café.

"We're here!" Megan squealed, hugging Derek.

I wondered where we'd find the *church in trouble*. Perhaps it was nearby.

Back in the foothills, Megan said, lived all manner of strange people—Mike's description. Left-over hippie types living in shacks and trailers busy with artsy-craftsy enterprises or lolling about philosophizing.

"Also a lot of people working the pecan orchards and mine," Lucas added.

Ahh, I'd feel right at home. If not with the retirees or middle-aged hippies, then with the blue collar workers. Mining was in my blood.

But so was music and religion, my mom invariably insisted. While I was growing up there was always this conflict, a struggle between two strong personalities. Dad favored rough and tumble sports and outdoor, blue-collar labor. Mom insisted on music and Bible lessons along with indoor occupations. Maybe that's why I sometimes felt my head was all screwed up.

Everybody tumbled out of the RV, including Hugo, who yapped at my heels and then whimpered as he pawed my leg. I knew what that meant. I bent to lift the puppy and tuck him inside my new blue windbreaker. He had me well-trained by now. The first blue jacket stayed in his box for naptime comfort. The second I wore as his home away from home. Both of course were zippered.

Matt and Mike hurried out the front door, their faces alight, their arms open for hugs. The Derrys were affectionate and demonstrative, I noticed. Derek Dolan stood to one side, a wide grin splitting his face. The Derry boys, tall, muscular versions of the pretty Megan, wore white tees with khaki pants. Now Megan would have a whole trio of men dancing attendance on her ladyship. Or perhaps it was mutual, she would nurture them too.

The only vehicles in the parking lot were Brother John's spanking new RV and one old battered red pickup. Ahh, *déjà vu*. I missed my old thing of dad's.

"Sorry we weren't with you for your wedding," Mike said to his sister following introductions all round. He said the pickup came with the café.

"We made a fast decision after catching a Greyhound down from Wichita," Derek replied, still grinning. "No time to call you ahead of time."

"We brought our parson with us," she said gleefully, drawing both Brother John and me into her circle of loved ones. "And the organist."

Lucas and I acknowledged her labels with nods and smiles. Hugo poked his white-spotted brown head over the zipper and said "Yap."

"Also their mascot," Megan added, giving Hugo a pat. He licked her hand.

"How's business?" Derek asked, shifting from one foot to the other.

Matt's smile faded. "Not so hot."

They invited us indoors, where Mike said the grill was hot, he could make hamburgers for supper. Megan laughed, a pretty little trill (so much like Patsy's).

"I can see you need a woman's touch."

"We're ready to roll up our sleeves," said Derek. "If you'll have us."

Relief bathed the brothers, much like the sun emerging from behind a bank of dark clouds.

I was tired from driving, manhandling that big rig despite its power steering. Hungry, too, for more than a sandwich. I walked Hugo and then fed him before checking the tires and engine. The puppy didn't want me to leave him. Back inside my light jacket, we returned to the café. No other customers. The graveled lot out front and the restaurant inside stayed empty save for family and the newlyweds' parson and organist.

Megan had built a huge green salad along with dessert, while at the grill Mike turned the sizzling T-bones. Great. I began salivating from the aroma as if I were Hugo.

"We've got to get on the road if we're going to find our church before dark," said Brother John between bites.

The Derry brothers said they could help, they were familiar with the area. Following the delicious dinner topped off with coffee and fresh blueberry tarts with cream, Megan's and Derek's contributions, they spread Lucas' big atlas on a bare table. I volunteered for K. P., leaving them at their study.

As I carted dirty dishes to the kitchen sink, I closely observed the establishment. The whole big dining room was bare. No window treatments or wall decorations, nor any advertising posters. A dozen wooden tables with matching chairs, an eight-stool counter, that was it. No wonder they had no diners. Nothing unique about the place. The name itself, Cat Castle, was a bit strange. Maybe they should design a cat motif or somehow carry forward the theme name. My hands in the hot suds, I thought about the Derrys. They could use a dose of imagination and a big advertising campaign. I didn't want to contemplate the creative ideas that immediately came to mind from my marketing class back home in Gillette.

I didn't aim to get involved. Enough paint on my palette already: launching my quest to locate Patsy, keeping body and soul together—mine and Hugo's, plus *factoting* at Brother John's side. In fact, I wasn't sure I'd stick with him. Instead, I might look into work at the copper mine or pecan orchards.

Finished in the kitchen, I sat at the counter with another mug of coffee while the others studied the map debating possible locales. Listlessly I thumbed through the paper. It was a bi-weekly out of Green Valley. Might as well acquaint myself with the retirees' activities. I started at the real estate ads first, gradually working toward the front page.

Right there, just below the fold, appeared an article warning naïve residents of a series of house thefts. The sheriff, said the article, was following up leads. Could be junkies after goods to sell to support their habit. Readers were admonished to lock their doors and get proper identification before admitting strangers to their homes. Apparently the thieves not only burgled empty dwellings but robbed people in broad daylight at gunpoint. One old lady had suffered a bonk to the head. When she didn't respond to phone or knock, a neighbor called the cops. She was rushed by ambulance to St. Mary's Hospital in Tucson, twenty miles to the north of Green Valley. She had a concussion.

I mused that it would be too much of a coincidence to think that Patsy's drug-dealing jerk could be behind this fracas. Possible, though. If not, the perpetrators, when caught, might lead me to Malcolm Barr. I'd have to produce some excuse to get me admitted, to get an interview with the perps. If caught.

Just then there was a great roar and a dozen or so bikers zoomed into the parking lot. I jumped off the counter stool as if shot from a cannon. Not again. What was it about graveled lots and half-dilapidated cafes that attracted bikers? Did they anticipate naivete, or think they could get away with murder? Silly me, exaggerating like that, but the wounds I'd taken in Gillette still smarted, if only in memory. As for temptations to horny leather-jacketed bikers, Megan was cuter and more delicious looking than Betty's Tina could ever hope to be.

Behind me at the front window crowded the Derry brothers. A quick glance over my shoulder and I knew what the others were doing. Brother John stayed put at the table with the map. Oblivious to the potential for danger, he smiled to himself and made a note. I guessed he'd found the church. Megan was polishing glasses and Derek was starting another urn of coffee.

I watched the motorcycle riders dismount. Wearing the typical gear of black leather jackets, pants, and boots, they doffed their helmets to head for the door. Gray beards and gray hair on the men who weren't already bald, salt and pepper or blond on the women. What in the world? Then I remembered we were a mere few miles south of the retirement community. Had the old folks home let the residents out for recess?

Noisy with laughter and chatter, these diners were nevertheless courteous. All of us pitched in, even Brother John, who acted as genial host. I grabbed menus and carried glasses of water around to the tables. The Derrys slapped ham and cheese sandwiches together. Megan, claiming in a whisper to me that she was fifth-generation "fast," dashed back and forth from walk-in refrigerator to kitchen preparation area tossing salads and opening cans of Campbell's soup while I tried to stay out of her way. Clearly I wouldn't be of much help. Waiting tables was apparently more my forte.

The old-timers shared highlights of their trip down south as far as Mazatlan on the coast. Later I stepped outside along with the Derrys and Dolans to say goodbye. Every biker, even the women, rode their own. Saddlebags and sophisticated luggage boxes mounted on the back carried the essentials.

"We're too old to rough it," laughed one cute little lady. "We stay in nice hotels, eat in good restaurants, and drink bottled water."

"And shop," squealed another woman; taller, with fewer wrinkles. "We ladies love to stop at all the boutiques and *mercados*, market places. Drives the men nuts."

Her mate stepped up to encircle her waist. "They're getting pretty good at bargaining, though. They rarely pay the prices offered."

I stared dubiously at their bulging packs. How much could they hold?

Their leader laughed. "We ship everything home."

I didn't tell this couple, apparently the group leaders, about the Green Valley article. They already knew. He had called home from Chihuahua. Laughing again, gray beard admitted that the neighbor supposedly responsible for watching their villa said they'd been burgled.

"You don't seem too concerned," I said, my face no doubt a picture of puzzlement.

His wife said they were planning a garage sale anyhow. The robbery saved them the trouble and the insurance money would pay for replacement of the essentials. "I'm so thankful we weren't home," she said, no longer smiling. "We might have been hurt."

"Or killed," said gray beard, grimacing.

It was then she said they were selling out and returning to Ohio to be near their daughter. She was expecting a child soon. "Which means we've got a couple of cycles to sell, too. Would you be interested?"

Surprised at myself, I realized I was. Unlike Las Vegas where I could walk down the street or hop aboard busses and shuttles, down here in the desert I would need transportation. Right there on the spot we agreed to a price and exchanged money and ownership. She jumped on the back of her husband's Harley-Davidson and they took off. Staring down at the used model, I laughed. Just like that I had become a biker. Candy apple red with shiny chrome, complete with saddlebags and comfortably cushioned rear seat. If Patsy were still mine, I'd take her for a ride.

CHAPTER 6

There was plenty of space indoors, but that's about all you could say for the old building that housed the Community Church in Christ, the name on the homemade weathered sign. Abbreviated, it was CCIC, sounding like *Kick*; could be an advertising gimmick, as in *Get a Kick out of Christ.* Irreverent, but that's how my mind worked.

We found the place on a narrow curving paved road across the Santa Cruz River from Green Valley and past the pecan orchards, but not up into the foothills. Once upon a time the big drafty structure had been a daycare center and then a safe house for battered spouses. Dr. Wallaberra, the present parson, took it over with some minor revisions, he said. Like sticking up on the roof what looked like a toilet plunger for a spire.

I could fix that. In an informal contract with my father's brother, I was apprenticed to my carpenter uncle after school and weekends from junior high through my sophomore year. By then I was captain of the football team and begged off carrying a job too. With my uncle I learned carpentry, which later led me into full-time construction, before I found steadier work and better wages in coal and then petroleum. I could build the parson a proper steeple. Indoors, the metal folding chairs didn't make a good impression, either. Constructing sturdy pews would take too long. Better to suggest a massive fund-raising drive. Then spend the money on pews, carpeting, and whatever else they needed.

One thing was needed for certain—a complete paint job. Graffiti that said nothing and meant nothing to us circled and swirled all over the front wall, up and over the door and windows. Plain two-paned windows, no stained glass.

Oh, oh, I could see it now, Brother John volunteering me for everything from providing the music to marketing and maintenance. I might do better by heading for the mine. Make better money and simultaneously steer clear of any heavy doses of religion. Except that I'd already met the preacher and liked the guy. I thought I'd like to get to know him.

"Outreach," said Dr. Paul Wallaberra, the young black pastor, admitting to innocence and ignorance with fiscal management and other business needs. "We need a program of evangelical preaching and music to increase our numbers, swell the congregation."

Older than I, but not by much, Paul Wallaberra was lean and thin. Perhaps we should feature ourselves as a singing trio in rendering soul music with a jazz beat. I neither caricaturized nor ridiculed for I was drawn to fine old gospel singing and hoped the brethren would allow me to feature it. His hair was cut close in a neat and compact scull cap. His skin was milk chocolate in color and smooth as velvet. Could have been first cousin to Denzel Washington.

One of the first things we wanted to hear was what the pastor meant when he wrote that his church was *in trouble*. Paul ticked off items on his fingers: vandalism to the church, items stolen from parishioners' cars, and a couple of middle-aged ladies who otherwise meant well battling like CIA and former KGB agents. Odd choice of simile, it seemed to me. At the time.

Right away and without conferring with me, Brother John volunteered me to solve the crimes. How'd he know whether I'd be any good at that? I couldn't see how recapturing his wallet by slinging tomatoes at a stupid kid counted for anything. That his counseling could alleviate the quarrels, I had little doubt. He was good at advising. Me, solving crimes? That would be a first.

Since my boss had put me on the spot, I figured I'd better start asking questions. What had been stolen, from whom, and what progress had the police made, if any? Lucas Wallaberra looked vaguely puzzled. He said the police didn't have jurisdiction out here, and I'd have to ask Sheriff

Truman my last question. The victims were still complaining, which must mean their possessions had not been recovered.

Against my better judgment I agreed to look into matters. I tried matching the pastor in vagueness, though, as this wasn't my kind of thing. I didn't want him and Brother John getting their hopes up or promising paradise to members of his flock, when I might come up with *Zilch*. I mean, if the sheriff couldn't solve these petty crimes, why should the preachers think I could?

Postponing a visit to the copper mine to check on job openings, I didn't get much of an opportunity, anyhow, and certainly not the time. With the RV parked beside the church, the electricity and plumbing connected, Lucas sent me to town for groceries. Looked like I would be chief cook and dishwasher. On the corner next to the church—and a vocational training facility for displaced workers next to that—sat a convenience store with gas pumps. We needed more vittles than they would offer.

I hopped on my motorcycle to pass an orchard and cross over a bridge on the road that led beneath Interstate 19 into Green Valley. On my immediate right lay a shopping center with a supermarket and a discount store among the boutiques, bars, and restaurants. I had brought a list, developed by the preachers under my advisement.

My kitchen repertoire wasn't extensive but the recipes came from mom. First stop, the hardware for a cast-iron Dutch oven. I was hungry for pot roast. Lucas and Paul would like that, I bet, as well as my

Sicilian Feast. An avid reader, mom had comprised the latter from Richard Condon's novels. Throughout his writing career, mom said, Condon had lived in sixteen countries. Besides writing one or two novels per locale, Condon liked to eat. His description of various ethnic dishes was extensive and included lists of ingredients. I could make huge dishes and freeze what the three of us didn't consume for later, when I was too busy to cook. For one thing, Lucas said, after confirming with Paul, they wanted me to paint the church, both outside and indoors. At the hardware I purchased several buckets of paint in addition to the cook pot.

On the way home from the store, I stopped to see the sheriff. "Dick Truman's the name, catching crooks is my game!" he yelled at me with a belly rumbling chortle when I'd introduced the theft topic. Pushing back an old, warped cowboy hat with sweat-stained rim, he took his booted feet off the scarred wooden desk to lean forward in his swivel chair. He didn't stand, though, just stuck out a callused hand. "So you aim to solve those petty thefts out at that black fella's church. I couldn't do it, but you, an amateur, can. That's what you're tryin' t'tell me?"

His face was craggy, as from adolescent acne, the square jaw chiseled. I couldn't help but think of *Dick Tracy*, of comic book fame. When he caught me staring at him, tongue-tied, too dry to swallow or speak further, he chuckled. "Cat got your tongue, eh? Meantime, you're thinking of *Dick Tracy*, I bet."

At last I admitted that the preachers out at the church expected me to do something. I was supposed to be a handyman, help out, whatever they needed. "Seemed smart to check with you, first, before running off half-cocked."

"You're dadgummed right, boy." Finally he stood to come around the desk, He slapped me on the back and walked me outside to my cycle. "You done right, that's for sure. Just keep right on checkin' in here. When I get news about them church robberies, I'll let you know."

Astride my machine, I said, "Wait a minute. What about those thefts in Green Valley? Also the vandalism down at the Cat Castle? Do you s'pose all these things are connected, were pulled off by the same thug or gang?

"Come again? Where's that?"

I told him about the new café the Derrys and Dolans had opened. Oh, yeah, he'd forgotten about that one. "Too much t'do round here, boy, t'cover the whole territory. I need a bigger staff." With that he turned away from me and went back to holding down the desk. Through the grimy, flyspecked window I saw him pour a mug of coffee, sit down, and prop up his feet. Down went his hat over his face again, to shade his naptime, I figured. So much for all that. Looked like I was on my own.

One of my first major jobs for the preachers had nothing to do with religion. They set me to looking after the garden patch, a huge quarter block. Two of the ladies, Dollie Martinez in partic-ular, demanded a flower garden. The parson wanted vegetables. He had contracted with a farmer to bring in several loads of good topsoil in his truck. Before we arrived, Dr. Wallaberra was using student help from the teenagers' Sunday school class—the Manson twins, George and Jack, and their buddy Arnie Somebody. Now I was doing the work of all three. Elise Goodman, Dollie's cousin, wasn't about to get her hands dirty, but she vied with Dollie in arranging the most beautiful bouquets for the church altar

Over the next few days I was occupied with painting over the graffiti and completing other pertinent handyman chores. The clergymen designed the evangelistic program and the advertising to support it, though they sought my reaction and input to their ads. (I didn't suggest *Getting a Kick out of Christ.*) Brother John was ecstatic. Next to counseling, he most enjoyed preaching and bringing lost souls to Christ.

I'd passed off the infighting Paul cited when first we arrived as par for congregations like this one that attracted a mixed group of parishioners. Working class people sat side by side with the affluent. Sprinkled throughout hunkered old-timers along with some of the artsy-craftsy, post-hippie types the Derry brothers had said were squatting back in the hills. Seasoning the mix was a number of Mexicans, recently or more distantly up from Mexico.

I was not asked to play the piano nor to sing solos. Thank God for the latter, as it felt like showing off and I wasn't happy under the spotlight. Elise

Goodman, the pianist, struggled valiantly to avoid mistakes, striking no more than half the full chords with her left hand. However, Dollie Martinez as soloist could have starred in a musical extravaganza, Hollywood style. Her rendering of the familiar old hymns was that excellent. Elise and Dollie were cousins and, once upon a time, good friends. Now they were the battling biddies.

Knowing my mom would demand a full description, I carefully scrutinized both of these middle-aged women. Remember *The Golden Girls?* I would remind mom. Dollie could have passed for Rose and Elise for Blanche. I didn't know about their personalities. Elise wasn't man-crazy like Blanche, but Dollie was sweet and naïve, though not as goofy as Rose.

Dr. Wallaberra strongly disfavored their squabbling. (Yeah, that's the way he put it, *strongly disfavored;* he's formal and aloof). Soon the other ladies in the congregation would be taking sides, Brother John predicted, aligning themselves with one or the other cousin. Then the church would be a battleground instead of a place of worship.

My next assignment was in advertising. When Brother John said this job would take several days, I decided to combine personal exploration with the distribution of flyers and posters advertising the upcoming week-long evangelistic series. I fed Hugo and pushed him back inside the RV with my zippered jacket. Then I hopped aboard my cycle. I was bent on exploring first.

Following the paved road on this side of the

river and along the back side of the pecan orchards took me first to Sahuarita where, among other structures, I spotted a grocery store and tavern. I would visit both later. Beyond the main junction crouched huge tin-roofed sheds for the processing of pecans, as announced by the signs out front. I continued along this road that might once have been the main thoroughfare between Tucson and Nogales, now used mostly for local traffic, I surmised. Houses, shacks, and trailers peppered the landscape along the way, with their cousins scattered among the cacti and scrubby trees to the east and on up into the foothills.

On the Papago Indian Reservation I discovered a bingo parlor. At that point I turned around and returned to the crossroads to travel west at Sahuarita to see what lay in that direction. A half-mile farther along, nearly to I-19, I spotted a large complex of brick buildings. Big yellow busses, youngsters running around the athletic fields on the near side and playing on swings and teeter-totters beyond, suggested that these were a couple of schools.

I parked my bike near the tennis courts, deciding to walk around a bit. No special reason. No reason for selecting the tee I'd chosen that day, either. Today's slogan read: *So wise so young, they say, do never live long.* I could hear mom whispering in my ear: *God's hand at work,* Son. *Providence.*

I saw a kid slipping out behind one of the busses. I sneaked right after him. He had a can of red paint and before you could say *Jack Sprat could eat no fat,* he'd created a nonsensical non-design. I didn't call out or run him down. Instead I followed him. Not back to school but to his car. From behind the corner of one of the campus buildings I got the license number, all except the last digit, before he pulled out, burning rubber.

Now I had something to report to Sheriff Truman. In the meantime, I'd be on the lookout for the kid and the car; the latter might not be his own. From Sahuarita I called the sheriff's office. He was out, said Tom, identifying himself as a deputy. Sure, he'd take my news, pass it on. Might help 'em nab the kid.

Enough of sleuthing. I needed to get busy with my job. But not before quenching my thirst with a good cold beer on this hot day. Time to hit the cross-roads saloon with the graveled parking lot full of vehicles, new and old.

In the dim light of the tavern, dark paneling and cracked vinyl booths, I perched on a bar stool and ordered a Pabst. From their rough clothes and talk it was obvious this was a working-class crowd. They and their cars and pickups matched the run-down appearance of the facility. Raucous laughter from insider jokes notwithstanding, I felt comfortable, at home among the denim-clad pecan and mine workers.

I didn't expect to make a connection with a dealer or witness the secretive exchange of bucks for dope. Not here. These men and women were more than likely God-fearing folk. They might not actually go to church, but I'd be willing to bet they were believers, in both God and the Bible. I couldn't guess whether they were likely candidates for my flyers announcing the upcoming services at Dr. Wallaberra's church, but perhaps they had family members who would be.

Should I scatter around the flyers I'd brought announcing the series of sermons scheduled every night over the whole next week? I didn't think so. But one never knew. I passed off to the barkeep a stack of flyers, finished my beer, and left to head for home. Time to feed and humor Hugo.

After lunch I was set on getting some posters into store fronts. In Green Valley that afternoon I didn't elicit much interest in the upcoming series of sermons to be delivered by Brother John. These senior citizens already had plenty of churches. There was the big Presbyterian structure on the hill, constructed in off-white stucco, appropriate to this hot southwestern country under the blazing sun. Then there were the Catholic, Lutheran, Episcopal, Baptist, Christian, and Mormon; also a few less familiar churches.

I got permission to mount posters in store windows. Then I hired a trio of boys on bicycles to stick flyers beneath windshield wipers in the parking lots of the shopping centers, at the senior recreation centers and the golf courses. I followed the kids awhile to check their reliability. Then I took off. Cruising a few miles north of Green Valley with more flyers, I hit the small village of Tomas and the intervening mobile home and RV park, the latter also exclusive to seniors. Then I headed back south.

Saving the Derrys' Cat Castle for last, I journeyed on past Tubac for Rio Rico, another small village. Up went more posters, under windshield wipers went more flyers. Another golf course tempted me. Another time I'd try it.

Two miles from Tubac squatted an exclusive golf and country club circled by expensive homes and mini-estates. If I had my directions right, one of those two church busybodies lived around here; Elise Goodman, perhaps. Maybe I'd play golf here someday, too, when not hitting the public links in Tucson or mingling with the seniors in Green Valley.

Tubac proved fascinating. At the bar where I stopped for my second beer of the day (man, it was hot!), I learned that of the no more than a few hundred people living in the village, the attractions nevertheless included forty or fifty art galleries, souvenir shops and craft studios. The place must be an outlet for the products created by the artsy people living in the hills. An historical monument and small museum also went on my back list to visit later. Nine times the town was destroyed and rebuilt, I learned, following several early history raids by vicious Indians bent on murder by spear and scalping or kidnapping, setting the whole village afire in the wake of their departure. Determined, the settlers continued to rebuild. Fascinating.

At the bar in Tubac I spotted what I was looking for, or thought I did—a drug deal going down. The exchange was so quick, I barely saw the brown envelope passed over beneath the newspaper. In searching for Patsy's whereabouts, I had decided to go undercover, hit the bars in South Tucson. I would pretend to make a drug buy. If oft repeated, it was possible I might stumble onto Malcolm Barr's operation. Dangerous, of course, as anything could happen. What I hadn't anticipated was running across that kind of action this close to home. My palms sweaty, from nerves as much as from heat, I clutched my cold beer, lifting the big frosty mug as a cover behind which to hide.

The man with the newspaper wore an expensive navy blue blazer with open white shirt, gold neck chains and one gold earring. Glancing about casually—yet suspiciously, it seemed to me—he left. I sat nursing my beer. Might look strange for me to dash out behind him, leaving half my beer.

My heart raced with excitement. A few moments later I exited, in time to catch the license plate number on the shiny red classic Jaguar XK120.

As the sun was setting, I hit the Cat Castle for a chat with the newlyweds and the Derry brothers. The two preachers could thaw pot roast or Sicilian Feast for tonight's evening meal. I was bent on relaxing with friends, though that might be a misnomer; *relaxing*, that is. I was all keyed up.

I couldn't believe it. While I contemplated a long, extensive, and complicated search of South Tucson, here was Fess Goodman dealing right beneath my nose? Yeah, I'd recognized the guy: Elise Goodman's son. He had stopped by the church a time or two while she was putzing around—arranging Sunday school materials, dusting, anything it seemed to avoid practicing the piano. Overhearing mother and son, he was invariably after money.

CHAPTER 7

The next evening I went into South Tucson. I was eager to case a few joints, pretend I was interested in making a connection for the purpose of discovering who might be dealing. I might run into Fess Goodman again. Even if I didn't, I was going to start asking around about Malcolm Barr, Patsy's jerk.

Instead I ran into a couple of brick walls called thugs. In bar after bar I asked if Malcolm had been around, my casual manner and questions designed to suggest we were friends. "Just looking for an old buddy," I said nonchalantly.

Not everyone was fooled. Somebody took offense. I'd had enough beers to launch the Queen Mary. Meaning I was pretty well sloshed and no longer as alert as I should have been. I paused near the alley to shake my head, get my bearings. That's when they hit me, first the little guy, then the one built like a Sequoia. Caught off guard I took a hit to the right eye and a sock to my nose.

That's when I came unwound, flailing my arms, slinging my fists, and whirling around to come in with a few solid hits of my own to jaws, cheekbones, eyes and ears. A crowd gathered, cheering on the neighborhood punks, I assumed. Sirens wailed in the distance, and the rednecks backed off. I too turned around. I intended to beat it before the cops arrived to question me.

As I wiped blood and sweat from my face and hands with the tail of my tee shirt, a voice in my ear said "Nuthin' personal." It was the bartender from my last stop, the tavern around the corner. "We don't know no Malcolm Whatever. It's just that we don't take kindly to strangers askin' questions round here. So you get on your bike and get out, ya hear."

I'd just been run out of town on a rail, old-West style! Ought to be jumping into a saddle so as to ride off into the sunset. Instead I mounted my faithful Harley-Davidson. With nary a glance over my shoulder, I headed home.

I could take the bartender's hint—for a week or so, while busy with the preachers. Meanwhile, I planned to follow up on Fess Goodman early the next week, after we'd launched the revival services and I caught my breath. Hah, I didn't know much about the religion game.

I had to make excuses for my cuts and bruises. When asked, I passed them off as injuries taken when the cycle flew out of control on the gravel roads, giving me a spill. No reason for the brothers to disbelieve, nor the two busybody ladies either. Fess Goodman didn't show his face and the cousins, Elise and Dollie, didn't talk about him.

At the church the next day I got another dose of the dowagers. Seems their squabbles harked back to Adam and Eve or thereabouts. I didn't know what their problems were and didn't care. Sounded like mom's soap operas. If Elise Goodman, the pianist, showed up with a bouquet of yellow roses from the florist, Dollie Martinez brought hot pink bougainvillea from her garden. When Elise selected loud, bang-the-piano hymns, Dollie argued for a selection of soft, worshipful songs. I didn't know where Fess Goodman fit in.

I didn't always cook and we didn't always eat in the RV. Periodically Lucas climbed on the back of my cycle for the ten-mile trip down to the Cat Castle. With her special dishes, Megan's cooking made you think you'd died and gone to heaven. Chewing the fat was nice, too. Today we headed south again.

I pondered how to bring the Green Valley house thefts into the conversation. More of interest was any gossip the Derrys and Dolans might have been privy to regarding drug deals in the vicinity. I wondered why Fess Goodman was operating so close to home, if drug dealing was what that sneaky scenario at the Tubac bar was what it appeared. These were not easy topics to intrude into talk of church and café operations. But I gave it the old college try.

"About those petty thefts at the church that Dr. Wallaberra spoke of," I said at last, when there was a lull in the chatter and Matt got up from the table to fetch the coffeepot for refills. "What else he tell you about that, Lucas?"

Mike leaned forward, his eyes agleam. "Yeah, we'd like to hear more. We've been robbed, too." I knew about that and their graffiti, but Brother John didn't.

"And vandalized," said Megan, screwing up her dainty features in a scowl.

Of course I knew the church troubles, too, but Brother John described the problems for their benefit. He said the collection plate had been robbed twice. Also, some of the more affluent among the congregation had reported cars broken into and car stereos stolen along with personal items—handbags and sports equipment—expensive golf clubs and tennis rackets; plus a fur jacket.

"In this climate somebody's carting around furs?" Megan was astounded.

"No accounting for the habits of the rich," Matt muttered.

"The same person or gang could have been responsible for all of it," I said, "the thefts at the church, here at your café, and up in Green Valley." Then I shared with the others my exchange with Sheriff Dick Truman. "He doesn't sound very concerned, excusing his lack of progress on his staff—not enough deputies."

The Derry boys said a deputy, Tom Something, took their statement. "We haven't seen hide nor hair of anybody outta the sheriff's office, since," Matt added, drawling, and trying to mimic the slow-talking sheriff.

My idea generated a lot more chatter. If the sheriff knew anything at all, he was keeping his knowledge from the press.

The robbery topic exhausted for the moment, we grew silent. The Cat Castle was empty of customers except for Lucas and me. The café was no longer bare. Megan had prevailed upon her brothers, she said. It was easier than arguing, Mike countered, with a grin and a nudge for his pretty blond sister. Matt mumbled about her notions taking their hard-earned cash. Nobody argued about that.

Green and white checkered tablecloths now adorned every table, with matching café curtains hanging half-mast on each window.

"Megan made them herself," said Derek proudly, one arm around her shoulders.

"Yeah, after we let her buy a sewing machine," Matt muttered.

Obviously he was the tighter-fisted brother. Her apron, with forest-green rickrack, she called the decoration, was made of the same material. Cute, I guessed, musing that her cooking would attract the hungry men while the décor should appeal to the ladies. So where were all these new customers?

"How about more variety in the menu?" I said. Brother John was talking church revival, drawing in the crowds. I mused that was the connection my subconscious made: people hungering for food to nourish the body; people hungering for preachin' to nourish the spirit.

"They'll come," said Mike confidently, removing his stained once white apron and apologizing for not ridding himself sooner of the offensive garment. When we arrived he was out back tending barbecue in the big barrel Derek had devised. "*Build a better mousetrap and the world will beat a path to your door.* Ever hear that one?"

Lucas grinned at me. "Not without an effective ad campaign," he proclaimed in his resonant pulpit voice.

That set us all off—on a drive to see who could produce the best, or worst, or most gimmicky ideas for marketing the café. "And the church as well," said Lucas. "Gotta advertise God too these days or people won't come."

That's when I introduced my *Kick for Christ* slogan. As anticipated, the idea didn't go over well.

"Our biggest competition is the Cow Palace up the road," said Megan, ignoring me and Brother John. "If we were to copy them, we'd have sing-alongs. With a great piano player." She stared hard at me.

I noticed Brother John sitting back, silent, a pensive expression on his face. Perhaps he was drawing a mental analogy—how to draw in and please the customers and how to *calm the savage breast* in the fighting dowagers, Elise and Dollie.

Abruptly the door opened and in walked Fess Goodman, once again wearing a single gold earring gleaming from his right earlobe and many gold chains. They lay over a hairy bare chest from beneath a shirt unbuttoned halfway to the waist. Behind him trotted his mother wearing a flowery print dress. He started across the room when Elise caught a look at our table. Blanching, she grabbed Fess by the arm and backed out, pulling him with her.

"What was that about?" said Matt with a growl. He motioned to Megan and Derek to sit back down. Both had jumped up from our table in readiness to cook and serve.

"That was Elise, our church pianist," Lucas said softly. "Guess she didn't want people she knew to see her with a young man dressed like that."

I held my tongue. After all, I didn't actually <u>know</u> it was a drug-for-money exchange I'd seen. I was surprised that Lucas didn't know they were mother and son. Then I remembered that he wasn't around when Goodman stopped by.

Megan laughed, a little trill with a snort on the end. Sighing, she re-sat herself. "What? She's married to somebody else and this guy's her toy boy?"

Lucas shrugged. "I don't know her personal particulars."

Derek pushed his mug aside to lean forward. He might have been imparting secret intelligence collected on the sly from the Chinese. "Maybe not, Lucas, but I'll bet she figures you'll tell Dr. Wallaberra. Right?"

Excusing myself I walked down the back hall, as if heading for the men's room. Instead I slipped out the back door and around the café. I wanted to check whether Fess still drove the Jaguar. He sped away, throwing gravel. Why the hasty exit from the café? Elise had spotted Brother John or the druggie had recognized me?

# # # # # # #

Lucas apparently forgot the incident at the Cat Castle, but I didn't. I had a lot to think about. Even if Fess was into drugs, that by no means meant he had anything to do with the recent thefts or vandalism; or, for that matter, with Malcolm Barr. My goal of locating Patsy still seemed nigh onto impossible. If I were able to devote more time to the search, I'd probably start by returning to the bar where I'd been warned off. Hang out in the café across the street, keep an eye out. That could take days, with no guarantee Barr was known around there or ever visited the neighborhood. The bartender who had threatened me could have been speaking the truth—nosy strangers weren't welcome. Time enough to devise and initiate a plan after the week of revival sermons.

I skipped prayer meeting that night. While sitting in a lawn chair under the RV awning, I watched Hugo snoop. Since landing here he had discovered rabbits. No special reason or plan to do anything in particular if he ever caught one. Instinct, possibly.

Having left the service early, the dowagers stood near the corner of the building on my side, away from the front door and side windows. I had no problem hearing them. Their voices growing louder, they could easily be heard in the still night with nothing much else to be heard but crickets calling mates.

From inside the church, voices wafted through the open church window on my side. No instrumentalists were allowed for the prayer and testimony meeting, so the congregation sang the hymns accapella. With half of them singing off key, they were murdering *Nearer My God to Thee.*

"<u>My</u> son will be graduating with his MBA next month," said Dollie. "How about <u>your</u> boy, Elise?"

Having seen Elise's *boy*, first in Tubac and again at the Cat Castle, I wasn't surprised when her mouth dropped open. I didn't think they could see me sitting back in the shadows. Conversely, every nuance of their body language and facial expressions was clear to me, for they stood beneath a light mounted on the corner of the church building.

"Now that's hitting below the belt, Dollie. You know I'm trying to get Fess admitted again to the rehab center. The paper work's been processed and approved, but he just won't go." Elise stood stiffly with stern demeanor.

"Yeah, well, you'd better get help with Festor before it's too late. Personally, I'm convinced he's already a lost cause." Dollie appeared angry.

With arms akimbo, Elise demanded, "Now what do you mean by that, Dollie?"

"You know perfectly well what I mean, Elise. Do something about your son before Festor gets crossways with the law and they send him back to jail."

I couldn't help it. I sat up straighter and leaned forward.

Elise flounced about, ruffling her hair with both hands. Then, like an angry and frustrated little girl, she stuck out her tongue at her cousin.

"I don't know what's got into you, lately, Elise. We used to be best friends. Now you pick on me every chance you get. Suffering from *the change*, is that it?"

"Oh, you're nasty, you are." Elise whirled to stalk off.

Man, these women were real cats. Elise was a bleached blonde, the color undoubtedly from a bottle or beauty salon. Dollie was physically fit and slender with thick salt-and-pepper hair crowning her head like a smoothly coifed cap. Preacher Paul had said one was married, the other divorced. I didn't know which was which.

Hugo barked. The women jumped, Elise's right hand flying to cover her mouth, and Dollie jerking backwards. Guilt was written all over their faces. They might have been caught with their hands in the cookie jar.

CHAPTER 8

"Lucas has a good sense of humor," said Paul. We were weeding the garden. Dr. Wallaberra attacked the weeds with his hoe. We were up way before breakfast. Already late spring, the days were growing hot. Good idea to get the outdoor work done early, he suggested.

"So do you," I said, referring to the jokes he made of next to nothing. Just now he had struck an analogy between weeding his own patch compared to his ancestors hoeing cotton for the *Massa*. He devised a joke from the big difference—working one's own property versus slave labor. I didn't get it.

The son of a Kansas City medical doctor, Paul was educated at the University of Missouri where he took his master's in philosophy and a doctorate in theology. He knew nothing of slavery, he said, beyond the history books. No stories had been passed down from his ancestors. He didn't know much about gardening, either. If I hadn't stopped him, he would have chopped off the budding okra plants along with the weeds. A recent widower, he had left the Midwest for a new climate and clientele, he said.

"I wanted to work with the indigent and disadvantaged, but not in the inner city," he said. He mentioned the poor Mexicans in this rural area. Across the state line and up north in New Mexico, the people of Mexican descent claimed a four-hundred-year residency. By contrast, much of lower Arizona, like Southern California, was populated with recent immigrants—true Mexicans, for many of them had not yet sought American citizenship.

Most of these people didn't speak English. So what was the point of advertising our revival services in the printed form, I asked.

"I speak Spanish," Paul said. "I'll interpret if we get any of those people."

Dr. Wallaberra's surname was a pseudonym he had taken while enrolled in an African-American studies course. He too was new to this region.

"So that's why you guys are sending me to Nogales with another batch of flyers and posters," I said, returning to his earlier comment. "You want to attract the Spanish-speaking Mexicans to your services and you'll do the translating, eh?"

"Sure. Why not?"

When he asked me if I'd picked up any clues to the perpetrators, I reminded him of the kid painting graffiti on school busses. "The sheriff hasn't called with any news, not about the kid and not about the thefts."

"I'd like for you to call the people whose things were stolen, Oliver. None of them have been back to church. Me thinks they're highly disgruntled."

Disgruntled? Yeah, I'd think so, especially with no good news reported by either the sheriff or the pastor. I promised to place calls; marketing, hump. I could do double duty, though. Proselytize, tell them they were missed, and simultaneously ask whether their insurance had reimbursed them for their losses.

Another thing I could do—go meet with the villa manager. Since a few villas in the retirement community had also been robbed, it was possible the home owners' association, with or without the development's manager, might know something. Somebody besides me must have been harassing the sheriff to get off his duff and solve these petty crimes.

Later I left Paul and Lucas to linger over their breakfast coffee and plot their preaching strategies. In the dog run that Paul had invited me to construct, Hugo romped and played, barking at butterflies and generally feeling his youthful oats. A roadrunner dashed by. A Gila monster slithered beneath the long flat flowering runners of the cactus Paul identified as Devil's fingers. A pair of quail coo-cooed beyond the garden, also fenced by yours truly.

Packing posters and flyers into my saddlebags, I hopped aboard and took off. This trip promised more adventure, as I had yet to cross the border at Nogales. Another country awaited.

My bike quit on me a dozen miles beyond Tubac. That was strange. I could have sworn I'd filled up the day before. Was there a leak in the gas tank?

Paranoid, I imagined somebody purposely siphoning off the gas. Who knew, besides the brothers, that I was on a mission to Mexico? Then I remembered. Elise and Dollie, either or both, could have overheard us talking when we went into the church to get the ads. The women were arguing at the time over some petty thing; who would teach which class. Yeah, that's what it was. Elise wanted the teens, not the middle-schoolers. Was Dollie's resistance genuine or merely a matter of principle? If Elise was actually listening to our conversation, she could have told Fess about my trip. Meaning Fess could have done the dirty deed, hoping to leave me stranded in the desert. Like the South Tucson punks who attacked me, was Fess issuing a warning—for me to back off?

What to do? I could thumb a ride into Nogales, U.S. of A. But what would become of my cycle? Couldn't leave it beside the highway. Shove it off the road, camouflage it with brush, maybe. Yeah, sure, my hands would be pincushions from hacking away at the prickly plants.

While pondering options, I stepped behind a Palo Verde tree to take a leak. Traffic along the four-lane divided highway rumbled by. Zipping up, I returned to my Harley-Davidson, shiny with chrome. I patted her, thinking I wasn't a very good steward. She was thirsty and I'd failed to provide sustenance. Silly metaphor. This religious stuff was getting to me.

Just then a semi-trailer truck pulled up, the cross-country hauler down shifting and mashing hard to brake the big rig. Ah, salvation. Except I still didn't know what to do with my motorcycle. The middle-height trucker wearing jeans and a thin plaid cotton shirt hopped out. Grinning, the tanned guy in the horn-rimmed glasses said his CB handle was *Gangly Guy*. A misnomer, that. Although slender and physically fit, he fell far short of gangly.

He stuck out a hand to shake mine. "Name's Brad Gifford," he said, openly and with the innocent trust of the neophyte who hasn't been in the business long. "Appears you could use some help."

It was then I noticed his Wyoming license plate. I introduced myself, thinking that home had come to me. He said he was his own boss, the trucking firm, with a single truck, belonged to him. Together we hauled the cycle over to the rear of the truck. He opened the back doors and pulled out a loading ramp. The trailer rig stood empty. With a heave and a shove and a few deep breaths we finished the job. I wouldn't have to abandon my bike after all.

"What's her name?" Brad asked as we pulled out and got underway.

"Whose?"

"Your bike." He tenderly patted the top of the dashboard. "This here's Polly Pew." Hah, more "P" female names.

We spoke of the weather: hotter than hot already in Arizona, cool in Wyoming this time of year.

Not that Gillette with all that blowing sand stayed cool in the summer. The nearby mountains with Devil's Tower off to the north offered a bit of escape when you could get out of town for some good fishing; hunting in the fall, skiing in the winter.

I asked Brad what he'd heard about drug smuggling out of Mexico. Interstate 19 was known as *drug alley*. He shared facts and figures, most of which I already knew from reading back issues of the newspapers at the Green Valley library.

"Drugs, illegal immigration, both give the border guards plenty to keep them busy. They can't be everywhere. Take Douglas, down on the border," Brad said, while downshifting and navigating a turn on a busy intersection in Nogales on the States' side. "I hear there are 550 agents stationed in that town alone. When the drug smugglers get scared off in Douglas, they spread out along the border. Same with here in Nogales. Can't watch every square inch."

We reached the border crossing and Brad pulled up in line. Looked like we could be waiting awhile. When I asked him which drugs were popular down here, he said just about everything, with cocaine, marijuana and heroin the first runners. I thought methamphetamine, sometimes referred to as crank, could be a runner-up, as it is in Wyoming. We talked about the small towns of our state—Wheatland, Cody, Powell, and elsewhere—where meth labs had been located and destroyed.

The line was moving. Soon we would reach the border crossing.

People running drug operations between Mexico and the States had used every ruse imaginable, Brad said, confirming what I'd read. Small-time operators smuggled on their persons. Others in cars and trucks often stuck the drugs up in the undercarriage or inside the doors. I wondered whether he had ever been suspected. He grinned and said Sure, every regular trucker passing this way was. That's why the inspection of trucks was so extensive and time consuming.

Brad said that years ago most of the illicit drugs coming into the country came through south Florida, where Colombian drug lords imported tons of cocaine. Since then the drug lines had moved rapidly westward, to Juarez across from El Paso, to Tijuana, south of San Diego, and to Nogales, over the border from Nogales. Confusing at first; made sense after you'd been down here.

"I don't know about now," Brad said, "but at one time it was estimated that as much as seventy percent of all illegal drugs were coming into America through Mexico. You can only guess how much of that is traveling the Nogales-to-Tucson corridor."

I grew quiet and pensive. I was thinking, as I had before, that drug smuggling was right up Malcolm's alley. Except I couldn't see him as one small cog in a big-time operation. He was strictly small time. Or had been, up in Wyoming. Come to think of it, he could have joined a gang down here and drawn pretty Patsy into the business.

No trouble passing over the border. Brad was a familiar figure and he was always clean, he said.

He invited me to accompany him on his rounds to pick up loads from several Mexican-based American companies to haul back up north. Sounded interesting. I was on no particular schedule. The distribution of advertising material could wait. I was eager to play Tonto to Brad's Lone Ranger. Besides, I might be allowed to distribute flyers to employees of these American companies Brad had mentioned. Or, perhaps not. Solicitors could be prohibited from hawking our wares. My product was God, an intangible service commodity, I concluded with cold-blooded business-oriented logic.

On the Mexican side we drove past blocks and blocks of *barrios,* slums. Brad said how different things were over here. Amazing, travel no more than a mile or two and we could tell the difference: trash and litter fluttering in the breeze, lining the roadsides; live chickens and goats pecking and munching their way across dirt yards; poorly dressed, hangdog types meandering along, head down, herding more goats, or merely studying their shoes as they shuffled. Windows rolled down, we could smell the difference, too—moldy garbage, unwashed bodies. Through the city proper it wasn't so bad. As in all cities, people crowded the sidewalks, rushing along, waiting impatiently for stoplights to turn green. Like their American counterparts, the affluent young adults carried cellphones at the ear and pagers clipped to the belt. They carted thin attaché cases or laptop computers. Obviously this Mexican city wasn't comprised of poor people alone.

We made stops at Stanley Leather Products and Conway Computers. I was right the first time. *No solicitors*, a prominently displayed sign at the front doors read, in English and also in Spanish.

Then we stopped at a Mexican-owned tile manufactory—their word down here for manufacturing firms. Brad asked for and got permission for us to tour the plant. Old machinery, what there was of it, with lots of manual labor apparent. The sweat-soaked, bare-chested laborers working outdoors hauled the red sand into wheelbarrows and on to the processing sheds.

Their low wages suggested to me they could be swayed by temptation. Get into the smuggling game, slip over the border to rob the affluent senior citizens in Green Valley; repeat their successes by tackling church members.

Indoors the women sat at rough wooden tables meticulously painting the finished tiles with small brushes and careful strokes to produce the beautiful designs. Actually, I couldn't see any of these hard-working people robbing us.

This plant also differed from the American manufacturers in that my flyers were welcome. So were my posters, which I mounted on lobby and restroom bulletin boards. I couldn't read them, for Dr. Wallaberra had cleverly provided me with two stacks, one written in the Spanish language.

Brad translated for me: *Ven a Jesus,* "Come to Jesus," and *Jesus te ama!* " Jesus loves you."

Who could guess whether any of these ads would garner customers for Brother John's enlightening (and comforting?) sermons. I couldn't imagine that any of Nogales' poor folk would be motivated to attend. I could be wrong, though. Transportation wasn't much of a problem as Greyhound regularly traveled between Mexico and the States, and our church was no more than a half-mile off Interstate 19.

At a fine Mexican restaurant, I insisted on picking up the tab. About to order my standard burrito and tacos, Brad recommended we start with quesadillas followed by chili relleno with steak. We drank *cerveza,* beer.

"You don't want to drink the water down here," Brad said, grinning. "Not if you want to avoid Montezuma's Revenge." I knew what he meant.

I was from Gillette in the northeastern sector of Wyoming and Brad heralded from the capital city, Cheyenne, down in the southeast. He had married into a Big Clan, he said, using an emphasis that sounded like capital letters. "An old frontier family," he explained, "descendants of Rose DuMaurier and Essie Deighton."

What Wyomingite hadn't heard of them? "You're related to Wyoming's secretary of state? That little short lady in the daisy-decorated straw hat?"

"One and the same. A third-cousin-in-law, something like that."

We had many stories to share from our common mountain-west ancestral history. The time flew and Brad said he must get hopping. Me too, I said.

We stopped at a gas station on the American side to fill up both vehicles, his Polly Pew and my Penny.

Yeah, Gifford had talked me into it. He said that bikes, like ships, cars and trucks, all went by the pronoun *She*. I had to pick a female handle. Avoiding *Patsy* like a plague (Megan, too; she might be offended), I chose *Penny*. She was my in-between girlfriend, about whom I still had pleasant memories. We had parted amicably without rancor because, we soon discovered, we had little in common.

Busy with refueling, Brad was unaware of the red Jaguar pulling up at the pump opposite. I nearly missed it, too, what with thinking sweet thoughts about Penny.

When the Jaguar pulled out, spinning gravel, I glanced up. That was when I caught sight of Fess Goodman, heading for Mexico. Nuts. Too late to trail him, try for surveillance. Maybe catch him in the act of stuffing that fancy car with drugs to smuggle back here to the states. Hitting eighty, ninety, perhaps a hundred, the Jaguar quickly disappeared. I turned back and finally caught up to Brad Gifford. He spotted me in his side mirror and motioned.

When he turned off at Rio Rico, I followed, curious. "How about a half game of golf?" Brad asked, grinning.

Couldn't pass that up. Before the sun started falling behind the western mountains we finished nine holes. We were well-matched, both usually playing in the mid-eighties. This time he pulled a forty-five for nine holes and me a forty-four. Can't beat golf for a good time.

I vowed to play more often, possibly with the Derry brothers and Derek or Megan. Not smiling, so I knew he wasn't joking, Brad said he hoped I wouldn't get caught up in the drug trade as an innocent bystander. We said goodbye.

Two things I missed, a buddy and a girlfriend. The afternoon spent with Brad made me realize I hadn't had a compatible chum, a confidante, since leaving Wyoming. That good buddy was my brother, the guy I'd stopped speaking to weeks before he died. The Derry brothers wouldn't do, they were too young and too busy with the café. Brother John was too old, more a father image than a close friend. Paul Wallaberra was close to my age, but he too was occupied with all the church doings.

As for a lady friend, I needed to put to rest this Patsy business before I could move on. Had I a buddy to bounce ideas off, he might suggest I was pining away for Patsy or that in my secret heart I wanted to get back together. Finding her was no abstract thing. What I really wanted, perhaps, was to pick up where we left off before my brother took her away from me? Good question.

On the other hand, maybe I wanted to see her pay for her sins. One thing was sure. I was after Malcolm Barr, who'd stolen her heart.

CHAPTER 9

W as I selfish? Reading and collecting news about the drug game, going after Malcolm, thinking he'd lead me to Patsy; Patsy, a ghost out of my troubled past. I should be focusing on the church, the upcoming revival, and practicing the piano. If I was after criminal activities, I could concentrate on the real crimes. Petty they might be, but the thefts from the church and parking lot, along with the internal friction, was what Dr. Wallaberra had called on Lucas for. Me, too, as Brother John's assistant. Pursuing my own nebulous quest was self-ish. Conclusion: better settle down for now and tend to church and revival.

The sheriff had no news and acted irritated that I'd put him on the spot. I reminded him of the kid spraying graffiti at the school and asked if he'd been arrested. Truman didn't know what I was talking about. His deputy had said nothing. So, okay, he'd get on it, call the school, see what the principal said.

I called each of the parishioners who'd had goods stolen, inviting their confidences, telling them we missed them and that the good brothers were praying for them. To a fault, they were disgusted. The sheriff had never visited them, the pastor had never mentioned their losses. What was the point of church, if nobody cared. I said I was working on the thefts, asking around.

"Snooping?" somebody said.

"Oh, you mean prying," was how another person defined my interest.

Heaving a sigh of frustration, I called my mom, next, apologizing for the small checks I'd been sending. Dismissing the amounts but not the thought supporting my gifts, she quickly changed the subject. I wasn't fooled. She was afraid I'd ask about Hernandez; was he working regularly, taking care of her. She asked after Hugo and my boss.

"I'm so proud of you, Oliver. I'm sure Brother John likes your last name."

I hadn't thought of that. We could have been capitalizing on my *Temple* handle. Or maybe not. The connotation is that of Jews and Mormons, not us. Better stick with *church*. The Community Church in Christ wasn't half bad, though I pondered the meaning of the "in" preposition. In the heart of Jesus?

Elise Goodman was down with a cold. "Too bad for her, but nice for us," said Paul laconically. "Now you can man the piano." What he meant was, her piano playing was poor, really bad.

Dr. Wallaberra had no organ and no cushioned pews as yet. He was counting on hefty contributions and tithe pledges in the collection plates for those. And for fixing the leaky roof. I could do the repairs but enough shingles to do the job right takes money. So does a proper salary. For me.

Again I retrieved and practiced songs I could use for preludes and interludes. The hymnbook would be my Bible. I especially liked the oldies, such as *Pentecostal Power* and *The Lily of the Valley*, with an English melody; also the spirituals, *Swing Low, Sweet Chariot; Lord, I Want to be a Christian,* and *Were You There when They Crucified My Lord?* Dr. Wallaberra said he liked, *It's So Sweet to Trust in Jesus,* so I added that one to my repertoire.

Mrs. Martinez stood at my side, hymnbook in hand. I would accompany her solos. She favored the 1923 version of *Holy, Holy, Holy,* words by Reginald Heber, composition by John B. Dykes. After rehearsing we decided to save this one for the choir, as Harold Hart Todd had arranged a choir piece in six parts.

Dollie's singing voice was similar in range, timber, and quality to Mickey Mangun's out of Alexandria, Virginia. I had heard her solo with the Pentacostal Messiah Singers. I asked her if she could do *He was Faithful unto Me*; or the one that said something about lifting up Holy hands in the presence of the Lord.

Dollie laughed, throwing back her head and delivering a loud guffaw. "I'll bet you like that chanting part at the end. The repetition of *We praise you,*

we lift you up, we magnify, we glorify, we adore you,
and a great big *Hallelujah* to finish off that chorus."

I grinned. "You bet. If that one doesn't stir up emotions, I don't know what will. You could do it, I'm sure you could."

She didn't have the music and neither did I. Disappointing, that.

With Dollie's help I agreed to audition and put together a choir. She had plenty of ideas. Sweet and cooperative without the cantankerous Elise to set her teeth on edge, she recommended a number of local singers.

"They can stay on key, at least," she said ruefully.

Dr. Wallaberra had his own contacts in Tucson. Soon we had assembled a fine group of mixed color rehearsing soul and gospel songs in lusty fashion.

Dollie—divorced, she had told me—commandeered a flock of women to contribute and arrange flowers from their lush gardens. She also organized the volunteers. We needed the phones manned, as calls were coming in now by the dozens. Our advertising was paying off? I'd believe that only when I saw the crowds pouring in, preferably with stuffed wallets and pocketbooks. The brothers were behind in paying my wages.

The two groups I didn't expect to see well represented were the seniors from Green Valley and the craftsy hippies from the hills. If the pecan orchard and copper mine workers didn't show, I'd bet a buck their women folk would. That left the Mexicans. Would our Spanish-language flyers draw them into the fold? We knew that a lot of Mexicans and young people worked in Green Valley. The seniors might be retired, into games, sports, crafts, and adult education classes, but somebody had to take care of them. For a population that hovered around twenty thousand, that adds up to a lot of store clerks and service people to man the decks.

No magical acts of healing were billed, no leaping and jumping or speaking in tongues. The message advertised was simple and clear: Believe; Come to Christ and be comforted; Repent and ask that your sins be forgiven. Brother John would feature some standard but everlastingly proven themes in his revivalist sermons. Love thy neighbor as thyself. Honor, respect, and live your daily lives in accordance with the Ten Commandments. No promises of fame and fortune if you did, nor threats of hellfire and damnation if you didn't. Come unto the Lord and Believe. Have faith. The brothers didn't even suggest that you could be saved by kneeling before the altar in supplication.

Apparently the only proposition was that you might feel better. Sounded like good psychology. Get moved by all that lively singing, and the preaching and praying if dramatic and kept short, could be palatable.

Okay, so I would hang around awhile longer; see what happened. Collect my wages and then decide what to do next.

The first night, to my mind, was next to disaster. Murphy's Law applied: everything that could go wrong surely did.

As seven o'clock, Zero Hour, approached, only a small number were trickling in, taking seats in the back and around the edges. Latecomers could only find seats by climbing over legs or marching up the aisle to sit in front.

Megan, Derek, and the Derrys didn't show, as they were swamped with diners, they told us by cellphone. Some of their customers could be among our stragglers, having decided to sample the Cat Castle's cuisine on their way to the revival.

Two choir ladies complained their robes didn't fit; one was too large, the other too small. Elise, who had crawled out of her bed still coughing and blowing and spewing her cold germs all over, told them to exchange robes. A trio of others complained it was too hot for such garments. Another, a big clumsy bass, kicked over a vase of iris, sending flowers and water to cascade off the edge of the podium. The same oaf, in an attempt to right himself, bumped into the lectern to be used as a pulpit, scattering Brother John's notecards and sending the pile to the floor.

Meanwhile at the piano I was thumping out *All Hail the Power of Jesus' Name,* followed by *When They Ring the Golden Bells for You and Me.* The old piano could use some tuning. The choir took their places. Brother John gathered and reassembled his notecards. Elise and Dollie bumped heads, and egos, as they vied for position and the best method to aright and reclaim the vase of iris.

More people walked in, hesitated, and finally found seats. We hadn't thought of enlisting some of the men to serve as ushers. We would before the second night rolled around. I wondered why Dr. Wallaberra didn't have people already designated as deacons, or whatever the title of reliable assistants. The church was too new as yet, I surmised.

Outdoors Hugo barked loudly in his dog run. Beyond puppy age (though still small), he no longer yapped.

This was like a show, a performance, a religious extravaganza. Naively, I hadn't realized how much there would be to do, how many tasks large and small went into this thing. I was learning. We all were.

His prior experience, Brother John later reported, was with established churches, where he merely walked on stage as the visiting minister. "Celebrity," I muttered. He scowled at my irreverence

By the next night we had learned a few things. The men responsible for manning the collection plates doubled as ushers. They tried valiantly to herd the back-row types up front, to no avail. They encouraged people to move in, fill up the middles. No soap. Edge people prefer edges, back people resist moving forward. No time to analyze this human propensity other than to muse that it must have something to do with basic personality or perhaps claustrophobia.

I was too busy at the piano. A new book refused to stay open. I needed a clothespin or a page turner. Megan hopped to the ready.

This second night of the revival Megan and Derek had begged off working at the cafe They wanted to see what all the hoopla was about. That's what Derek called my massive ad campaign that included radio spots and news articles that I'd gotten placed with the Green Valley media, both of which covered southern Arizona.

That first night the Cat Castle had enjoyed after-service visitors as well as pre-service diners. So the Derrys and Dolans were privy to secondhand news. While people streamed in that second night and between turning pages, Megan whispered that the revival was gaining interest.

"They really liked the music, Oliver, both your piano playing and Dollie's solos. Others among our diners raved about the choir."

Music to my soul. Mom would be proud.

Megan didn't mention reactions to Brother John's first sermon and I didn't think to ask. At the time I had noticed little beyond one of the scriptures he used. Later that night I searched Second Corinthians and found it in Chapter four, verses eight and nine: *We are troubled on every side, yet not distressed. We are perplexed, but not in despair; Persecuted, but not forsaken; Cast down, but not destroyed.* Hmm, that seemed rather a dismal text. Not remembering how Brother John elaborated, I vowed to pay closer attention after that.

The second night was better, though still not perfect. Some people shouted Amen inappropriately, startling Brother John. Discombobulated, he again lost his notes.

No matter. He was good with ad libbing.

When a whole family of folk rose from their seats to march up the aisle and kneel before the altar, both Lucas and Paul nearly lost their cool. "Praise the Lord!" Brother John shouted, collecting his wits. "All those who want to give their lives to Jesus, please come forward."

Simultaneously the conductor jumped to his feet and raised his arms. At his nod to me, I flipped to a new page in the songbook. Following my short and snappy prelude, the choir burst forth with a lively rendition of *His Eye is on the Sparrow.* They leaped up to stand and sway with the beat while glorifying the Lord with their words: *I sing because I'm happy, I sing because I'm free*; *I know He watches over me.* Talk about improvising.

At first hesitant, soon a whole parade of people streamed up the aisle. Brother John relinquished his notes about loving kindness and nurturing each other in God's name. Both preachers stepped to the edge of the podium.

A few kneelers lifted their heads, closed their eyes, and opened their mouths like baby birds awaiting worms. They anticipated wafers to the tongue?

Megan slowly turned pages, giving me time to give each hymn a quick eyeball. We both spotted a quiet, worshipful tune. Nodding to Megan, she held the page steady.

Not to be found wanting, knowing not what to do next, the two brothers stretched out their arms to lay hands on heads.

"Bless you, Sister."

"Praise the Lord, Brother."

Obviously satisfied, each kneeler in turn arose and left the altar to be replaced by others from the long line awaiting.

Yup, looked like we'd done it. My assessment was confirmed when the money started rolling in. People dug down deep. The collection plates over-flowed.

Unfortunately, before we could count it at the close of the service, somebody robbed us of the whole cache.

CHAPTER 10

"**O**hmigosh!" exclaimed Derek. "Who would steal from a church?"

Sweet innocent Megan sobbed, both small hands covering her face. Brother John was too sad to speak. Dr. Wallaberra was mad as a wet hen.

"I'm mad as a wet hen!" he said. He paced back and forth in the big room while we awaited the arrival of Sheriff Dick Truman.

Immediately following our discovery I had run outdoors. I was searching for Fess Goodman's red Jaguar. No such luck. If he were responsible, he was long gone. I had no other ideas and neither did the Dolans or the preachers.

Derek said he and Megan would keep their ears open. The culprit might happen by the café and succumb to bragging.

That gave me an idea. *Liquor's quicker*, they say, usually in reference to mellowing out a woman so a guy can get her in the sack. The ploy could also work for loosening lips. The Cat Castle served no booze, but the Cow Palace did. I planned to hang out in the bar side, nurse a couple a beers. Like Derek, I would keep my eyes peeled and my ears open.

Half the choir also quit. Their excuses lame, we figured they didn't want to be involved with a church that got robbed. Put another way, maybe some of them were; involved, that is, either singly or collectively responsible for the theft. Dr. Wallaberra reported this supposition to the sheriff.

Still later that night the preachers went into Tucson to scare up more choir members. Paul had contacts in an African-American church whose Tuesday night choir practice usually ran late. He was able to recruit several good gospel singers, who promised to show up early the next evening for practice.

Alone that night I put on my recording of Eva Cassidy singing the saddest version of *Autumn Leaves* I've ever heard. Made me feel like bawling, I missed Patsy so much. Withdrawing her photo from the back of my wallet, I stared at that lovely face. Showing her picture around the Tucson bars might work.

We may have lost all the cash we'd taken in Tuesday night, but the theft worked to our advantage nevertheless. We got plenty of free publicity. The public, including nonchurch-goers, was incensed at the news reported from the Tucson television and radio stations and in newspapers from Tucson to Nogales. The rest of the week we were swamped.

People poured in, and so did their money. Whether from pity or proselytizing, what did it matter (to me)? Our coffers were running over.

Elise insisted that she was the designated piano player and the preachers gave in. She took over. Her well-worn music books lay flat, so Megan wasn't needed to turn pages any longer. With the strength of the choir, including the new voices from Tucson, plus the enthusiastic singing of the worshipers, I doubt that people noticed how many notes Mrs. Goodman missed. She made few mistakes. I assumed she had practiced her little heart out while home with her cold and out of the stream of church doings.

Megan traded off with her brothers, each of whom showed up for a single night apiece. The Cat Castle was humming with business, both before and after our services up the road. I dutifully attended services every night but I sat in the back, bent on running security. We had learned our lesson. The collection plate money was promptly stashed in the locked safe. Nevertheless, I continued to watch for suspicious activity. Which meant I didn't listen much. I do recall a scripture from Ephesians, Chapter two, verse ten: *We are his workmanship, created for good works in Christ.* When I shared that with mom, she agreed that I was doing good, sticking by the reverend. I didn't tell her I planned to apply for work over at the pecan orchard as soon as the revival was over.

Whether out of curiosity or a genuine desire to worship, the old-timers showed up; also a handful of artsy-craftsy hippy types. Whole families of Hispanics arrived, too, along with Looky-Lous from Tucson. Good turnout.

By the close of the week, with so many good hearts surrounding me, with the fine preaching, and so much outpouring of the Spirit (or whatever), I found myself praying too: that Sheriff Truman or his deputy Tom would catch the collection-plate thief; for mom and even her hubby, the shiftless Hernandez; and especially for Patsy. I prayed with all my heart that she had found the Good Life. I didn't want to finally locate her only to discover she was on drugs or into prostitution; or worse, dead.

No leads about the thief. The media and the fickle public soon turned to other news and pursuits. Having met the sheriff, I thought to trade on his good will, if any. I was eager to discover what progress his county office, or the Green Valley cops, might have made. The town was also in his jurisdiction, with the police legally responsible to him, although apparently nobody paid any attention to that. At any rate, Truman could have been privy to the insider's news and clues, if he'd bothered to ask. The earlier thefts, the ones that had brought Brother John and me down here, still hadn't been solved. Whatever the reason, Truman wasn't talking to me about Green Valley crime.

Sheriff Dick Truman, laconic, seemingly uninterested in what happened in the retirement community, shrugged his disdain. "A few rookie cops and some semi-retired old coots over there.

They don't know nuthin'," he said, his booted feet as usual propped atop the desk. "Me thinks the victims filed their insurance claims and forgot it. You know what they say, *The squeaky wheel gets the grease.* They don't squeak, then who cares." Another shrug.

I asked about drugs and whether he'd caught anybody dealing here abouts. He looked surprised. "I s'pect that goes on, too. Anyplace you know about where it don't?"

"What about around the Sahuarita High School?"

"That's the principal's and parents' responsibility, that's what I say."

He was what you'd call laid back. I wondered what it would take to shake up this guy. The frustration mounting, I turned to leave.

"You hear anything about the collection plate theft," he called after me. "You let me know, ya hear."

Early mornings I repaired the roof with the new shingles, sweat pouring from every pore like water over Niagara Falls. An exaggeration, but I longed for home and the comparatively cool climate of Wyoming. What I wouldn't give for an afternoon with fishing rod in hand and a cold mountain stream full of trout and bass.

Later I suggested to the Derrys that they needed a break. Mike and Matt readily agreed. They grabbed their fishing gear with a spare rod for me and the three of us took off for the mountains. At this time of year the Santa Cruz River, near the church, was running low, a mere trickle. In the Derrys' old red pickup that reminded me of my dad's, we headed east for a cool mountain stream.

Before the revival I had constructed a rather nice looking church spire atop the roof, if I do say so myself. Soon the shingling would be complete. Brother John spoke of leaving but he had no particular destination or plans, so we lingered. Dr. Wallaberra pleaded with us to stick around awhile. He had made arrangements with the vocational training center next door to rent their facilities on Sunday mornings. With all those classrooms, each equipped with chairs and chalkboard, the adjacent building made a nice Sunday school center. Volunteers, including Elise and Dollie, lined up to teach classes.

Paul assigned Lucas the early morning worship service with all the attending tasks and responsibilities. Young couples sought his premarital counseling and middle-marrieds in trouble sat for his advice. Brother John was happy as a laughing hyena. In short, Paul kept Lucas and me plenty busy.

The Cat Castle prospered. Prevailing upon me to help brainstorm, the Derrys and Dolans produced a cat motif on the walls, tables and menus. Fearful they might offend cat haters, Megan suggested setting off a section of the room to be called *The Dog House*, but nothing came of that idea.

In my free time I haunted every bar throughout the region. I was listening for news of Patsy; and, incidentally, watching for a braggart with loose lips and looser wallet. No luck.

On Penny, my bike, I continued exploring. Curious about the battling dowagers, I found where both lived; Dollie Martinez in a small Green Valley villa, Elise Goodman in a mansion-size house in the exclusive golf club development north of Tubac. What was with Elise? She had everything: husband, money, clothes, jewels, and a luxurious life style. Why must she pick on her poor cousin? For that matter, what motivated Dollie to respond in kind?

I didn't sneak about. It wasn't an undercover job of surveillance I was doing on the two ladies, each of whom was nice enough when separated. On Penny I geared down as I passed the Goodman residence the second time. Elise sat out front on the shaded veranda, fanning herself and sipping a mint julep, maybe an iced tea. I waved. She waved back, immediately standing to grab glass and glossy magazine to quickly disappear through her front door. What was that all about? I didn't propose to enter her inner sanctum.

Actually, I was hoping to spot her son's red Jaguar. He was still my number one suspect for the church thefts—prior and recent. No sign of Fess Goodman in any of the bars. Not at the Sahuarita Junction tavern, nor in Green Valley or in Tubac. He had moved his operations, if any, to Tucson? I should return to the city. Lot of territory to cover up there but I wasn't ranging far from the church these days. Not with all my early-morning construction jobs, the Derrys and Dolans to visit, and Hugo to tend and play with. Was I avoiding the neighborhood where I'd been warned off? You bet.

Dollie's definition of hospitality was an improvement over her rich cousin's. Spying me idling at curbside, she motioned for me to join her. Gratefully I accepted a frosty glass of lemonade and we settled down on the porch.

"Let me escort you around," she said, as if her two rooms and walled patio constituted a show-place. The private cemented patio—with a Palo Verde tree in the corner and roses blooming along the narrow flowerbeds edging the chest-high wall—nicely extended her living space. An awning over a table in the center and a chaise lawn chair beneath the tiled roof on the porch completed this delightful picture of outdoor living space. In a protected corner of the porch sat an easel, stool, and a side table full of paints, brushes, and palette. Nice hobby for this little lady, I mused, praising her half-finished canvas depicting the desert floor with various cacti in the foreground and mountains rising in the background.

Indoors, one large room decorated in earth and sand colors combined living, kitchen, and eating areas. Dollie then showed off her large, airy bedroom with big picture window looking onto the patio. The decorative aqua and pink bed coverlet with a heap of matching pillows appeared new. So did the curtains. Through the half-open closet I spotted a fur jacket, a set of golf clubs, and tennis rackets. These too looked expensive.

All of which was a puzzle. If Dollie was as poor as she made out to be, how could she afford such luxuries? Pretty costly hobbies—painting, golf, and tennis; plus the fine furniture and decorations, topped by the fur jacket.

What was Dollie's source of income? Not old enough for Social Security, she didn't hold a job, either. Was Martinez, her ex-husband and whatever else he was, paying her alimony? I couldn't think what questions to ask that wouldn't sound rudely inquisitive.

I was eager to leave, get away to ponder these questions and return to the church to interrogate Paul. The pastor should have been privy to personal information about his soloist, the helpful woman so eager to volunteer her services, from singing to cleaning, from teaching children in the Sunday school to selecting flowers from her garden.

Before I could decently excuse myself, Dollie suggested a tour of the area. All alike, built in sets of four adjoining dwellings per section, the villas differed widely in patio decorations and the flora chosen to grow within the sheltered and walled patios with their small garden plots. Each of the common grounds, as Dollie referred to the sandy areas just beyond each villa section, was beautifully landscaped with varying cacti, many old tall trees, and a few green lawns. Everything was exquisitely maintained. By a paid staff of mostly Mexican laborers, Dollie said. The funds for this service along with the replacement of roofs and hot water tanks, plus maintenance of the swimming pools, came from their monthly dues. It seemed to me that despite the villas' small size, the residents got quite a lot of amenities.

A large development, the villas stretched for several blocks along both sides of La Canada, a main thoroughfare running parallel to Interstate-19. Moreover, the villa district lay within walking distance of banks, pharmacies, medical offices, at least one church, and a large outdoor shopping mall.

"Serving the villas are a half-dozen neighborhood swimming pools," Dollie said, suggesting further that we return to her place to change into swimsuits. Martinez had left his, she said, smiling sweetly.

On such a hot afternoon I couldn't resist. The azure pool, water shimmering in the heat, invited me like a desert oasis beckons to and tempts a man crawling across the desert and dying of thirst beneath the blazing sun.

Also walled and landscaped, a lanai at one end of the pool offered a shady respite from the sun. Comfortable chaise lounges mingled with a couple of card tables. Several residents wearing swimsuits and sunshades rested and read or chatted. A foursome seated around a card table played bridge. I got in a couple of dozen laps before leaving.

Dollie hated to see me go. She said her golf game wasn't that hot, but perhaps we could play some time. Elise was once her regular partner. "Until she got mad at me."

"Why was that?" I asked cautiously, sounding, I hoped, merely mildly interested. I wanted to grab her and pump her, try to get the gossip out of her like water from a well.

"When you solve that puzzle, let me know."

Back on Penny and heading for home—the RV and the church and Hugo—I studied my suppositions. Instead of getting answers, I was racking up more questions.

I decided to head for the Cat Castle soon. I'd like some input from the Derrys and Megan and Derek.

CHAPTER 11

My mind working overtime on the puzzle of the cousins while feeding Hugo, I didn't pay much attention to the little guy. Sadly neglected lately, he must have sensed my preoccupation. He resumed his puppy habit of yapping. Not satisfied with my petting, he nuzzled my leg. Half his supper remained untouched.

As the shadows of early evening stretched long and lazily across the sandy yard in front of the RV, I asked him what he wanted. Yap, yap, he said. Retrieving my thin blue windbreaker, I slipped it on and connected the zipper at the bottom. Jumping up and down, Hugo went into a frenzy.

Of course. He needed comfort and reassurance, just as Dollie must. Whatever had happened to tick off Elise, she was no longer *there* for her once beloved cousin. I pondered anew this mini puzzle. Brother John might know what to do. His counseling heretofore limited to marriages, upcoming and long standing, he could branch out. He could listen to, if not advise, the cousins, whichever would sit still for his admonitions and prayers.

Walking down the lane to the river with Hugo warmly ensconced against my chest, I decided to organize the clues. If Dollie had acquired the golf clubs and tennis rackets specifically to play with Elise, the time sequence suggested this was before they had their falling out and before Brother John and I arrived.

Down by the river I let Hugo out. He romped and ran, dashing back to my side every few moments, as if to ensure I wouldn't leave him. Feeling like a kid out on recess, I sat down on the sandy bank to remove sneakers and socks. I waded in, tickled at the cool mud oozing between my toes.

Brother John no longer stayed in the RV. He was old enough to qualify for residency in Green Valley so he rented a house and Paul moved in with him. However, I saw plenty of both preachers at the church during the day. They'd said earlier that they were going into Tucson to shop at the mall, eat dinner, and catch a movie. I declined their invitation in favor of the Cat Castle. I was after input. Not about Patsy and Malcolm. My search for them and whatever they were doing remained my secret. Megan in particular was interested in the church gossip. She said it beat the TV soaps. The Dolans and Derrys had all met the battling dowagers and I was keeping them posted about the ladies' ongoing quarrels.

At the café a waitress failed to show or even call in with an excuse. Once again I stood in to serve as substitute waiter. By now I was familiar with the menu, the establishment, and the routine. We were far too busy to sit and chat.

Discarded were various menu gimmicks, among them *Cat Food—Fish and Foul;* also *Big Cat, Lion Food—Steaks and Prime Rib.* Instead, they had opted for standard items plus the Chef's Special— Megan's daily dishes, featured Monday through Friday and a traditional Sunday specialty. The latter was my pot roast recipe and Friday was another of mine, mom's rather—Sicilian Feast. I told mom, to make her proud. She had little enough joy in her life. She could just as well have been married to *Andy Capp*, Hernandez spent so much time on the couch.

When I called my mom to tell her about the Cat Castle recipes, she had news of her own. Betty Ortiz and her daughter had returned to Mexico, mom said. Their café a mess, Betty couldn't afford the repairs. She had no insurance. After a series of jobs including waitressing and house cleaning, she decided to pack it in. With a loving family across the border awaiting her return, perhaps she would be okay. In a postcard to my mom, Betty said she was working at the American Conway Corporation. Tina had settled down, too. Back with her cousins, she was having fun acting like the kid she still was.

Up at 4:30 the next morning, I was back on the roof with the shingling. When I had checked with the orchard people they said they weren't hiring right now. I had yet to visit the mine office. Time enough later to decide what to do.   I decided to renew my survey of Tucson. Maybe I'd luck out next time and get a lead on Patsy Parsons, if not Malcolm Barr. This time I carried her photo. I had decided on a new approach. Shove Barr to the back burner. If anybody had seen Patsy, surely they would remember the luscious blonde.

Maybe we would get back together, see the sights as a couple.

Dream on. What had happened to my desire for vengeance? Too big a dose of religion from the revival week? Forgive and forget? Not bloody likely. But somebody had to pay for Arlo's death. My brother didn't get into the drug scene all on his lonesome. Somebody was responsible for baptizing him.

On my motorcycle I passed El Con Mall and then Randolph golf course. Would Patsy learn the game so we could play together? Hah! On Wilmot I turned north, crossed Speedway Boulevard, and continued on to Tanque Verde Road and Sabino Canyon. Beautiful rural area right within the city limits.

Having done that, I backtracked to hit the bars along Miracle Mile, followed by checking at restaurants and saloons up and down Oracle Road, which switches to Sixth in the center of town to continue on into South Tucson.

Might as well forget every street and byway, as nobody admitted to having seen Patsy. Women shook their heads No. Some men leered, a few making lewd remarks until looking into my face and eyes; serious, somber, eyes sparking with anger and threats if they didn't shut up.

Another night, after recalling that Patsy had once worked as a motel maid, I tried those too; also hitting the big fancy downtown hotels and the resorts out in the northeast quadrant. Then it occurred to me she might have hit bottom. Working alone or with Malcolm pimping, she could have gone into prostitution. If she was a fancy call girl pulling down big bucks, the hotels would be a place to look. Either way, hooker or maid, somebody should have seen her.

No Patsy. By now she could be in Phoenix or Los Angeles.

Hanging out in all those saloons and cafes with the crowds, I picked up something. A virus, probably. I wasn't feeling well. Back home in the RV I stretched out in the back on my bed. With the temperature in the nineties I should have been hot, ready for the air conditioner. Instead I was freezing. My eyes bleary, I nevertheless fed Hugo and caught up on the bookkeeping.

Concerned, Brother John suggested I needed a break, some time off. "You've been working seven-day weeks for over a month, Oliver."

Yeah, right. He didn't know about the double life I'd been leading, heading for Tucson in late afternoon, and returning home well after midnight. Should I confess? No, of course not. Both preachers would be appalled. Right off the bat they would commence their preaching at me and praying over me.

The next day I felt better. Down at the Cat Castle in the middle of a quiet Sunday afternoon, Megan had news. Clapping her hands and squealing, she said she was pregnant. Derek grinned shyly, his smile rather like the *Mona Lisa*'s, I thought. Suffering from morning sickness, Megan had quit the kitchen until the evening shift. Derek had taken over for breakfast and lunch as the chef with Mike manning the griddle.

Up to now all four of them had been living together in a trailer out back. The mobile home was large enough for them, but a child demanded permanence. Or the Dolans thought it did. Together the Derrys and Dolans had bought an adjacent acre and their new home was now under construction. The property was well shaded, with cottonwoods, Palo Verde, and weeping willow. They would all continue living together. They got along like peas in a pod.

"We'll have six bedrooms and four bathrooms. Plenty of room," Derek said. "For the uncles, too." The marrieds grinned at the singles.

Again feeling woozy, I figured I ought to leave. Whatever I had could be contagious. Before I could excuse myself, they wanted to talk clues, Matt said.

"Let's put our heads together. Maybe each of us has seen or heard something that taken alone made no particular impression at the time." Matt had one hand on the back of my chair, as if to restrain any sudden departure. He laid a stack of note cards on the table in front of us.

Mike fetched a pot of hot coffee. Derek poured a glass of milk for Megan and opened a small package of peanut butter crackers to set on a plate for her. The lovebirds held hands.

Sigh. I wished I had somebody besides Hugo to look after. I recalled Brother John's advice to the Dolans during their pre-wedding counseling session. All about loving your partner more than yourself, putting him or her first; open communications, talking and listening; trust, faithfulness; coordination and cooperation; understanding and appreciating differences while reveling in similarities. One piece of advice I particularly liked was to nurture and allow, not resist, the personal growth and ambitions of each other. All that made good sense—marital and psychological, if not theological.

It also made sense for me to forget Patsy, and especially Malcolm. Put all that behind me, like shooing away *Satan*, think of it as part of my personal history. Bury it. Commence my search for somebody else to love. Patsy and I never were all that compatible, come to think. Had we been, would she have deserted me for Arlo?

By then the quartet around me had filled at least two cards apiece. "What do you have to contribute, Oliver?" Megan asked gently, smiling between tiny nibbles on a cracker. I knew she meant to draw me back from woolgathering, but she was too nice to suggest I was sitting amidst them as my solitary self.

"Let me see what you've got," I said, thumbing through the cards.

Matt reached for a blank three-by-five and sat poised with a black fine point pen by Pilot. "You talk, I'll record," Matt offered. He took each of the completed cards as I finished reading. "Let's add dates, if known."

Thus we lined up the cards chronologically. First came the earlier collection plate robberies, then the thefts of personal items, also at the church.

Mike left the table for the back room. "I keep old newspapers," he said upon returning. "Don't ask me why."

From culling those, we learned that the Green Valley thefts and the old lady knocked unconscious had happened before the Cat Castle was vandalized. Finally, the church was robbed again of contributions during revival week.

"Nothing since?" I asked, surprised and stymied. A fortnight had passed since then. "Makes no sense."

"The thieves moved on?" Derek suggested.

"Maybe they attended the revival and got religion," Megan sweetly proposed. Suddenly she pushed back her chair and ran out of the room, Derek fast on her heels.

"Her doctor says the vomiting should stop soon," Mike said, thereby explaining their quick departure.

I debated how much of anything to contribute. By the time the Dolans returned, chatting happily as if nothing unusual had happened, I'd decided to share a few things. Not much, just enough to satisfy them that I was a willing member of this amateur sleuthing team.

I showed my hand when visiting Dollie. Even that much sharing made me feel like a traitor. I wasn't sure why. Because I liked her and wanted to protect her? If she were the culprit, or one of several, she deserved reporting, though, so why the reluctance?

"Oh, that reminds me," Megan interrupted, after tut-tutting about my discoveries. She, too, rejected the notion of Dollie Martinez as thief, despite the golf clubs, tennis rackets and fur jacket in her closet. "If I felt better, I surely wouldn't have forgotten. Dollie's cousin, Elise—uh, Mrs. Goodman—left her wallet at the cash register after eating Sunday dinner here. I should have called her right away. Forgot. So sorry." Megan covered her face as if in remorse.

She arose to fetch the Goodman wallet from beneath the cashier counter.

"Let's have a look," I said, not at all disturbed at the notion of prying. I didn't like the woman. Elise was a pain in the rear.

Megan gasped, still clutching the fine-grained maroon leather wallet. "Oh, dear. Do you think we should?"

Disgust in his voice, Matt reminded his sister that she had already searched the thing. To find the owner's name, Megan objected, still resisting. "That's the only reason I opened it."

"Anybody ever hear of a *Mr.* Goodman?" I asked. "What if he's the perpetrator and that's how he finances their lifestyle—through robberies and fencing of the goods."

"Come on, Oliver. Don't be silly," Megan protested. "That's reaching, isn't it? Besides, whether either or both the Goodmans were stealing, that doesn't explain how the stolen goods got into Dollie Martinez' closet."

"A gift from Elise to Dollie?" Mike proposed.

We tossed that idea around awhile, like playing five-man basketball. Oops, amend that; a five-*person* team. At last realizing she was outnumbered, Megan slowly passed the wallet across the table toward me.

I opened the billfold, gingerly thumbing through the contents. What we found was the usual stuff: credit cards, driver's license, receipts, and a hefty stack of twenties, fifties, and hundreds; plus a medical card stating that Elise was a diabetic. We raised eyebrows at one another. None of us had known.

"No photos?" Megan eagerly asked, leaning forward now.

"Wait a minute." From inside a flat packet I extracted a thin plastic-covered envelope. On the one side was Elise with a man, Mr. Goodman we presumed. On the back side was the same man with two boys; not one, but two. The teenager on the left was clearly Festor Goodman, taken a few years earlier, obviously. The boy on the right could have been Fess's twin, they looked so much alike.

I passed around the plastic packet. "Who's this other kid?" I asked the table. "I thought Elise only had the one son."

Mike, Matt, and Derek shook their heads. They couldn't answer me.

Megan hardly needed to scrutinize the photo. She knew. "That's Dollie's son. The one completing his MBA." She glanced around the table at all of us. "Dollie and Donny, as she calls him, came in after lunch this past week. While I was alone on duty. She's clearly very proud of her son."

CHAPTER 12

Before we could ponder or try to interpret the physical likeness of the two second cousins, Elise's and Dollie's sons, a lone diner interrupted us. As usual I handled the job of carrying menu and water to the table. The mid-size fellow shaped like a rectangular block of wood ordered coffee and a BLT.

Mike and Matt jumped to the ready, Mike frying bacon, setting out lettuce and tomato, and bread to toast, and Matt pouring coffee.

"Black is fine," said Juan Garcia, introducing himself. He worked in Green Valley, he added, passing out business cards when I asked about his job.

When he said he managed the villas, I realized this was the guy I'd intended to question about the crimes in the area. He had a nice smile that showed off an even row of white teeth in tan face. Black wavy hair with black eyebrows and matching mustache set off fine facial features arranged symmetrically. He wore a dark blue Ralph Lauren golf shirt, matching navy pants, and a golf cap with Nike symbol. His easy-going courteous manner and fit physique reminded me of Tiger Woods.

Garcia's office was in the outdoor mall next door to that section of the villa development situated to the east of La Canada Boulevard. The maintenance and repair sheds sat to the rear. His department, Juan explained between sips of hot coffee and while awaiting the sandwich Mike was slapping together at the grill, was responsible for collecting and accounting for the monthly dues paid by villa residents. All management activities were under his departmental domain, including working with the villa association president and officers, fielding resident complaints, and supervising the maintenance staff. His management degree came from the University of Arizona in Tucson, he said.

"Six hundred individual villas, with a lot of absentee owner-landlords plus tenants and on-site owners keeps a guy hopping."

Mike served the BLT with French fries. Then he joined the others at a nearby table where they could hear. Juan dug in.

I noticed he seldom used personal pronouns. He said the *villa office* or *department,* and referred to himself in the third person as *the manager*, or *a guy.* Self-effacing, humble, or just shy? I paid close attention. Beyond an idle courtesy to a Cat Castle patron, I was particularly interested because Dollie lived in one of those villas. Perhaps I could pump Juan into revealing secrets he didn't know he had. The others occasionally glanced knowledgeably my way.

Devious, too, that's me. Besides, Mr. Garcia was a likeable guy. Unfortunately, I didn't get a chance to question him further as I was feeling sick again. Whatever I had, I didn't want to risk infecting Megan.

I excused myself to Juan, and to the Derrys and Dolans, and left. Back on my motorcycle, I ran out of gas again, halfway between the café and home. Not again! This wasn't paranoia. This was real. I easily recalled when I'd filled the tank last; that same morning, at the convenience store with the pumps near the church.

It occurred to me that somebody was sending me a warning. Not the South Tucson bartender this time, threatening my limbs and my life if I ever showed up again in his saloon. Somebody closer to home. Right off I thought of Fess Goodman. Question: under his own initiative or in response to the command of his mother?

No love lost between Elise and me. More than that, there was the competition. Dollie preferred my accompaniment for her solos, and the ministers used every excuse to keep Mrs. Goodman off the piano bench. Nevertheless, commanding Fess to take care of me seemed extreme. I couldn't see the meticulous lady who would sooner eat worms than get her hands dirty poking about in the dark of night siphoning gas out of my bike. Elise complained when she found a speck of dust on the piano and wiped imaginary dirt from a folding chair with her hanky before seating herself among the congregation.

By contrast, Dollie regularly dug in to scrub toilets, mop floors, and muck around in the flowerbeds standing guard on each side of the church entrance. Mrs. Martinez as culprit, then? No way. Dollie's nature was as sweet and caring as Mother Teresa's. Or at least as considerate and nice as Megan's.

All that supposing raced through my mind as I stood by my bike beside the highway. Again cars, trucks, RVs and SUVs thundered by, not a one slowing or stopping to ask how they could assist.

Until Juan Garcia pulled up in his green pickup. *"Carumba!"* he squawked. He had left the café shortly after I did, he explained. The maintenance department truck carried extra gas, he said, grinning. Lucky for me. He filled my tank from his five-gallon gasoline can.

"Maybe you have a gas leak," he suggested. "I'll follow you home."

Garcia and Hugo immediately hit it off, my dog licking Juan's hand and all but swooning from the friendly petting. Was I jealous? Not at all. Hugo's assessment of Juan confirmed my own. This was a nice guy, his friendship worth cultivating beyond my first devious motivation.

I showed him my living quarters, glad I'd made the bed that morning. With a treat for Hugo and a pitcher of iced tea in my hands and our drinking glasses in his, we vacated the RV to sit in lawn chairs outdoors beneath the shade of a cottonwood tree. Hugo ran around us both before settling down at Juan's feet to gnaw a bone I'd brought from the Cat Castle. My friends saved them for the dog, my best friend to date.

Hugo finished his bone and yapped at me, paws on my knees. He expected seconds? I shook my head No and Hugo whined, retreating from my petting hand to rejoin Juan. Flopping down on the far side, Hugo was distancing himself from me in disapproval, I guessed.

"Too bad," I said.

"Yeah."

We lapsed into a comfortable silence. After awhile he asked whether I'd visited Old Tucson, a restored old-timey town west of Tucson proper.

"That tourist spot?"

"Also used as a movie set for westerns. Bruce Willis is out there now."

"What's the movie?"

"Don't know. Wanna go out?"

"When?"

"Now. There's a cute blonde with a bit part. Like for you to see her."

I grinned. All I had revealed was that I too had lost a girlfriend, a *cute blonde*, up in Wyoming, who might have come down to these parts. "Too big a coincidence," I said, not moving a muscle beyond my lips.

"I wasn't thinking of that."

"What, then? A substitute?"

"Maybe. Maybe not."

We sat on, neither of us stirring.

Brother John and Dr. Wallaberra arrived and I made introductions. Lucas asked if I was playing for the song service and preaching that night. I hadn't told him I didn't feel like it. Sounded sissy.

"If you've got somebody else," Juan said, "that would be nice. I've invited Oliver to join me this evening. They're shooting a night scene in Old Tucson."

Paul scowled and rubbed his head with the short, tight mat of kinky hair. "That means," he began, when Elise pulled in the church lot and hopped out, to take quick mincing steps over to us. Was I imagining things or was she surprised to see me? Like I might have met with an accident while stranded out on the highway?

Leaving Dr. Wallaberra to deal with Elise, Brother John bent over to stare in my face. "You're not looking well, Oliver. What's the matter with you?"

Startled, I felt like going indoors to stare into the bathroom mirror. Was I pale? Yellow with jaundice?

Suddenly everybody was gathered around me, staring silently. What was this? I was a fascinating animal, captured from the wilds of Africa to stick in a zoo? In that moment of silence, Elise looked with bitter eyes into my own before turning aside.

"That settles it," she said, flouncing and twirling her full flowered skirt. "I'm playing the piano tonight."

"I'm okay," I said, with great determination,

while running a hand across my face and standing. "You've got Mrs. Goodman for tonight, so I'm taking off with Juan. With your permission, Sir."

What could Brother John do but agree? It was he who had suggested I needed time off. Juan sat still, grinning silently, as if he'd just won the battle at Waterloo. I put Hugo, protesting, inside the dog run and closed the gate.

In Juan's pickup we left for Green Valley. He said he was returning from Nogales with a load of fertilizer for the villa lawns when he'd stopped at the café. Now he wanted to switch vehicles, take his own car into Old Tucson.

Except that we ran out of gas before reaching Green Valley.

What in the world? While we were sitting sipping tea outside the RV, Juan's truck was parked on the far side of the church, out of our sight. Another siphoning job? But why? What was Juan to Elise or Fess, if they were in fact responsible?

Little if anything made sense. Neither the church nor the Cat Castle had been vandalized lately. Why, suddenly, both my cycle and Garcia's pickup?

Juan laughed. "Sorry. I should have filled up in Nogales before leaving. No problem. There's still enough gasoline in the can to get us into town."

Feeling better after hearing it was a common enough mistake rather than a malicious act, I nodded and smiled, but said nothing. He might think me crazy.

Then I bit the bullet and questioned him about the villas and his suppositions.

He shrugged. Like the sheriff and Dr. Wallaberra, he said he assumed the victims' insurance had covered their losses. "As for on-going security, we're not in the business. As you know, the villas are small. Many of the residents are snowbirds with their major residences elsewhere. Or they're impoverished, like Mrs. Martinez. Either way, few people have much to steal. I'm not making excuses, I just think it was a fluke, those few robberies."

"So you haven't done anything out of the ordinary to help protect them from future heists?"

He glanced at me, a question on his face. "No, but sounds like you think I should. I don't have the staff, Oliver, to put guards all over the place."

Understaffed. Reminded me of the sheriff.

We followed our schedule. Fascinated with Old Tucson with its dirt streets, wooden sidewalks, and batwing doors on the saloons, we ambled past the Spanish church and down the short two-block street. They were shooting a movie scene at the far end of town, out near the train depot and wooden water tower. Beyond the town the usual cacti grew, with foothills rising beyond, providing a good backdrop for just about any western or Mexican movie.

Staring from a distance at Bruce Willis and the blonde Juan pointed out, I must have looked like a gawking greenhorn. The bit player was cute, all right, no doubt about Juan's judgment. She wasn't Patsy, though. I hadn't realized it until I saw the little stranger, but I must have been holding my breath, thinking, This time it will be Patsy!

It didn't occur to me until later that my Patsy might have been on staff or working as a bartender or waitress in one of the saloons or cafes designed to replicate the Old West. By the time I thought of it, we were long gone.

We looked no farther. Again I felt hot and feverish, or it could have been the warm day compounded by my heartache. Juan drove me home and I went straight to bed, the off-key voices of the congregation and Elise's many piano mistakes lulling me to sleep amidst my sorrows.

CHAPTER 13

The phone rang, awakening me from a cold sweat. It was Brad Gifford, the cross-country hauler who had rescued me and Penny my bike the first time. He was back in town, Tucson, he said. At the Doubletree Hotel, across from Randolph golf course.

"How about a game early tomorrow morning?" He didn't have to be in Mexico until late Monday afternoon.

The way I felt, I must have been mad to agree, but I did. After breaking the connection I went outdoors to check on Hugo. His whimpering and clawing at the chain link fence was getting to me. I let him out and put him in the RV. After his defection, choosing Juan Garcia over me, I needed the comfort of re-bonding as much as Hugo.

Before turning in I got another idea. Notwithstanding Juan's running out of gas, counted as an accident, there seemed no point in taking chances. I rolled my cycle into the dog run and closed the gate. Then I went into the RV to look for my windbreaker, the good one. While in Green Valley after groceries the last time, I'd also stopped at the hardware store to make a special purchase. Now I unzipped the side pocket to get the combination lock. With that on the gate and the Harley-Davidson inside with Hugo, I might be able to foil the vandal.

Hugo whined when I left him and he whined when I returned. Something to do with the windbreaker? Feeling faint, I sat down on the cushioned booth bench at the RV's eating table to pat the dog. Hugo's front paws on my knee, he continued to whimper. What? I wasn't good enough for him, after Juan?

"No, Hugo, No! You can't have this jacket. You've got your own." Gently I turned his head to face his box bed. "See? There it is. You can't have mine."

Still he nuzzled, poking his nose all over the jacket I continued to hold. Crazy mutt. Was he trying to clone himself after me? Suspecting danger where none lurked? What was it with this little guy and zippers? I held out the windbreaker I sometimes wear so he could sniff it. Then I bent over to retrieve the old one that was now his.

"Smell the difference?"

He whined but I held steady with my resolve not to give in to him. There was no reason he should have two zippered jackets and me none. This time I hung my jacket in the closet, patted him, and told him to go to bed. Tough love, firm and consistent discipline, that was the ticket. Must remember this, if I ever had a child. Perhaps Brother John also provided parental counseling and would advise the Dolans about child rearing.

Amused at the meandering path the human mind can take, I dosed myself with Tylenol and went to bed. But not to sleep. If animals often seemed almost the opposite of humans, what was Hugo trying to tell me? I'd be willing to bet his mind didn't wander all over the place. Smell something strange, tell your master. Clear-cut logic from A to B, with no detours or hidden meanings. Could be Hugo's actions were that straightforward.

Any other time I might have gotten up out of bed immediately to give my zippered jacket a thorough once over. Not this time, for the medication took hold and I was out like a snuffed candle.

CHAPTER 14

Monday morning I was up and out of bed before dawn. Staring in the bathroom mirror, I couldn't see anything wrong. Whatever Lucas had seen the day before was gone or in his imagination. I felt pretty good, better than I had for several days. A shower and shampoo, a shave, and a boiled egg with orange juice and toast, and I was out of there.

Hugo didn't appreciate the dog run but this time I tossed in the old windbreaker from his box to keep him company. Fresh water and dog food, a few kind words and a pat, that would have to do it for now. I could hardly take Hugo into Tucson to the hotel and golf course with me.

I used my key to unlock the side door of the church and left a note for the preachers on the pulpit. As advised, I was taking the morning off.

Golf, great. Playing with Brad Gifford, the guy whose scores easily matched mine, would be a challenge. Fun, too. Great guy. As compatible as Juan Garcia.

Riding Penny into the city, the wind in my face against my blue goggles, golf clubs tied on the back, I was feeling pretty good about my life. Time enough later to *settle down,* as they say, when a guy gets a permanent job with a decent salary, finds a girl, and asks her the big question. Then come the babies, the mortgage, all the stuff you gotta buy. For right now I guessed I was sticking by the preachers, doing something useful. That's what mom said.

Mom would be happy to hear I'd made friends; not only with Brother John, my *Father Figure* as she called him, but also with the Derrys and Dolans and now Juan Garcia. Nice as he was, Brad Gifford hardly counted. He didn't get down this way that often. Or perhaps he did. Have to wait and see.

I exited Interstate 10 on Twenty-Second Street, coming up on the back side of Randolph Park, turning left on Swan. The Doubletree Hotel sat on the right facing the east side of the golf course.

Brad was waiting for me in the lobby. Polly Pew, his truck, was parked on a side street, he said. We went straightaway to check in at Randolph and hit the links. This time he beat me good. His score, eighty-two; mine, in the low hundreds. I couldn't believe it.

"You don't look too hot," Brad said, loading my clubs with his into the truck cab for safekeeping. "You sick?"

"Maybe. Or hungry."

The hotel served a nice luncheon buffet, he said, recommending we stop in the lobby bar for a drink first. I didn't object, although I thought I might barf.

"You sit, I'll fetch."

I chose a fat chair next to the big window overlooking the pool. From there I could see that the hotel offered the amenities to snowbird tourists, to business travelers, and also to avid amateur golfers and the professional golfers and their entourages in town for a golf tournament across the street. A placard mounted on an easel to the side discreetly announced an art show, to open that evening in the ballroom beyond.

Brad was coming toward me, carrying two frosty mugs of beer, when I spotted her, dressed to kill. No illusion of oasis in the desert, there she was in glowing, glimmering real life, walking across the lobby, alone: Patsy Parsons!

Quickly I stood to dash across the lounge, down the carpeted steps, and across the lobby to throw myself at her feet, if it came to that. Instead, I fainted.

CHAPTER 15

When I came to in the white room with the white ceiling above and the white sheet covering me, I thought I'd swooned dead away; that I'd died and gone to heaven. No Patsy Parsons hovering over me like an angel, though.

The good Brothers John and Wallaberra sat near the window, staring out at blue sky and white drifting clouds. The Derry brothers sat in chairs, quietly talking to each other while Derek paced. Idly I pondered why Dollie wasn't here, or Mr. and Mrs. Goodman. Come to that, where was Elise's elusive husband? Closing my eyes, I vowed to unravel that mystery, too, one of these days soon.

After a few moments I again opened my eyes. "Will somebody tell me what th'hell is going on?" I shouted, or thought I did. Actually, it came out as a weak croak.

I must have been really sick with something awful because Brother John didn't even correct my language, nor did Dr. Wallaberra scowl. Both men arose from their chairs but nobody came near. All five men stayed stuck a good six feet beyond me.

"You've got infectious mononucleosis," Lucas said.

"Compounded by a bad case of shingles, also highly contagious," said Paul. "Which is why Megan isn't here."

"We shouldn't be here, either," said Mike. "They're going to kick us out."

"Yeah, you're going to be quarantined," said Matt. He told me that my trucker friend had called nine-one-one for an ambulance from the Doubletree Hotel. I was taken to St. Mary's Hospital, out west of the Interstate on St. Mary's Road. I must have come to, because Brad Gifford got Brother John's name and the church's telephone number from me before I passed out again.

"Wait a minute," I gasped, edging up on one elbow. I wanted to sit straight up and shout, jump out of bed and stomp. "I can't afford this."

"That's right," said Brother John. "So we're taking you home."' And they did, which is when Paul brought in his friend, an old fellow from Green Valley, who must have practiced medicine back when Noah built the ark. He didn't seem to know a lot, or it could have been the reverse. He knew way too much and was determined to saddle me with every disease in the book—all contagious. First he diagnosed this stuff as tuberculosis, scaring me to death by predicting the disease would soon spread from lungs to brain, kidneys, bones, and lymph nodes. Then he switched to sporotrichosis, a skin disease caused by fungus or mold that lies in soil. Well, I had been working in the garden, but so had Paul. Both Lucas and Paul disagreed with the doctor's diagnosis and he was dismissed. So it was back to the prognosis from St. Mary's Hospital. Mono was bad enough, dumping on a body a big case of weakness and requiring mostly bed rest. Adding shingles, generally conceived of as an old man's disease, was heaping injury on top of insult. I was told that it was the result of infection by the herpes zoster virus, the same virus that causes chickenpox. During a case of the latter, the virus can get to the root of a nerve in the brain or spinal cord to lie dormant.

The Tucson doctor had said it wasn't known what can reactivate the virus, possibly stress. With the uttering of this word, he'd stared at me ruefully, one eyebrow raised, as if a young man, a blue-collar worker, couldn't experience stress? I could expect to experience intense knife-like pain in the nerve where the virus was lodged. This severe burning pain, he'd said further, often precedes the rash of blisters that erupts. Oh, man, looked like I was in for it.

The cure? Rest and medication. Lots of rest and sleep. Quarantine.

Megan cooked for me and Derek or one of her brothers brought the meals in covered dishes to set on the step of the RV. Megan's notes the first couple of days suggested I might enjoy her stuffed cabbage and pasta-broccoli salad. Actually, both were too heavy. I preferred her homemade chicken noodle soup. Sick as I was, I washed the dirty dishes thoroughly in scalding water and lots of soap before setting them back out there to be picked up. I felt like an old-timer and the Cat Castle was my personal *Meals on Wheels*, with personalized delivery. If I was up and felt like it, the Derry brothers, one or the other, paused long enough for the occasional visit through the RV's screen door.

The silly part was the accelerating competition between the cousins. They competed over who would do my laundry. I only had two sets of white sheets but with all the bed rest, my flopping about and alternating between cold chills and fever, I drenched them daily. Then the ladies began providing their own sheets, pink and green flowers from Elise and blue and white stripes from Dollie.

Their sons made pickup and delivery, which meant I figured to *make hay while the sun shines* in getting Fess Goodman to talk. No way. No matter what I said or asked him, I got merely a Humph, Yeah or Naw, in return. As for Donald Martinez, he was even more taciturn. He said nothing at all, just dropped off his mom's bundle and ran.

Then the cousins competed with time, so that while Fess was delivering flowered linens, Donny was retrieving stripes. Then they switched, with flowers from Dollie and stripes from Elise. I lost track.

Meanwhile, Elise couldn't cope with the unruly teenagers in Sunday school class, and Dollie wouldn't take them after that. She was no second best, she said. Paul had pleaded with me to teach them, but I too had refused. What did I know? Brother John was devious, I figured. If I had to study the Bible to teach the youngsters, I'd be learning for myself. No thanks. Now four teens—a gal and three guys including the Manson twins—volunteered to take over my jobs. Why was that, I wondered. I turn my back on teaching their class and they demonstrate Christ's love by turning the other cheek?

I couldn't lie around all the time. Not bothering to shave, I took an occasional shower. I exercised some by walking the RV aisle. Even that small amount of exertion brought out a sweat to send me back to bed, flopping crosswise. Curious about the youngsters, I sometimes sat on the table bench to watch the girl work the flowerbed out the side window. Or I climbed into the passenger seat to spy on the boys through the RV's front window. The three boys hammered, sawed, laughed, and played their stereos.

I couldn't believe it would take four people to substitute for me. The guys were assigned to prop up and paint the old shed out back. Starting out, it leaned from southwest to northeast. After hammering for days, it leaned from southeast to northwest. So much for that. The girl's work was just as peculiar. After digging up a flowerbed, she planted a flowering geranium horizontally bloom and all, in the ditch she'd dug and covered the whole thing with soil.

Weakly, I called to ask what she thought she was doing. She replied that everywhere a flower bloomed or a leaf stuck out, if buried one got a flower. "I don't think so," I said. She insisted this was her grandma's advice. I wanted to mutter *Old wives tale*. Instead, I returned to bed, shaking my head.

Standing outdoors and looking in, Brother John laughed by way of explanation. "You're fast and you're good," he said. "We thought you knew that." I guessed that was supposed to explain why they had hired four teens for me.

He installed a second television set in the RV, this one mounted up high in the corner at the foot of my bed. Didn't matter. I wasn't much into TV. In the fall I like football, the Denver Broncos, the Kansas City Chiefs, the Seattle Seahawks and some college games, like the Nebraska Cornhuskers and my own state's university team, the Wyoming Cowboys. But this wasn't autumn and the golf tournaments took up only a few hours on the weekends. Otherwise, it was catch the news over breakfast and supper and tune into the occasional documentary. That was my typical television fare and it didn't change now. I saw a segment on TLC, The Learning Channel, on the construction of bridges, and another on the Nature Channel on worms and whales. Otherwise I slept or looked out the window. Until I began to prowl Brother John's bookcases.

Then I read, choosing literary authors. My mom was into literature or, perhaps, to be more precise, into language. She gave to me an appreciation for words, the many words one can use to express ideas and feelings and things. To describe how I was feeling these days, I would say that I was spiraling down into the bowels of inactivity and inadequacy. Franz Kafka's opening line from *The Metamorphosis* came to me, which was how I felt half the time these days: *As Gregor Sama awoke one morning from uneasy dreams he found himself transformed in his bed into a gigantic insect.* Everything hurt, more so than before, meaning I was getting worse, not better? My legs felt heavy and they ached. So did my belly and abdomen, no matter how lightly I ate. Retching came easier than swallowing. My head ached, too, and sometimes I thought my eyes would pop right out of my head.

Another of Kafka's lines appeared on the screen of my memory. Brother John would no doubt say the quotation reminded him of a similar Biblical reference. If I remembered it correctly, Franz Kafka put it this way: *You do not need to leave your room ... be quite still and solitary. The world will freely offer itself to you to be unmasked.* Possibly that came from his reflections in *The Great Wall of China*.

Attempting to lie quite still was a problem, though, with so many aches and pains. Besides reading and quiet contemplation, I watched the world beyond my cell. For a prison cell is what the RV was to me these days.

Although Brother John visited me regularly, Dr. Wallaberra did not. At the window he once quoted to me some scripture. My lethargic response could have put him off, for he never returned. I did catch sight of him a few times out in the back garden with his hoe. I could have been reading something foreign into his behavior. It seemed to me that he occasionally glanced furtively over his shoulder, in my direction, as if I might catch him again cutting down plants instead of weeds. What did I care? I wasn't judging him on the basis of his ineptitude at gardening.

More people were joining the congregation, Lucas said. Probably the result of the revival; word-of-mouth advertising. I watched them troop into the old building with the four coats of fresh white paint, thanks to yours truly. They arrived in old cars and new, in SUVs and pickup trucks. A trickling of balding men and gray-haired ladies showed from the retirement community. Not many arts and crafts people, but some. The brothers didn't mind how their parishioners dressed so long as they were respectful. More orchard and mine workers arrived, plus a number of Mexicans with their families large and small.

I lay on my bed, eyes closed, listening to the music. The congregational voices were okay, though I heard no solos. Dollie couldn't tolerate her cousin's accompaniment and Elise wouldn't agree anyhow. Listening to Elise's rendition of the old hymns at the piano reminded me of my schooldays when boys played pranks by scratching fingernails to screech along chalkboards. With the newcomers and more volunteers among the women, the cousins fought over which support committee each would chair. Some of their followers took sides, but not all of them.

Besides Megan, Elise and Dollie occasionally cooked for me. The cousins, when not battling among themselves, were also busy plotting their culinary campaign in pursuit of feeding the brothers. The widows and divorcees along with a few marrieds regularly carted casseroles and pies to church. Neither Brother John nor Dr. Wallaberra gave out their home address; they would have been besieged. At my window they said they'd like to chuck the pair of busybodies, Elise and Dollie, who had started all this cooking and volunteering commotion, as their battling was not one bit Christian. But the ministers agreed they could hardly act so unchristian themselves as to dismiss the ladies from meeting their Lord at the Community Church in Christ.

The sheriff stopped by. To report, he said; to gloat, I figured. Based on an anonymous tip, Truman said, he'd picked up Arnie Olsen as the graffiti artist. Gave his dad a good talking to, then let the kid go.

Had he confessed to all the local vandalism? That's what I wanted to know: "Here at the church, down at the Cat Castle?"

The sheriff looked startled. Guess he hadn't remembered everything.

Juan Garcia and I started e-mailing each other. I could only take a few moments at the computer, morning and afternoon, but it was enough. Lucas popping up at the window and Juan on the computer comprised my major company. The Derrys or the dowagers' sons left food and picked up the dishes, but they came and went so quickly I hardly counted any of them. Fess and Donny weren't my buddies, that was certain.

Brother John let Hugo out of the dog run and into the RV. Ecstatic, he was all over me. However, we kept Hugo's visits to a minimum.

I had forgotten his frenzy over the now closeted windbreaker pocket.

Mike or Matt also fed Hugo. He couldn't understand the rejection—my failure to come outdoors to play, or our insisting that he stay in the dog run. Juan felt sorry for Hugo and took him home. Now I was really devastated. What would I do without Hugo? By the time I recovered, the bonding would be complete. Hugo would be Juan's dog.

Juan started to stop by the RV in person. He sat in a lawn chair on the far side of the RV, the side opposite the door. With this plan I could sit on the cushioned bench and lean my elbows on the table, hold up my head if it came to that. Through the open window we talked. Rather, he talked and I mostly listened.

Mom would have come, I was sure. Only where would she stay and what would she do that wasn't already being done for me? I simply didn't tell her; didn't call, just waited. Soon this thing, whatever it was, was bound to go away.

My defenses down, or perhaps while half hallucinating from fever, I guessed I had confessed more to

Juan than I planned. For in a subsequent conversation, he had ideas of his own that led me to believe I'd spilled the beans. Maybe not every last bean in the pot, but quite a few.

"I've got master keys, Oliver," he said the next day. He stood from the lawn chair to reach into his pocket and pull out a set of keys. Jingle, jingle, right in my face. "How 'bout I get into Dollie Martinez' villa while she's in church and prowl through her things? Photos and such. Look for clues."

"To what?"

"Anything."

Caving in again, I returned to my bed and my wadded up sheets, sprawling across and not even bothering to pull up the covers until the cold chills sent me diving beneath blankets and comforter. Had I agreed or disagreed with Juan's plan? What did it matter. Too sick to think, again I closed my eyes and finally sank into the blessed sleep of oblivion. I even forgot to take my pills.

That afternoon Juan was back, again on the far side of the RV where nobody looking out a church window could see him. He held up a page of color photos. "Bingo!" he said. "I took them to the copy center to have color duplicated. So don't worry your bloated brain." Here he paused to laugh at his joke, meaning, I trusted, that he referred to my sick head not my normal state. "Dollie will never know I was there, either to find the photos or to return them."

I pushed out the screen to reach for the pages. Trying to focus, what I saw made no more sense than anything else: Fess Goodman with Elise, Fess with Mr. Goodman (probably), Dollie with her son Donny, Donny and Fess, and finally the same man with Donny. So what? In these pictures, there was less likeness between the two boys, the second cousins. Donny was a brunette and Fess was a blonde, but I already knew this, for hadn't I been seeing the both of them every day? Not that they hung around. I was lucky to glimpse the back of them as they dashed off. Staring at Juan's page of photos reminded me of the boy's differences, not their similarities. In the meantime, I could have sworn that in the photo Megan found in Elise's wallet, both boys were blond as teenagers.

Like switching TV channels with the remote control, I tuned back into what my buddy was saying. Juan had another idea, he said. He would snoop around the Doubletree Hotel, where I'd spotted Patsy. Wearing his golf clothes, he would be taken for a guest and could freely roam the lobby bar, the buffet luncheon, and the ballroom where the art show was now in progress.

"Then I make the switch," he said, grinning. "In my carryall, which could be taken for a sports bag, I'll have a blue shirt." He showed me. Over the left pocket, in red stitching on a white background, was the single word, *Maintenance*. "Wearing this shirt, I'm free to go anywhere because I'm invisible. Maintenance people, of any race and ethnic group, always are. The customer's mind blanks out."

So that was the plan. In two different personas, Juan could go just about anywhere with *carte blanche*. Whether Patsy Parsons was a guest or an employee, Juan ought to come home with some concrete evidence for me. Except that as a guest, wouldn't Patsy have checked out days ago? I hoped Juan would get lucky.

CHAPTER 16

"**P**atsy! Patsy!" Drenched with sweat, I awakened with her name on my lips. Night after night this happened, and I ached for her. Only today it was different. This morning it was a nightmare that brought me sitting straight up. It wasn't love that made me scream, it was hate. In the dream I was running after her with a knife in my hand. I'd caught her, knocked her down, and was raising the long sharp hunting knife to strike when my eyes popped open.

I wiped my damp face with the sheet and lay back down. Think about somebody else, I told myself.

Dr. Wallaberra remained an enigma to me. The man I had initially thought would be nice to know never got closer to me than *preacher;* anybody's Sunday minister. Nice enough, but distant, aloof. Perhaps he resented my lack of spiritual commitment.

Yet I couldn't bring myself to play dishonest, pretending to feel something I didn't.

I tried to picture Paul as the perpetrator and all this religious stuff as his cover so he could steal from the members and their contributions. Naw, too far fetched. I still couldn't figure his furtive manner in the garden. Unless he was growing illegal poppies or marijuana plants. Absurd notion, unless that was the whole purpose of the garden—use it as a cover-up. Because he would have to know that sooner or later I'd be well enough to get back outdoors and would recognize any foreign plants he'd recently added.

Time to move on. To stop imposing on the brothers' hospitality, meanwhile working for a pittance. Hugo didn't even need me any longer.

That's when I decided to go home. I had enough money in the bank to cover the price of a plane ticket, and a credit card to put it on. Despite my friends here, I felt so alone. As Joseph Conrad said in *Heart of Darkness: We live as we dream—alone.*

Mom would take me in and nurse me back to health. I could tolerate Hernandez awhile. He never had given me a hard time, personally; he did sense my resentment. With me in the way, he would have to let me have the couch, which meant he might get up off his daytime cushions to go out and find work.

Lying on my back staring at a fly strolling leisurely across the ceiling, I mentally ticked off my accomplishments since arriving in Arizona.

I had designed and constructed a church spire, single-handedly managed the revival's advertising campaign, played the piano, kept the books (singling out the pledges and following up on these by letter and phone call), painted, cleaned, gardened, run errands, shopped, cooked, and laundered. Sounded like housewifery.

Then I counted my failures. I had not identified the thieves. I hadn't rooted out the cause nor helped to stop the squabbling dowagers. Dr. Wallaberra might resent my lack of progress along these lines. At least the sheriff had identified the vandal, though I doubted Arnie had been alone. More failures, personal: I hadn't located either Patsy or Malcolm.

That's when Saul Bellow's *Seize the Day* came to mind. In writing of man's shame and impotence, he wrote: *Maybe the making of mistakes expressed the very purpose of his life and the essence of his being here.* Bellow could have been describing my life right about now.

Time to pack it in, head for home. Wyoming's cool summer climate beckoned.

A bout of coughing sent me to the toilet. The Green Valley doctor, the old retiree, had said I'd also picked up a staph infection and could expect trouble with coughing, sore throat and lungs, watery eyes and nose. What was this, the battle of the bacteria versus O.D.D. Temple?

Propped up on pillows, I fiddled with the remote, searching for a golf tournament. More coughing, me clutching my chest as if to keep it from exploding.

More sneezing, running eyes and nose, me rubbing my pounding head. My legs ached, too. Made me wonder every time I tried to stand if soon my only navigation would be on hands and knees. I felt like a wounded toddler.

A roar outside, sharp braking, doors slamming. I glanced out the window in time to see Fess Goodman leave his red Jaguar to disappear around the opposite corner of the church. I read him as sneaky. Maybe he was a spy.

Elise came to the door, knocked, and yelled through the screen. "Hey, Oliver, I've brought your laundry. I made you a nice dessert, a blueberry tart."

She left without waiting for a Thank you. I didn't for one minute believe she was sincere in doing nice things for me. She hadn't even invited me up on the porch when I passed her house. It was all a matter of competing with Dollie.

Soon I could expect to hear Elise pounding on the piano or arguing with her cousin, who was already indoors. Dollie's old white baby Cad was parked out front. She hadn't stopped by to say hello or to compete with her sheet game. Oh, well. Not caring what either woman was up to in mid-morning of mid-week, I was right the first time. Elise immediately began mangling *Beneath the Cross of Jesus,* followed by an incredibly bad rendering of *The Old Rugged Cross.* I didn't know Brother John's sermon topic for the upcoming Sunday, but something about crosses could be expected.

Dollie stormed through the little used church door on this side to stride around front. She jerked open the door of her Cadillac, jumped in, slammed the door behind her, started the ignition, and roared away. Not in time to stop or question her, Paul Wallaberra came bursting out the front door to run down the steps. Gravel and dirt flying, Dollie left behind merely the flash of red taillight as she braked at the corner by the convenience store. Paul scratched his head, scowled, and returned to the church, as Elise was pounding out *When I Survey the Wondrous Cross*. Yup, the next preachin' would address crosses.

No sign of Fess. I couldn't imagine what Elise's son was doing at the church, anyhow. Like me, he was no believer. He seldom showed at the church except as his mom's chauffeur.

It was at that moment, after all the hubbub with the cousins died down, that she arrived at the RV. Not blond Patsy Parsons, but the cutest little tanned brunette bundle a guy could ever hope to meet. And me a mess. She was a new waitress at the Cat Castle, she said, and had offered to deliver my meal on her way home, up Sahuarita way.

She introduced herself as Vanna Solano. "Yeah, I know what you're thinking, and you're right. Mom was a *Wheel of Fortune* fan first off." Her laugh was a light trill, like a little bird. She grinned and walked right in.

"Hey," I objected. "I'm under quarantine."

"Yeah, and I'm a two-headed orangutan." Vanna set down the covered tray on the table. Then she went back to the top step to get my laundry and Elise's blueberry tart before seating herself on the cushioned bench. "I'm not afraid of you. You aren't going to knock me down and beat me up, are you?" When she grinned, she dimpled—left cheek and mid-chin.

No, I felt like saying, *but I'd sure like to get better acquainted.*Cute girl, great sense of humor. Still, I kept my distance, backing down the RV aisle until I tripped over the throw rug in front of the sink. She pretended not to notice my clumsiness or my blush. My face felt so hot, either the fever was coming back big time or I was blushing red with embarrassment.

"Boy, howdy, that café is so busy these days, we're all hopping around like Mexican jumping beans," she said, as if we were talking about the Cat Castle all along. She lifted her eyes from studying her shoe to smile shyly at me. I could smell her lovely fragrance from across the kitchen counter and table. Not French fries; more like *White Diamonds*, something nice like that.

As Thomas Mann said, *Beauty can pierce one like a pain.*

I knew I should put up more resistance, get her out of my contagious little home, but this was the first time in days I hadn't felt like a leper, and I hated to see her go. Vanna was so nice. Dollie hadn't bothered to stop by to pick up my soiled laundry; too mad at Elise, probably, or else Mrs. Martinez had turned over the dirty job to Mrs. Goodman. So when Vanna offered to take it away and do it, I let her. She said she was majoring in hotel and food management at the U. I assumed she meant the University of Arizona in Tucson. She was working to earn tuition money for the fall term, she said.

"Tips are great at the Cat," she added, using the nickname that was coming into vogue. I could see why she'd pull hefty tips. Who wouldn't feel good, want to tip big, with a waitress like the sweet and attentive Vanna hovering? She asked if there was anything else she could do for me. I wanted to say *Yeah, hold my hand,* but I shook my head No. She promised to return.

Same time tomorrow, she said. I could have been Hugo and she'd promised me a bone, she'd made me that ecstatic. By then I would look and smell better, what with forewarning and time to grab a shower, shampoo, and shave. After eating all that I could manage and putting away the uneaten meatloaf with mashed potatoes and green beans for supper that night, I returned to the table and reached for the tart. After nibbling at that, I sat a few moments longer at the table, staring out the window. I felt dizzy.

Staggering to my room, I collapsed on the bed, disheveled and annoyed. Couldn't be helped. The doctor said this terrible fatigue would go away eventually, but meanwhile I must expect to be weak and exhausted. Okay, sure, I had felt this way before, but dizzy, unbalanced? What was happening to my equilibrium? I slept awhile.

Awake again, this time disoriented, I nevertheless decided to initiate a mild exercise program. I could do leg lifts while in bed. Tomorrow I would try arm lifts while clutching cans of corn and hominy to rebuild strength.

Meeting Vanna had given me all kinds of incentives beyond cleanliness and muscle building to force my body back into motion. I must also improve my attitude, practice smiling more often. I tried to recall some jokes to tell this funny girl. Of course she probably already had a boyfriend, a whole stable of them. Maybe a husband and two kids. Plus a dog.

Did my missing Hugo make me think I'd heard him bark?

"Hi, Oliver," Juan said, opening the screen door and poking his head in. Hugo bounded down the aisle to jump on my bed. "I've been meaning to ask you, Oliver. What's your middle name?" He sat on the booth bench, leaning over to look down the aisle at me.

I sat up to swing my legs over the edge of the bed, nearly toppled over, and stretched out both arms behind to hold myself in place. Bare-chested, I gritted my teeth. I'd been saved this particular embarrassing question for awhile, as neither of the preachers nor the Cat Castle folk had ever thought to pry. "Two middle names, actually: Daniel and David. Oliver was my dad's father's name. Mom had a father and a stepfather, both of whom she adores, so she couldn't choose between them. So she didn't, she used both names." I thought that if I talked fast enough, Juan might not decipher the silly part.

"So your initials are O.D.D. With your last name, that's Odd Temple."

He was quick, all right. "You got it." He could have guffawed, made some rude joke. But he just smiled, as if appreciating my discomfort.

He and Hugo had stopped by, Juan said, to report that they had no report. "*Lo soiento*; I'm sorry." He stepped back outdoors to pull up his favorite lawn chair just beyond the screen door and sit down. "I showed Patsy Parson's photo all over the Doubletree Hotel, making a big nuisance of myself, no doubt. Nobody recognized her. So she doesn't work there. Then I thought she might be the wife or girlfriend of a golfer … ."

"A guest, you mean?"

"Maybe, if the golfer was a professional from out of town. Not necessarily an overnight hotel guest if they were locals. Nobody at the front desk could recall seeing her check in or out, alone or with some-body. No record of her name in the computer, either."

"How do you know that?"

"Ah, remember my blue collar? I changed shirts in the men's room, picked up a mop, and walked behind the counter. Checked the computer myself."

I raised one eyebrow. Juan took a big chance. But maybe not. What could have happened? Somebody order him to leave? Call the cops and press charges, more likely.

"If Patsy was registered as a *Mrs.* Somebody, I couldn't tell," Juan said.

I wondered how he'd got all those people to sit still for questioning, or what it had taken, really, to get behind that registration desk. Then it dawned on me. "How much are you out of pocket, Juan? For bribes."

"Uh, no matter."

"I insist. I'll reimburse you." Before I could get him to render an accounting and submit his bill, we heard more cars drawing up. Fess and Elise were leaving and Vanna was arriving.

I didn't get a shower before seeing Vanna again, because there she was, in my face no more than a couple of hours after departing the first time. "What's up?" I asked.

"Nothing. I just thought you might be lonesome. But I see you've already got company." She turned to leave.

Quickly I made the introductions, which both Juan and Vanna let me go ahead and do. Then Vanna grinned. "Juan and I have known each other since middle school, Oliver."

"You could have said."

She ignored my attitude, which I'd promised myself to change; if not from vinegar to honey, at least from beans to T-bone. While she stood just inside the door and Juan outside, I turned my back to don a fresh pajama top from the laundry Elise had delivered. "I repeat, Vanna, you'd better not come indoors."

"You come out, then."

Juan repeated her suggestion, so I did. While I slipped into jeans on top of my pajama bottoms, I felt a sharp pain in my gut. I doubled over, gasping. Grabbing the open door to the bathroom, I stayed that way, bent over, heaving, for several moments before the pain backed off, to hide in a corner if not depart. My feet in slippers, I couldn't think where my robe could be. Elise washed it but forgot to return it? I needed to dress half-way decent and I was shivering with cold again. Ah, the zippered jacket could substitute for the missing robe.

Vanna Solano and Juan Garcia, *friends since middle school*, arranged chairs in the dirt yard out front. She reached into a wicker basket to withdraw a thermos and brightly colored plastic glasses. "Party time!" she caroled lightly, flipping back her thick dark hair. She quickly added that she meant iced tea and vegetable crackers. "Soothing and good for you."

Hugo at last paid attention to me. But not in the way I expected, with his nose on my leg, his eyes pinned on mine to plead for petting. No, not today. I could have been a stranger, an unfamiliar guy with a nefarious plan and Hugo must jump to the rescue of his new master, Juan. First Hugo leaped up, then he ran in circles at my feet as if chasing his tail, then he ran from me back to Juan and back to me, again. He barked. He howled. He leaped at me. Vanna and Juan looked from Hugo to me and then at each other. The dog's behavior was purely a puzzle.

"It must be something in your pocket, Oliver," Juan said. "Look how he keeps trying to bite your jacket on that side."

Then I remembered how he'd acted earlier, when I was too tired and sick to wonder why this particular windbreaker, and the side pocket zipper, especially, drove my poor dog crazy. "But it's empty," I said, patting the flat pocket from the outside. Hugo was a mystery. Besides, he was wearing me out. Juan caught on quickly.

A single sharp command and both Hugo's barking and his jumping abruptly ceased. Juan led him to the dog run. Hugo whined, nevertheless obeying. The gate closed behind him, Hugo headed for the corner (the one on my side), where he flopped down, his nose pointing in my direction and resting on his paws.

Looked like he might obey Juan. But I didn't think Hugo was going to forgive me. Whatever had I done to him, except feed him, pamper him, and treat him like my best friend? I couldn't believe an animal could pout because he couldn't have two zippered windbreakers.

I watched Juan and Vanna eyeing each other. Just my luck. Find a girl that makes my heart dance after nearly a year of celibacy, and what happens? Turns out she's Juan's lady friend? Listening to the pair of them banter, watching them poke or sock each other, I told myself they were just buddies, like two guys. Nothing romantic going on here.

Hope springs eternal, Brother John had said back at the wedding chapel when he longed to provide young people with premarital counseling. Now the phrase came to me as a reminder of how dopey a guy could get. That's all I needed, to repeat my own history—fall for a gal who was falling for my buddy. Must I again go through the pain of betrayal?

Suddenly I had a new thought. Juan and Vanna obviously knew each other long before I arrived. If they were or were about to become lovers, who was betraying whom? Not them to me; but me, intruding on their twosome.

Which led me straight to another idea, one that had never once occurred to me in all the time Patsy and Arlo were together. What if the Patsy-Arlo coupling happened before, not after, I came into the picture? What if I had betrayed Arlo by temporarily stealing his girl, and not the reverse?

I shook my head in disbelief and puzzlement, bringing on another fit of coughing and hacking, plus the dizziness that was so bad this time I thought I might vomit and topple right out of the chair, or both. I leaned over to hold my poor head in hands propped on my knees.

"We'd better get out of here so you can get back to bed, Oliver," said Juan. I didn't like the sound of that *we* word. Not much I could do about it, not even raise an objection the way I felt. Silently I nodded. Then he twisted the knife, while sending a grin flashing first at Vanna and then at me. "This here's my friend, *Odd Temple*, Vanna."

Yeah, some friend.

CHAPTER 17

I watched the taillights until both cars turned the corner. Ready for bed, another coughing fit hit me. And me out of both cough drops and cough medicine.

When Vanna asked what she could get for me, my cough should have reminded me. Instead, I'd been distracted. When Juan told Vanna he and I were friends, I could have remembered what betrayal felt like.

Not so sure what to do about budding friendships, I turned my mind to cough medication. I told myself I could easily fix that problem, notwithstanding the quarantine. Forget it. Good time to shop while I was already dressed. I could surely walk to the grocery down there on the corner, make my purchases, and return home. I didn't open the screen door on the RV. No need. I kept my wallet in the glove compartment. I opened the passenger door, retrieved the wallet, and meandered on down the road.

I never made it. Just then the RV blew up.

CHAPTER 18

Word travels fast. I thought everybody in the world was arriving: Sheriff Truman, the fire-fighters, the preachers, the Dolans and Derrys, Juan with Hugo in his car, Vanna, a few reporters, tourists too. But no dowagers or their sons.

It felt like hell revisited. When my pickup was set afire in front of Betty's café, I had lost all my worldly goods except the clothes on my back and a nearly empty wallet. With the explosion of my RV home, I again lost everything but pajamas, wallet, boots, and windbreaker. The *God of Fire* must have something against me. Scratch that. This time I was also left with a dog and a motorcycle.

Between the authorities and the gawkers came the press. This time I couldn't escape the interrogation of both. Unlike back home in Gillette, I had no friends in high places. The explosion, a great fire-ball, was seen on this side of the retirement community, the sound echoing up and down the valley. Word of mouth reached my café friends. The others, closer in, saw and heard the commotion or tuned into the news.

Fortunately, the church didn't burn, and neither did Hugo or my cycle. However, the bushes and trees on the far side of the RV caught fire. So the firefighters had plenty to do. A sheriff's deputy held back the crowds and managed the traffic simultaneously. Little kids pointed at me and teenage girls giggled. You'd have thought this was a circus and I was the head clown.

No, I told both the sheriff and the reporters, I didn't know anything. I was out for a walk when it blew. No, I wasn't cooking at the time and I had no idea what caused the conflagration. I couldn't say whether I had any enemies.

Elise taking revenge for my competition with her over the piano sounded childish. My reply brought a line of furrows to the sheriff's brow, deep enough for planting. "What do you mean, you don't know whether you have enemies?"

I shrugged. It was a slip of the tongue. I had no intention of mentioning Elise. That it could have been the South Tucson bartender and his thugs who'd warned me off my search for Malcolm sounded too far-fetched, too. Just whose slop I'd stumbled into—that was the question.

What didn't occur to me in the way of enemies was the graffiti kid from the high school. Blowing the RV, that was serious, too deadly for Arnie Olsen.

While those thoughts ran through my head like a river, I scowled and pursed my lips, anything to stall for time. Recalling the brothers' expectations of me, and of the sheriff, I again reminded Truman of the Green Valley and church thefts. He countered by reminding me he'd caught Arnie, the vandal. "Keep your nose out a my bid-niz!" Dick snarled at me. "Solving crimes takes time."

How long did he need? Months had passed with no progress. This time next year he still might not have caught the RV bomber. Weak, worried, I could no longer muster the energy to care.

Dr. Wallaberra scowled, scratched his head, and looked puzzled. Neither he nor Brother John could produce any reasons for this extreme case of vandalism. That's what Paul had called the explosion that sent the RV into *Kingdom Come* with one big whoosh, "the work of vandals." The sheriff said he'd direct his deputies to take statements from people having business near the property. Although that included the Goodmans, mother and son, and Dollie with son Donald, there was no sign of any of them.

"The cousins probably haven't heard the news yet," Brother John whispered to me. I sat on the front steps of the church, the lawn chairs having disintegrated along with my little home.

"Sheriff, this man's sick," Megan said to Truman while tugging on his sleeve for attention. "We can take him down to the Cat Castle with us for the night. We'll bring him back tomorrow if you need to speak with him again."

The café? Where would I sleep, on the grill or tables after hours? Their new house was still under construction. The whole quartet of café operators were still crowded into an undersize mobile home out back of the Cat Castle. Besides, I was under quarantine. Wouldn't do for me to get close to food or diners, and certainly not to Megan. I had risen from the steps, but now backed off to plop back down. I felt like *Raggedy Andy*, with no bones.

Brother John stepped forward, opening his own mouth as if the idea had only just come knocking at the door of his brain. "We'll take him home with us."

Juan immediately countered with the hospitality of his home. I accepted.

Shaken, from the illness and this whole miserable experience, I was eager to get away from all these people, to hit the sack. Vanna returned to Juan's car to pet Hugo, his nose poking through the crack in the window. At that moment I wished I were the dog. Vanna read my mind. Smiling, she returned to my side, to reach out a hand and stroke my arm. I still wore the windbreaker.

"How did you know to turn around and come back here?" I asked her.

"I didn't. Juan and I were having a beer up at Sahuarita when I got a funny sensation; peculiar, that is. 'Let's go back and check on Oliver,' I said."

"Oliver, not O.D.D.? You didn't call me ODD?"

She poked me. "Don't be silly. That's your secret. And ours. We'll keep our lips zipped. What are friends for?"

I could have grabbed her right then and taken off

for the bedroom and a sweet cuddle. No bedroom, no bed. Probably too soon anyhow, even if I were well and she were willing. Backing off, I reminded Vanna of the quarantine

"Sounds like an *Old Wives Tale,* to me. With that old maid of a doctor hovering round you, it's no wonder you're sick. With his various diagnoses, it's a wonder you haven't up and died by now. He's probably got you thinking you've come down with everything in the book."

She saw me as a hypochondriac? I'd read about psychosomatic illness. "I'm not really sick, I just think I am?"

"Not at all. Of course you're ill, but perhaps not all that contagious."

Good. I could catch a plane home without putting people at risk of catching whatever batch of germs and ailments I'd collected

The firefighters put out the fire, including the brush and a half-dozen trees. The sheriff said he would send out a team tomorrow when it was light to investigate further and the fire chief's team would search for evidence of arson or an explosive. With little if anything left to see, the strangers who had come out to gawk got in their cars and left.

Mike approached. "I hear Juan is putting you up at his house, Oliver. Be sure to drop by the café when the doctor lifts this blasted quarantine."

"Yeah, we've missed you," said Matt.

"I'm going home," I said, blurting out the half-formed idea as if my plans were already set in cement. "To Wyoming."

"Sorry to hear that," Dr. Wallaberra mumbled, coming up on my other side. "We were just getting to know each other."

The Derrys and Dolans, the preachers, and Vanna all crowded around Juan's car as I climbed into the passenger seat and he behind the wheel.

"We'll miss you," Megan bawled, overcome with emotion.

"Hurry back here," said Brother John, his face as long and sorrowful looking as an old hound dog.

"Bye," called Vanna, as Juan started the car.

"Woof!" said Hugo, suddenly jumping up and down and all over the back seat like he'd just contacted rabies and would shortly start foaming at the mouth.

"What's the matter with Hugo?" I yelled over all that doggy racket. "You been feeding him sugar treats? He's acting damn hyperactive."

He crossed the Santa Cruz River. "I believe it's that jacket, Oliver. You're wearing the same one tonight that made Hugo crazy this afternoon."

I slipped down in the seat to lean my head on the headrest. "Dog's nuts. He can't need both zippered jackets."

Juan's home was decorated in quietly soothing earth tones. The single story townhouse, though larger, reminded me of Dollie's compact and pleasant villa. I stood in the center of the big living room with kitchen and eating areas to the end and one side. Tidy as *Tidy Bowl Man.*

"Take a load off, Oliver, while I make us some coffee." He stopped mid-step, remembering. "Or would you prefer herbal tea? Or warm milk?"

"Yeah, sure. How about affixing a cap with a nipple on the milk bottle?" I bit my lip, annoyed with how easily I got irritated these days.

"Knock it off. I know you're sick, but that's no excuse."

"Right. Pardon me." Saying I was sorry was galling. So I kept it light.

Juan retreated to the closet after a stack of sheets and blankets, a pillow teetering on top. He dropped them on one end of the sofa, then backed off to stare at me. "You want, I can check with *lowfares.com* on the Internet. See if we can get you an inexpensive rate for your flight to Wyoming." His offer to make pretty host noises from the kitchen apparently withdrawn, I simply nodded. Without a word I stood to make up the sofa bed.

I left my blue windbreaker in Juan's car. I was sick of listening to Hugo howl over a jacket or a zipper, whichever was making him crazy.

Again I had no personal possessions. Juan gave me a fresh toothbrush, a clean tee and pajama bottoms. We stuck my stuff in the washer. I'd slipped on jeans over the PJs and the windbreaker over the tops for the trip to the store.

We sat up late talking while my clothes traveled through the washer and dryer cycles. Vanna called to "check on me," she said. I felt like a kid sick to my stomach on the first day of kindergarten.

"Losing your home like that, on top of being physically ill, could shake up a guy," she commiserated. "I know it would me. I'd be devastated."

It was then I told her that Juan got me on a flight leaving first thing in the morning. "I'll probably be back here in a month or so, though." I don't know why I said that. I hadn't been planning to return at all. Meeting Vanna might make the difference, but I also dreaded leaving things half-finished, from the leaning church shed to the robberies; also the overt warnings to my person.

"I made a good impression on you, eh?" she whispered in my ear. "Sick as you are, you did, too, Oliver." A little giggle came tinkling over the line.

The next day early, there was Vanna again, determined, she said, to see me safely on the plane. I wanted to believe she was actively pursuing me but it could be Juan she was really after. One of mom's cliches echoed in my head: *A woman will chase you, trip you, and then fall down on the floor under you when you fall,* to make you think you're the pursuer. Had Vanna been an old hag, an offensive ugly warty crone of a witch, I would have objected. Since I already liked her so much, I didn't mind her escorting me into Tucson. I smiled.

At the airport Juan pulled up at the curb in front of my airline. "You've got an e-ticket," he said, as I climbed out of the back seat.

We'd left Hugo at Juan's. At my insistence, Vanna sat up front with Juan; to avoid my germs, I reminded her. She waved goodbye to me as Juan pulled away, so quickly I didn't get to thank him.

At the ticket counter the wait was short. I would transfer planes at Denver, I noticed from the attached itinerary, arriving in Casper by noon. Following the signs, I took an escalator up one flight of stairs and headed down the concourse toward the security check. The procedure routine and the attendants bored, I didn't notice much else until all hell broke loose.

A pair of security guards ran up, pulled their guns, and grabbed an elbow apiece. That was enough, but then a big German shepherd (a K-9 cop?) leaped forward, both front paws crashing against my chest. Down I went, expecting to be eaten alive. Instead, the big dog went for my windbreaker, the same zippered pocket that made Hugo nuts.

"Drugs!" shouted an approaching fellow, the one holding the dog's leash with the letters DEA on his jacket. "Down, boy. You caught him. Good boy!"

CHAPTER 19

Sweat poured off me, leaving my brow awash and running down my neck. Getting hauled out of line and dragged off to the security office was no picnic. If I'd thought that quarantine in a small RV was like a cell, I didn't know what I was thinking. This was far worse, and we were only in the office—me under a bright light, the authorities hovering over me. Maybe they'd catch my germs. Voices harsh, eyes suspicious, they obviously doubted my innocence.

Allowed one telephone call, I reached Juan on his cellular. He said they would return immediately, adding that Vanna would try to reach Brother John.

Time is such a strange variable. It could have been hours, even days, before they showed. I didn't know what anybody could do to rescue me. The big K-9 had sniffed drugs on me, the remnants of marijuana, I supposed. I wasn't sure because nobody was explaining anything. Instead, they asked me every question in the book. Who was I, where was I from, what was I doing, where was I headed and why was I so eager to get out of town? Who were my contacts, was I selling or buying, was this a one-time thing or a habit? Why was I sweating, did I need a fix, and what was that awful stench coming from my body? They could have offered me coffee or water, a chance to use the facilities, but no. Poke their faces in mine, bang the table, pace and scowl. Where was the *good cop, bad cop* game, or perhaps neither the Drug Enforcement Agency people nor the airport guards subscribed to such a thing.

Juan and Vanna arrived. I knew because they were soon invited into the airport office; perhaps not an office, nor a plush conference room. Could have been designed for interrogation and intimidation. Garcia was asked to identify me, which he did, with pretty Vanna nodding her head seriously and emphatically. Yes, they knew me. Yes, they could vouch for my honesty.

Sometimes things work in one's favor, sometimes not. I wouldn't believe it, because too many bad things had been happening to me lately, but the DEA fellow in charge let me go. No apologies. No smiles or offers to shake hands. Just a nod to the guard at the door, who opened it for me, albeit reluctantly.

As we walked down the quiet hall, empty except for the three of us, I wondered if this was what it felt like to stare down the corridor toward the execution chamber. No, of course not. I was free to go.

Turned out Juan and the chief of airport security were chums. If Juan said I was okay, then I was clean.

"Except it wouldn't hurt you to get a bath, son," said the DEA old-timer.

Mechanical troubles had delayed the plane. I didn't miss my flight after all. As I waved goodbye for the second time that morning, Brother John came running up, his long lanky legs loose like I imagined Ichabod Crane.

"I hurried as fast as I could. Are you all right?" Lucas grabbed me by the shoulders for a big hug.

Juan said he would explain things to the preacher.

I rushed toward my plane. Would this day never end?

CHAPTER 20

Mom actually sent Hernandez away. Not for good, just for awhile, she said. That was after he met my plane in Casper to drive us up to Gillette. We didn't talk much. Luis never had, I was too sick. A fresh bout of hives had broken out, not only on my torso but also on legs, arms, and shoulders. I figured all this stress was too much for my immune system, what there was left of it. My head ached and now a case of sniffles was attacking along with the continual coughing and hacking.

"How you been?" I asked, when we were in the car and headed north on Interstate 25 toward the cut-off.

"Okay. You?"

"Fine." If he believed that with all the evidence to the contrary, I had a Stradivarius I'd offer him for sale cheap. "And mom?"

"Fine."

The flat land with the scrubby grass and sage brush of the high plains sped by; the reverse, rather, as Hernandez mashed the accelerator. Finally, mom's taciturn second husband had another two words for me. "You stink."

I should have worried about infecting him with my half-a-dozen ailments, but if I'd willingly sailed right through airports and airplanes without a shred of remorse, why fret now. "Medications. Sweat, too, I guess."

Briefly the dark-haired, swarthy-skinned man glanced my way. Wearing khaki pants with clean white shirt on this pleasantly warm day, his hair and body smelled fresh, of shampoo, soap, and aftershave lotion. Hernandez was fastidious, I'll give him that. By contrast, my nervous perspiration must have been purely awful.

Luis rolled down the window. "You wanna stop at my brother's for a bath before you show up at your mother's?"

Man, this was terrible. My nose must have been stopped up, too, for I detected no more than an occasional offensive whiff. "Okay. Thanks."

After a shower, shampoo, and shave, I dreaded donning the same odious clothes. Out in the bedroom of the modest two-bedroom cottage, Luis rummaged in his brother's bureau. "Cal won't mind my lending you a pair of his shorts and a tee shirt."

I wondered why Luis was being so nice to me. He must know how I felt about his marrying my mom. Unless it was her feelings he wanted to protect. Mom had a sensitive nose and a soft spot in her heart for her only son.

I thanked him and, behind the bathroom door, slipped into jockey shorts. "Yowl!" I yelped, immediately jerking them back off. "Too tight, too rough against these shingles," I called out. "Gimme back my pajama bottoms." The thin cotton with the drawstring that I could leave loose felt better.

"Whew! Let's get you over to the house and into bed. Margaret will do your laundry and I'll go shopping for fresh jammies."

Jammies! Yeah, that's what he'd said, like I was a six-year-old kid instead of pressing thirty. In fact, my birthday was next week.

Ignoring the danger of contagion or the offensive odor, mom gathered me in her arms like a hen with a new baby chick beneath her wing. She sobbed, real tears. I took it this was more than a woman's emotion at welcoming home her son, this was desperate weeping.

"For cryin' out loud, son. You look half-dead." She had no formal medical background but you could say she was self-taught. Mom's a midwife.

Luis said he was off to work and then he would stop over a few days with his brother's family. Mom accepted his peck on the cheek, returning her husband's affection with a vague wave. Petite, about five-one, she's as tiny around as she is tall. Wavy, salt-and-pepper hair topped a sweet face, her habitual nice, really *nice*, expression now etched permanently on her features.

She dished up fresh pajamas along with her home-made chicken noodle soup and a pot of green tea. "Climb into bed, Oliver. I've made up the spare room with fresh sheets. Now, don't fuss. But you're my son, I raised you, changed maybe a couple thousand diapers, bathed you and kept you healthy. I'm going to examine you all over, so get your clothes off."

I grimaced and protested, to no avail. Margaret Rose Vicente Temple Hernandez would have her way with me, and that was that. One descendant among many of frontier settlers, she had a long history of dominance and determination. I obeyed, removing pajamas and throwing back the sheet, lying back down and closing my eyes. I didn't have to watch her probing my flesh, I could feel. The hives itched worse than ever.

"It's not shingles you've got, Oliver. It's a bad case of poison ivy."

Casually tossing the clean top sheet over my nakedness, she turned to leave. "Gonna get down my medical books," she said. "Then I'm calling in reinforcements."

Besides her well-worn books and brochures, pamphlets and such, Mom had other resources—an herbalist and a retired medical doctor. *Déjà vu.* Another old geezer who'd likely come up with a prognosis straight out of the fifties. Couldn't be worse than the Green Valley doctor's diagnoses.

The old doctor came, he looked, and he too probed. Without a word to me, he left my bedroom with Margaret mincing quickly after. Soon a woman showed, armed with more references. Mom introduced her as an herbalist with a specialty in poisons. Poisons?

I don't know how long that cute little trio of senior citizens conferred, because I fell asleep. My body bathed and now coated with soothing calamine lotion, I felt peaceful, protected, and safe.

Presently I awoke to the aroma of steaming, fresh-brewed coffee, sizzling bacon, and eggs. Mom returned with a tray holding toast and orange juice. "Doctor wants to ask you some questions after you eat, Oliver."

I couldn't believe how hungry I was for mom's food. In Arizona I'd been eating Cheerios for breakfast, with Megan's *Meals on Wheels* for lunch and Dollie's or Elise's casseroles for dinner. I guess a boy always misses his own mother's familiar cooking. I dug in. Megan could cook, but the cousins could both use a few lessons.

Although the day was waning, *breakfast* tasted good. When I say "tasted," I mean I could actually tell flavors, it was all that delicious.

Doctor too wore a happy face. His full head of white hair topped a consistently pleasant expression in counterpoint to the nose that ended in a round blob of a schnoz. His steps quick and short, his voice a staccato, I rather thought he could have been a rooster pecking round the hen house.

My meal finished and a trip to the bathroom—one among many over that night and the following day—the group convened. The foot of my bed quickly became their conference table. The questions they asked, one right after the other, reminded me of the Tucson airport interrogation, only this session was benign, designed to root out information they needed to make me well. First, said the doctor, they had to get the evidence so they could make a proper diagnosis. Then they would proceed to administer remedies. Their questions were precise and straightforward. Mom recorded my replies.

"Describe your recent habits," the doctor said softly, pulling up a chair at bedside. "Who prepared your food and who stopped by regularly and what did they do?" Sounded like strange questions. I'd already told him I was under quarantine; doctor's orders.

Nevertheless, I tried to be accurate, recalling those who had dropped off and retrieved things at my doorstep. The cousins had vied for food and laundry duty. Fess and Donny had made the deliveries. When Megan cooked any of her three guys delivered. Derek, Mike, or Matt could have cooked. The tray with its array of dishes could have sat untended on a counter awaiting delivery. I supposed that anybody familiar with the routine could have had access to and tampered with my meals between the Cat Castle's stove and my place.

Meanwhile, first one and then another probed, pulling up my eyelids to stare deeply into my eyes, poking my chest, belly, and abdomen, and asking how each part of this physical examination felt. *Pain, ache, hurt*, these were insufficient responses, said the herbalist. "We must know more," said mom. "Please be explicit, son."

They asked about my menus, every dish, any scrap of memory I could dredge up from every activity, no matter how slight and seemingly irrelevant to me. They wanted to hear about plants indigenous to the locale and specifically to home-grown gardens. I named the cacti, grateful for their names and descriptions as told to me by my friends.

At that point another vision flashed across the screen of my consciousness. Dr. Wallaberra in his garden, his furtive glances over his shoulder at me making him appear damn suspicious. This wouldn't be the first time I'd pondered upon what manner of plants he was growing out there; until now I'd thought of illegal substances, drugs. Instead, he could have been nurturing plants with poisonous fruits and seeds.

I spoke of the thefts and vandalism in the area and at the church and my quest to identify the culprits. It seemed too silly to mention but I described running out of gas to be left stranded on the highway, not once but twice.

"Somebody meant to send you a message," said Doctor. "Get out of town or else."

"The *or else* signifying stronger retaliations," added the herbalist.

"He, she, or they kept upping the ante," said mom.

With the effort of trying to recall everything, I completely forgot to mention the zippered pocket on my windbreaker, the one that sent poor little Hugo into a frenzy every time he got near it. Later I would remember to ponder whether the puzzle of discovering remnants of cocaine and marijuana also had something to do with my would-be murderers. (I don't know why I kept thinking in the plural.) *Up the ante*, eh. If they couldn't kill me with poison, if they couldn't get me sent away on a drug charge, they would just blow me up! It was pure coincidence that I had left the RV to head for the store. I had never left it before, not since the St. Mary's Hospital doctor had imposed the quarantine. (By the time I remembered my zippered pocket and its implications, it was the dead of night when, time after time, I had to go potty.)

The herbalist spread out a batch of notes on herbs and plants over the foot of my bed, where they all took a gander. Intermittently they mumbled, conferring in low tones as if I were comatose, as they continued passing pages back and forth, raising eyebrows, shaking or nodding heads.

"Am I not long for this world?" I asked, unable to resist.

"Good thing you came home," mom said.

"Or you'd soon be, that's for sure," Doctor said.

That evening before they left, another batch of people arrived. This time they prayed over me. They prayed and prayed and sang the old hymns. I drifted in and out of sleep on the wings of song, *Blest Be the Tie that Binds* the last notes I heard. Then two men dressed in suits and ties conducted the laying on of hands ritual, using consecrated oil, mom whispered in my ear. I felt four rough-worn ministerial hands on my head and felt a great peace descend as if a dove from heaven.

CHAPTER 21

Miraculously I awakened feeling fine; not cured, of course, but a whole lot better. Having returned to my bedside, the team agreed there could have been several things poisoning my system. The oil of poison ivy leaves rubbed inside my pajama bottoms could simulate the hives of shingles. Pneumomycosis, I was told, was caused by a variety of yeast-like and mold-like microorganisms, resulting in symptoms resembling tuberculosis. Antinomyces hominis attacks the lungs, jaws, and alimentary tract.

"The latter alone is usually fatal," doctor said, shaking his head. "Whoever did all this to you must have been pretty disgusted that you didn't die straight off."

"Thanks to his good health and strong constitution," affirmed my mom, smiling with pride like an architect staring at a fine completed structure of her own design.

"But where did these symptoms and diseases come from?" I demanded. Still abed, I was propped up with feather pillows. Instead of the proverbial weak tea and toast, mom had scrambled eggs laced with ham and brewed strong coffee. I pushed aside the tray with the plate licked clean.

"Poisons!" the herbalist squealed, hitching up her chair and clapping hands; almost, I could have sworn, with glee. Nice to have one's knowledge vindicated. "Many otherwise harmless plants, including some of the most wholesome food plants, contain traces of substances which in concentrated form can produce violent poisons."

Startled, I recalled Dr. Wallaberra's furtive gardening habits. He might not be the bumbler he wanted me to think he was.

"Yes, indeed," she continued, getting up to stand at the foot of my bed. "Certain botanical families of plants contain many poisonous species, all of which produce similar action. Nearly all species of the nightshade and poppy families produce narcotic alkaloids. Dogbane and nux-vomica families also contain heart and nerve poisons."

My mind was bouncing all over the place. Poppies and narcotics hit home. If not the pastor growing illegal substances, could have been Fess, or those teenagers, using their shed fixing and garden digging as excuse.

The team still huddled and babbled around me. "You could have been served a whole smorgasbord of harmful substances," mom said. Her mournful expression spoke volumes, suggesting she should never have let her little boy leave home. As if anything she said or did could have detoured me from my initial goal of following Patsy and Malcolm down to Arizona.

The herbalist had more: "In many plants the poisonous principle is contained chiefly in the fruit or seed, as in belladonna, bittersweet, henbane, or strophanthus. Also in nux vomica." My head was whirling. To check all this stuff out, plus the perpetrator who'd fed them to me, I needed specificity. I asked her to make notes.

The doctor interrupted with more ideas. Looked like he and the herbalist were in competition. I sighed and reached for my empty mug. Mom took the hint to refill it with more of the steaming brew from her Mr. Coffee machine.

"In other plants," said the herbalist, "the poison is found chiefly in the roots or tubers, although other parts of the plant are also poisonous … ."

"Yes," said mom, determined to get in on the act. "As in the ailanthus, larkspur, wild cherry, lily of the valley, and mountain laurel."

Doctor leaned back to rub his scalp and stare at the far wall. He could have been talking to himself. "If you had actually contracted mycobacterium tuberculosis, that belongs to the same genus as the organism causing leprosy."

I jerked, splashing coffee down the front of my clean jammies, as Hernandez labeled his offering. Doctor continued: "TB was isolated in 1890 by the German bacteriologist, Robert Koch. TB is very contagious."

I recalled Thomas Mann's *The Magic Mountain*, and was thankful I wasn't being ordered to languish atop an alpine mountain for months, the recommended cure in those days. I wouldn't be able to identify my would-be murderers from that distant place. Sitting up straighter, I again jiggled the coffee cup. This time mom removed the mug from my hand, muttering that if I wasn't going to drink it, I didn't need to flang it around. I submitted easily, ready to toss back the covers. I had to get out of here and get going.

"Never mind all that. What's the cure?" I demanded.

The trio of conspirators exchanged glances accompanied by a full choir of grins, smirks, and guffaws. "Notice anything different about last night?" the doctor said.

"You mean the trots?"

Another chorus from the singers of Truth. "We dosed you with stuff to initiate purging," mom said smugly.

"Too late for an emetic," said the herbalist.

"To encourage vomiting," doctor blithely added.

"What about my abdominal cramps? And my legs? The way I felt, I thought sure I'd be crippled for life."

"Arsenic," said the herbalist, relying on her knowledge of poisons. "Probably very small doses, but frequently administered."

Ohmigosh. Who and how many people were responsible for all this? Must be a whole gang. I had to find out. Couldn't let it lie or the killers go free.

"Oliver Temple, you just be still," mom commanded. "I'll be right back."

I obeyed mama. Doctor stared at the wall. The herbalist stared at the back of his head. When mom returned she handed me a tall glass of milky looking stuff. Reminded me of Juan and his offer of warm milk. "What's this?"

"Never you mind. Just drink it."

Didn't taste half-bad. Could use a shot or two of whiskey, though. "Eggnog? And it isn't even New Year's Eve?"

"Raw eggs with milk. Plus a little sweetener and nutmeg."

"*A little bit of sugar makes the medicine go down,*" I sang gleefully, imitating Julia Andrews playing *Mary Poppins*. I emptied the glass like a good little boy.

"Get some sleep," said the doctor. "In between the runs." He actually giggled.

It was mom's turn to stare. "No, Sir. My drink is supposed to stop the diarrhea."

"What?" he yelled, knocking the glass out of my hands. "Not yet!"

I would have cleaned up the mess, but I still had no strength. I fell back onto the pillows. Mom did the duty.

At last I was left alone. I gazed around the walls of my old bedroom, everything still arranged exactly as I'd left it a decade earlier, before moving into my own place, a trailer out east of Gillette in the sticks near the village of Rozet. Closer to the mine where I'd worked at the time. Now I thought about sneaking next door to the guestroom where mom had set up her new computer, to get online with Juan. But I couldn't lift my head from the fluffy pillows. The Sandman was calling.

Later, following another half-dozen trips to the potty, mom produced the "doctored" eggnog I was at last permitted to drink. Soon, I concluded, I would be ready to get control of my life.

Over the next couple of weeks the emails flew between Juan and me. Took awhile for me to summarize my medical history and pose questions for Juan to ponder, for I was still very weak.

A sweat broke out, the perspiration running off my brow and down my sides from my armpits. Between us, Juan and I recapped what we knew for certain before progressing to share conjectures.

Meanwhile, Juan said he would investigate. I warned him to watch his Ps and Qs. "Don't forget what they did to me as punishment for my prying."

Elise and Dollie had done my laundry along with some of the cooking, which meant that both had access to sheets and pajamas. "But their sons did, too," I reminded Juan. "Fess and Donny both retrieved and delivered the goods." Sounded like we were discussing contraband instead of jammies.

I shared my suspicions of Dr. Wallaberra's sneaky gardening habits. Later Juan said he'd gone to church, actually attending prayer service. Neither cousin had shown, he said, adding that he made sure he was the last to leave, driving off into the shadows to park and outwait the departure of both preachers.

He'd examined the garden by flashlight. "Fresh digging there, and an empty square patch, with plants missing," he wrote, leaving me with an ominous feeling. I was afraid for his safety. I could see Juan tugging at his black mustache, white teeth gleaming in his tan face.

"I hope you kept a sharp eye out for Fess Goodman's red Jaguar," I pecked out on mom's keyboard.

Back came Juan's reply. He remembered something else. "Didn't Dollie take you on a walking tour of the villas? My maintenance men plant and tend a big variety of flora throughout the common areas. Mrs. Martinez wouldn't have to be growing poisonous plants in her own small patio garden. She could go outside her own place. Or, how about this? She likes to walk in the desert, though I've personally warned her about the potential dangers out there—snakes, gila monsters, the possibility of stumbling and falling into a prickly cactus. Ever get your rear stuck full of stickers? Hurts like hell, and they're the devil to get out."

The next day he had more news. "Dollie's son Donny—guess what his undergrad degree was in. Botany!"

"How did you learn that?" I tapped back.

"Asked him. Not to worry, I was casual. He came in the office this morning to pay his mom's villa rent. We got to talking. I asked what he planned to do when he graduates this summer with his MBA. 'Look for a good job,' he said. Taciturn, that's Donny. Which was when I asked about his B.A. major."

"Botany! Which means he knows all about plants."

"Right. And poisons, no doubt."

"What about Fess Goodman?" I reminded Juan of the conversation I'd heard between the cousins while eavesdropping from Brother John's RV. "Dollie claimed Fess was into drugs, going to a rehab center, something like that. Elise didn't deny her cousin's accusations."

"Which means Fess must have contacts in the drug world. Whether a junkie or a dealer, he would know something or somebody, or both."

"Motivation?"

Before I could reply to Juan's single-word question, mom interrupted. I fully expected her to send me back to bed—after making sure I drank another eggnog. I was starting to hate those things, though I had to admit that drinking them slowed down my endless trips to the toilet.

Instead she smiled and handed me a full set of daytime clothes. "Get dressed and come to dinner."

I could smell the delicious aroma of broiling steak. "Does this mean I'm well? I can be a man, again?"

"You tell me. How do you feel?"

I signaled goodbye with a "talk later" message to Juan and switched off the computer. Then I stood to walk around the room and smirk at myself in the mirror at the healthy face grinning back. "Like a million dollars."

CHAPTER 22

That night with a full belly and no more extra potty trips, I should have slept like a baby. No way. Too many suspects and suppositions rolling around like marbles inside my head. These thoughts were compounded with worries about Juan's safety, and longing for Vanna in my arms.

She had called a couple of times, wanting to assure herself of my improving condition, she said, lightly tossing off her concern. When was I returning, she asked.

Soon, I said, surprising myself. Any sane person would certainly take the hint, delivered in the worst possible way short of getting shot in the back or my throat slit or my guts ripped open.

I flipped and floundered in my bed like a fish out of its bowl, rumpling sheets that, thank the Lord, were no longer drenched with sweat. In all our emails, plus a couple of phone calls both ways, neither Juan nor I had once proposed that the Derrys or Dolans were responsible. Yet Megan too had prepared my food.

Startled, I sat straight up in bed. What did I know about Mike and Matt, after all, except that they were Megan's brothers. One or the other usually delivered my meals. Sometimes Derek Dolan. Then Vanna. Hey, not Vanna!

I reconsidered the Derrys. What if the handsome, look-alike blond brothers were into drug trafficking? From next to nothing the Cat Castle was an overnight success. Now the Derrys had so much money they could afford to buy not only the building they had first rented but also the acreage next door. The six-bedroom house under construction must have cost them a bundle, too, requiring a hefty down payment any banker would demand before signing off on the dual mortgages.

Another flip-flop, more tossing and turning. Too many suspects. I ticked them off on my fingers. Dollie and son, Donny; Elise and son, Fess; Dr. Wallaberra. Now Matt and Mike? Better to keep it simple, stop including everybody under the sun, especially Megan, Brother John, Juan, and Vanna. A guy had to trust somebody and I would swear on my life that these four were clean. Call them friends, if not bosom buddies.

Past midnight and all was quiet. Mom was a deep sleeper and Hernandez was still bedding down at his brother's house. Time to leave, let Luis return to his home with mom. Abruptly I felt ashamed of my selfishness. Mom had a life beyond playing nursemaid to a grown man. After my birthday party a few days hence, I was out of here.

Birthday party, indeed. Like I was a scrawny six-year-old giggling over balloons, clowns, presents, vanilla ice cream and chocolate cake. Well, I wouldn't say No to the latter. My appetite was returning in full force. I could eat a horse. As for a gift, how about Vanna Solano? She needn't come wrapped in gold foil and glitter. The pretty brunette gleamed and glittered just with her presence and her smile.

Early the next morning to the tune of sizzling bacon on my end, Vanna called. Following a lot of chat over not much of nothing, she asked what she could do for me. Seemed strange, from that distance. I was thinking of a sweet cuddle, when she added, reading my mind and laughing, "I meant about helping Juan find the bad guys."

That's what she said, *bad guys,* like in an old B-rated cowboy movie. Across the room mom was motioning to me, pointing to the eggs, sunny side up in her blue and white speckled granite skillet.

Before cutting the connection, I stammered, "Uh, eavesdrop? Only be careful, Vanna. I don't want you poisoned next."

She admitted to reading some of my emails to Juan. (When? Where? Under what conditions? My heart ached with envy and jealousy.)

"Eavesdropping, eh. Good idea," she said in my ear as mom forked up crisp bacon and scooped two eggs onto my breakfast plate. "Neither of the cousins nor their sons have been into the Cat lately, but maybe they'll return soon." She paused. "Oh, hey, I nearly forgot to tell you. Brother John made a public announcement Sunday. He told the whole congregation that you're recovering and will return to the fold shortly."

I groaned. Although I didn't by any means know everybody at Dr. Wallaberra's church—not to call them by name—they knew me, I supposed. When Elise didn't play the piano, I did. It was me who'd cultivated and weeded the big plot of land the pastor used as a garden. I was also the painter, the maintenance man, the marketer, the book-keeper, and the bus driver. The preachers now had a bus, a spanking new, bright yellow school bus. Before falling ill and going under quarantine, I was driving it all over the rural community three times a week to collect children for the Sunday School and to pick up and return the old-timers and the poor with no transportation of their own for sermons and prayer meetings.

Yeah, they would remember me.

"They cheered, Oliver. Right there in church, people cheered and clapped their hands. Everybody misses you, Oliver Temple!" She didn't say whether she counted herself among them. I felt like crossing my fingers.

I appreciated mom's hearty breakfast, and all her cooking, and told her so. She let me eat a few bites before planting herself in the chair opposite me across the square wooden table. She likes raisin bran by Total, with two percent milk and a dab of cream.

"All right, Son, give. Who is this Solano woman and what is she to you?" Mom had taken Vanna's calls.

"Just a friend."

"The soloist, Dollie somebody?"

"No. Vanna's younger. Younger than Mrs. Martinez, younger than I am."

"Ahah." She added more cream to her bowl.

"What's that supposed to mean?" I said it but I didn't look at her. Busy sopping up egg with the last corner of toast, I kept my eyes on the plate.

"It means you're blushing, Oliver. That's what it means. Are you and Vanna lovers, yet?"

"Ma-ma!"

"Don't tell me. I can see for myself. You're like a kid with a schoolboy crush. If you'd taken her to bed already, you'd be more sure of yourself. Am I right or am I right?"

She didn't wait for my flustered reply. Margaret Rose Vicente Temple Hernandez pursed her lips as preface to the standard line I'd heard since childhood. "Can't fool your Mama!" Now she merely looked smug. She knew that I knew what she was thinking.

I washed the dishes and put them away. Although I had bought her a dishwasher, mom used it for storing pasta and crackers. That afternoon I had an appointment with an old chum, Bill, a police officer now.

CHAPTER 23

That afternoon I met with the cop, the fullback player on our high school football team. After Bill got off work we met at the Starlight, a saloon out on Highway 16. Attached to a Mexican restaurant, the bar was quiet. Another thirty minutes, when Happy Hour commenced, it would be hopping, but for now I had ample time to visit with my cop friend. A big guy with a neck like an oak tree, a bent nose and a short kinky haircut, Bill played fullback when I was Campbell County High School's quarterback. After exchanging the usual niceties, hearing about his wife and two kids, boy and girl, Bill asked about the drug trade down in Arizona.

He could have been reading my mind. That's what I wanted to pick his brains about—drugs. "Haven't heard much."

"Guess you wouldn't, seein' as how you're a civilian and all." What was Bill, military? I paid for another couple of Coors.

"What about up here, Bill? You ever hear of a Malcolm Barr into drugs, especially dealing?"

He leaned his elbows on the bar top and twirled his can of beer around and around. "Small timer. We caught him with a small bag of MaryJane. He's been in jail for, oh, four or five months. Just got out."

You could have knocked me off the bar stool with a dead dandelion fluff. All this time I was looking for him and Patsy down in Arizona, Malcolm was stuck up north in the slammer. So who had Patsy left Gillette with, if not Barr?

"Forget him," Bill said. "He's clean, now, or so I hear." Bill reached down the bar to fetch a huge handful of popcorn out of a wicker basket. Munch, munch. "That what you wanted to jaw about? Malcolm Barr?"

"Uh, him and drugs, I guess. Or something similar going down."

Crunch, crunch. "If it's criminal stories you want, Oliver, I got a good one for ya." Between munching and crunching, Bill described an illegal immigrant who kept returning to Gillette from Chihuahua. "Galarza keeps sneaking across the U.S.-Mexican border, even though he's been deported seven times. He told the judge at the sentencing hearing that he'll keep coming back like a bad penny 'cuz he's got family up here. This time the judge threw the book at him, gave him a dozen years for illegal entry."

I whistled, the noise akin to a *Whew.* "Long time."

"Yeah, but he's been convicted for burglary, assault, trespassing, aggravated assault, disturbing the peace, criminal impersonation, loitering, driving while under the influence, drug possession and trafficking."

The first was all color. My ears perked up at the latter. Another Whew. "Bill, you said something about dealing down along the Arizona *Drug Corridor*, namely, I-19, between Tucson and Nogales. What do you know about that?"

Bill grinned at the woman behind the bar; cute, with a nice friendly smile, wide as an ax handle in the behind and over the hill in the face. "I'll tell you another story, Oliver, about a three-point-seven million dollar drug bust. See, its like this. All the high-tech surveillance equipment in the world can't protect against human greed. Colombian dealers who work out of South Florida have also discovered Mexico. Officials from the Justice Department learned that a major drug trafficking organization in Southern Arizona was planning to offer bribes to U.S. immigration officers in exchange for their cooperation. The Colombian and Mexican cocaine kings wanted immigration documents and assistance to smuggle in one-hundred-kilo loads of cocaine into the States. It's now estimated that Mexican government officials and law enforcement personnel took in as much as five-hundred-million per year in bribes from drug dealers."

"Wow!"

"Yeah, well, that's not all that's happen', man." Sometimes he liked talking Black; otherwise he sounded more like the educated guy he is.

"How do you know all this?" My second Coors sat untouched, growing warm, while the huge man in plain clothes beside me ordered another. I took it he was off duty. The second hand on the clock above the saloon mirror clicked over. Five o'clock. Soon the place would be packed. Down at one end of the bar a young thing in a tight short skirt and low, revealing bodice turned out another big batch of popcorn in the enclosed glass-fronted machine. Two more skimpily dressed cocktail waitresses came on duty. Midway along the bar an old-timer replaced the rumpled gray fedora on his head, slid off the stool, and shuffled out the door.

"I gotta get home," said Bill, gulping his third beer. "Wifey will guess where I'm holed up."

I didn't want to let him go. "You were saying?"

He struck me on the back, simulating a friendly slap from a grizzly. Nearly knocked me off the stool. "Can't say too much, Oliver. But I got connections all over the place, old buddy. After high school I played ball first with the Nebraska Cornhuskers and then with the Dallas Cowboys. Some ex-players, like me, went with the police. Others into the military. One guy is with the DEA."

I knew some of Bill's personal history, but by no means all. "Yeah, so?"

"So you watch your step if you're heading back that way. There's a big sting operation on the horizon, boy. Can't say just when. But I mean t'tell ya, really big. When it comes down, it'll blow your freakin' mind. So watch yourself. I'd hate to see any innocent bystanders hurt. Especially my old quarterback. Keep your ears to the ground, and stay outta the way. Don't get involved."

The big black man left, shaking his head back and forth, and chortling. From his tone, one of pure devilment, he could have personally pulled off the biggest prank of the decade. As for the sound coming up from his throat, it could have been a freight train rumbling out of the tunnel.

CHAPTER 24

I had promised mom I would be home for dinner, another big T-bone, and I was. This time Luis joined us. Diffident, he deferred to me by pointing to the chair at the head of the table. I declined by deferring right back. A big grin splitting his face, he took the seat of honor and assumed his role as head of the house.

Just like that, everything was okay between us. Casually he spoke of his job and the new set of houses going up out west of town. "Out there in the hills, the ritzy ditzy area," Luis said. "Company's name is Ashbery Homes. And get this: it's owned by a woman. Pretty little slip of a thing, hobbling around half the time on a crutch. Says she broke her leg in seven places out at the skate park. She was rollerblading with her granddaughters." Luis hee-hawed, while helping himself to mashed potatoes, the top part of this mini-volcano sunk in, with a huge pat of butter melting into a golden puddle. "She named her business after both little girls—Amber and Ashley. Get it? Ashbery."

That was more talk than I'd heard out of him since his marriage to mom. Guess he felt comfortable with me, finally.

When I said I would be returning to Arizona after my birthday, mom threw a fit. I should have waited until we'd finished eating. Talk about insensitive.

"Oh, no! Not back down there where they tried to kill you. Oh, Oliver." My pretty, petite brunette of a pug-nosed mother appealed to her husband with a sharp look.

"Huh?" he muttered.

Apparently she hadn't shared the details of my various ailments with Luis as yet. Reeling from my bad news, she did now. That took up the rest of the dinner hour. Hernandez, handsome with dark hair and swarthy skin covering a strong, physically fit body, tried to avoid taking sides. He could see mine, too. Mostly he tried to comfort mom while raising an eyebrow at me.

Following a healthy serving of her Decadent Chocolate Pie with pecans in an Oreo cookie crust and topped with heavy cream, I asked to be excused. Declining dessert herself, mom hunkered down with both hands gripping her coffee mug. "Be careful, Oliver," she whispered, bringing a tender pat from her husband.

On the way back to the bar where I'd met Bill that afternoon, I got to thinking again about motivations. Rubbing my PJs with the leaves of poison ivy would be easy if Elise or Fess used plastic gloves to protect themselves from contacting the rash. Except that, how would the Goodmans get access to arsenic or any of those poisonous plants, and how would they know how much to administer? Or, how about this scenario: Elise, with or without her son's knowledge, could be aware of Fess's activities and be set on protecting her son. Particularly if she even suspected a drug deal was about to go down.

Braked at the stoplight on busy Highway 59, I didn't notice the light turn green until the line of cars behind me commenced honking. Plenty of good memories around here: Baskin & Robbins and Wal-Mart to the left, the big high school off to the right, coming up the huge recreation complex with swimming pool and gym. Despite the flat, wind-swept terrain and cold winter climate, Gillette's not a bad place to call home, to raise a family in. Fleetingly I pondered on whether Vanna could adapt. I might return to the oil field or the mines if good pay was her Number One job criteria for a husband. If she wanted to hear me play church music, I could volunteer at mom's church. Warm thoughts enveloped me like a cloud, with Vanna central to my future.

I had no particular plans that night; nobody to call, nobody to meet. My only goal, to get out and about, leave the Hernandez lovebirds alone. At last I could sympathize with mom's need to find love again, even if it did seem rather soon after dad died when she'd latched onto Luis.

Besides, after the imprisonment of the quarantine, it felt good to be released from my cage. I'd been a captured parrot whose wings weren't really clipped, just pined down for awhile. Now I was free again. To come and go, do anything I wanted. The only thing I could think of was another beer, in the same bar as I'd left earlier. I couldn't even go out to Betty's familiar old drafty Mexican café. Neither she nor her daughter Tina was there any longer. I hoped they had found happiness down in Mexico.

Back on the same bar stool I'd warmed that afternoon, I chatted with the barmaid until she got busy. Happy hour over now, the place was fairly quiet until a trio of loudmouths arrived. They ordered and waited at the bar for their beers, served frothy and foaming in frosted mugs, which they carried with them to the pool table in the rear.

Turning to the bartender, the same woman who had served Bill and me earlier, I asked about the newcomers. "That dark-haired guy in the middle. He looks familiar."

"That's Malcolm Barr. Just got outta jail."

I sauntered over to kibitz. The guys' game over, Malcolm approached and challenged me to a game. I won, not so easily, but by a legitimate margin. Enough to make buying drinks a natural move.

Settled on bar stools over our Coors, I casually broached my purpose. "You ever hear of a girl named Patsy Parsons? I been outta town awhile, but I'd like to get in touch with her. We knew each other in school." Drat, I'd dragged out my question with way too much verbiage.

Malcolm fired a Marlboro, not bothering to glance up, not looking suspicious or particularly interested. "Yeah, I knew her. Cute little blonde. Haven't seen her in months."

"Where was that?"

"Huh? Well, I been in jail awhile. Last I saw her, me and her were heading south to Arizona, but she got mad over sumpin', I fergit what. We parted afore we ever got out of Wyoming, down at Wamsutter. You ever been to that stick-in-the mud little burg?"

"Yeah."

"Well, she asked the manager at a café there if they was hiring. They was, and Patsy put on an apron and went to work. That very minute. With not even a by-your leave t'me. I was yesterday's news. I come back home. Why? You fixin' to find Patsy?"

I shrugged.

End of story.

Until I figured out how to write another chapter.

CHAPTER 25

Again Juan and I talked on the phone. He didn't mention having seen Vanna and I didn't suggest that the Derry boys might bear watching. I asked about his work and he replied *Bueno*, good, maybe so-so, before wishing me happy birthday. When I said my mom was planning a party, Juan asked, chuckling, if that meant balloons and a clown. Clairvoyant, that guy, our two minds again traveling the same highway. At least he made no reference to ODD Temple.

Then he said he was busy training Hugo, giving him puppy lessons.

"Oh, yeah?" Like I couldn't make my dog behave.

"You know, house training. Curing him of destructive chewing and inappropriate jumping."

"Hey, Juan. Hugo's jumping all over the place in a frenzy of barking <u>was</u> appropriate. He was trying to warn me that the contents of my zippered pocket was <u>very</u> inappropriate. Or had once been."

That must have been another scheme dreamed up by the perps, no doubt to put me out of action. If the poison ivy and poisoned food didn't send me running back to Wyoming and screaming for my mama, then they'd sic the authorities on me to come down on a cocaine charge. They had also tried to blow me up along with the RV! And before all that was the siphoning of gas out of my Harley-Davidson. To carry that scenario further, perhaps a member of the drug gang was supposed to have caught me stranded out in the desert to beat me up. Or give me one more in a series of warnings. Shoot me dead, more like.

Juan was still talking in my ear. Something about taking Hugo to a professional trainer. "Diana's been training in conformation to professional activities, and her experience working in herding, tracking, guarding, and search and rescue." I didn't ask who Diana was; he'd probably already said.

"Hah. Hugo's already a tracker. Of cocaine, remember."

Juan chuckled and rang off before I could ask him about Vanna. Of course I didn't really want to know. About Vanna, yes; about whether he had seen her, no. I didn't want to discover they had gotten together without me.

Already Vanna had replaced Patsy in the forefront of my head. An amazing revelation until I recalled that old cliché: *Out of sight, out of mind.* I still wanted to locate Patsy, even though I now knew she wasn't with Malcolm Barr. Curiosity, call it. After all, I'd spotted her once. At the Doubletree Hotel. Don't tell me that was a sick hallucination. It was real life.

Brother John called next, with another good birthday wish. And then a question about my estimated time of arrival. "Paul and I and everybody else we know are tired of trying to sing along with Elise's playing. We need you. We miss you."

Brad called after that. Man, the phone was starting to grow to my ear. Mom smiled when she passed it over. "You're one popular guy, today," she said, wiping her hands on the lace-decorated apron tied around her waist.

He was in town, he said, and wondered whether I was free to get together. "And feeling up to it. If so, we'll hoist a few afterwards."

I declined, but countered with an invite to my party, feeling silly, but delighted nevertheless with the prospect of his company, which was fine with mom. Now there would be five of us for the hamburgers Luis would grill in the backyard. Five, counting Mom and Hernandez, Bill the cop, me, and now Brad.

No balloons, no clown, no lemonade; tall cool cans of Coors, which went well with the burgers and mom's own potato salad recipe. Bill's wife and kids showed in time to eat, with their son eager to clamber aboard Polly Pew, Brad's truck. When the little girl discovered the neat little "play house" in the back of the cab, she too wanted to crawl in with her dolly for a game of pretend. Bill Junior sat behind the wheel making vroom-vroom noises. Gifford opened his wallet to share photos of his tiny blonde twin daughters, Brianna and Brittany. "We call them the BBs, for short."

Mom shot an accusing glance my way. I knew what that meant. She wanted grandchildren. She wanted me married and "getting on with my life."

It was a fine, compatible group. Had Juan and Vanna joined us (preferably not together), the party would have been perfect. Mom invited Brad to spend the night. He agreed, with no reluctance, because we had already arranged for me to ride with him. Following a stopover in Cheyenne to see his wife Beth and the BBs, he was taking off on another run to Arizona.

I was pleased there were no presents. Only a silly card from Bill and family. His wife bought it, the ex-football player turned cop said sheepishly, excusing the remembrance with a shrug as if to say, "You know, it's a girl thing."

Then mom had a big surprise. "However, Oliver, it's not a gift from me and Luis. It's your inheritance, son! From your great-grandfather. It was in his Will. To be given to you on your thirtieth birthday!"

"What? I don't see anything."

She handed me an old yellowed envelope with a proper seal—a blob of red wax now cracking at the edges. Grandpa had died twenty-eight years earlier. I couldn't remember meeting him. "What in the world?"

"I'm going to hazard a guess, Oliver," mom said.

"Your two cousins got huge gold nuggets when they turned thirty last year. I'm betting your share will be even bigger. You were his favorite."

"How could that be? I was two years old when he died."

"Right. You hadn't had time to get in trouble yet, or raise his ire."

Standing to the side, Brad grinned. "Gold nuggets, eh."

"Maybe a brick of bullion," mom said. "Grandpa was a rich man. He found gold."

CHAPTER 26

Before the bank even opened and I could get to my grandpa's safety deposit box, I headed for the Wal-Mart with my plastic clutched in a sweaty hand. I needed new clothes. What hadn't burned up in my pickup out in front of Betty's café got blown up in the RV; rather, the few duds I'd bought in Tucson, plus mom's tee shirts, as a replacement for my original wardrobe.

Passing a used car lot, I stopped to browse and touch and drool. A man and his car can develop an affinity I'm not sure a woman can understand. Like man and dog. Or a man and his woman. Yeah, I know we're not supposed to think of a lady friend as a chattel, a personal possession. It's true nevertheless. Not that this was a topic I'd ever discussed with another man. I just knew, like getting one of those gut feelings.

As I stood there in that new car showroom,

stroking the smooth shine on that car, what flashed through my mind were some of the ideas I'd formulated while lying abed under quarantine. Back in the days when men were known to prize a virgin, a guy wanted to think he was first. And only. Something about purity, pride of possession, exclusivity. Then you could think of a woman's very private spot as a temple, a place that you alone could visit, find comfort and joy in. I'd tried explaining this feeling once, just once, to Patsy Parsons, the only woman in my life I had ever wanted to make my own. Until now.

Patsy had laughed in my face. Said it was hers, not mine; no more important than an elbow, and she'd damn well do with it whatever she pleased. That was when I first suspected she might already have lain with my brother. I saw red. I could have killed the both of them right then.

After that I started paying more attention to animals, like on television's Animal Channel. I couldn't see how the male human was all that different from the bulls and bucks, moose and elk. Nature endowed such animals with horns, some with such great huge racks it must be tough to carry them around on their heads. They used them, too, to battle each other on behalf of the female population. Each male seeking to build his own harem or, for those seeking exclusivity, to be the only favored buck chosen.

Apparently it wasn't possible to explain all that to a woman so she'd understand. Another man, though, you didn't have to tell. He knew instinctively what could motivate a guy to move heaven and earth, if that's what it'd take, to get your woman back by your side. Which was probably why I'd felt so driven in searching for the lost Patsy. (It could also explain, if not excuse, why over-zealous ex-husbands and ex-boyfriends turn into the stalkers and even murderers among us.)

Malcolm Barr had said they weren't together when Patsy took off, possibly for Arizona, he said she'd said. Question: would I continue my quest when I returned to the state? Better to give it up as a lost cause; admit she was never right for me in the first place, or that I'd grown beyond my aching need for her. When the big buck scents another female crossing his path, does he cease his wrangling over the first prize?

I hoped Vanna Solano was more than a mere distraction. If I had in fact inherited a fortune, I could afford to go after Vanna, make her my own. Was that what I wanted, a permanent relationship with her?

Naturally I didn't think all this stuff while standing there, fondling the new car with my mouth gaping open. While feverish and half coherent in bed, I must have conjured up all that psycho-babble. Now this all came rushing back to me in a flash.

Mom had said she would meet me at the bank. She wanted in on the big surprise. I was amazed she could keep the secret as long as she had.

"It wasn't that long," she'd said over coffee that morning. "Yes, your great-grandfather's Will only came to light after his death. Even then we didn't think much of it, as he died practically penniless in the VA home. As a veteran of World War II, his benefits included care for his last days. It was only when your two male cousins reached their thirtieth birthdays, one right after the other, that we heard of the gold nuggets. He must have saved them from his gold-mining days back in the fifties. He went prospecting down in Arizona after the war."

"Arizona!" I blurted.

"Right. So your trips down there aren't so unusual, after all. *Déjà vu*, in a sense. History repeating itself."

"How much were the nuggets worth? The ones that Jack and Jeff got."

"Fifty, sixty thousand, in that neighborhood."

Jeez, that was more money than I'd ever had, all at once. Not a fortune, but enough money to buy a used car, plus to live on temporarily, so I wouldn't have to play *general factotum* to Brother John and Dr. Wallaberra for awhile. I could concentrate all my energies on my search. This time not after some elusive, romantic dream over Patsy, but for my potential killers. If they thought they could drive me away, they had another think coming.

Luis was up early that morning. He'd had breakfast and was out of the house before I awakened. Mom too left early, telling me she wanted to get her one-hundred-fifty salads made in the hospital kitchen where she worked during the summer. She promised to be finished by the time the bank opened. That left Brad Gifford.

We had taken Polly Pew to Wal-Mart and before stopping at the car lot. "What was your great-grandfather's name?" he asked, when we were back in the truck.

I turned to stare at the quiet guy with the dishwater blond hair and horn-rimmed glasses. When I had asked him how he knew where to find me, he said he'd called the church from Cheyenne. That's when Brother John gave Brad the whole story of my illness, plus mom's name and number.

"Just coincidence I was booked into Gillette to pick up a quarter-load bound for Tucson." No rush, though, he added, saying he would gas up Polly Pew in Cheyenne before leaving the state. "Most of the time I'm dashing all over the place. Only now and then can I lay back, catch my breath … ."

"Get in a game or two of golf," I said, completing his sentence. I wondered whether he *had one in every port*.

"Woman, you mean? Naw. I'm the faithful husband. You'll meet Beth and the BBs in Cheyenne."

"Okay, a buddy, then. Golf partners scattered around the country."

"Two or three. No more."

I didn't press. Just because he was a sociable guy, seemed to appreciate company, didn't mean he wasn't as private as the next fellow. I liked him. That was enough.

Brad found a place to park the truck in the graveled lot down by the railroad and said he'd stick with Polly Pew. My purchases tossed in their plastic sacks in the compact sleeping quarters in the back of the cab, I took off. A few blocks to the old downtown bank, a quick jaunt. I said I wouldn't be long.

He said he had a book to read, one of Richard Condon's. Ahah, one of my all-time favorite authors. Gifford was a quarter-way through *Vertical Smile*. I rolled my eyes, conveying a fan's critique—one of Condon's super but incredibly goofy books. If Brad liked that one, he'd go ape over *Bandicoot*. Richard Condon was dead now, but he had left an interesting though weird legacy.

Gifford grinned. "I knew we had more in common than golf."

I met mom outside the bank. I couldn't remember when I'd seen her so excited, not even at her wedding to Luis.

"You were grandpa's favorite," she said again. "He might have left you a million dollars worth of gold," she whispered.

"Get real."

Clutching a pink purse, mom led the way through the big glass door I held open for her. Soon we were closeted in a tiny booth with two chairs and a small table but no windows. In front of us sat my birthday present, in the form of a long, narrow, shallow safety deposit box.

"Can't hold bullion, Mom. Not deep enough."

"Hurry, hurry. Oh, Oliver, I can't wait." The Kleenex tissue she held to pat her brow with was already shredded. "This could be your *Ticket to ride!*"

Startled, I stopped fiddling with the clasp to stare at her. She was into country music, now? "What happened to Verdi and Chopin?"

"Luis agreed to hear my music if I'd listen to his."

Nice trade off. I could do the same with Vanna. Check out her tastes when compared to mine.

"Just think, Oliver," said mom. "With a fortune, you can afford to take a bride." Mom's old-fashioned, she thinks a man's totally responsible for bringing home the bacon. Well, why not, nothing wrong with that. "Time you started giving me some grandchildren," she finished.

Ahah, the woman did have a devious bone deep down inside all that sweetness. Mom hadn't met Vanna yet, nor heard more than a few suggestive words drop from my lips. Unless, while still hallucinating, I'd coughed up my secret longings.

Inside the box we discovered but two small envelopes, one thin and flat, the other somewhat lumpy. Sure enough, three gold nuggets tumbled out of the latter. Mom was so disappointed I thought she'd bawl. She gasped and covered her mouth.

"That's all? I'm so sorry," she sobbed, as if she were somehow personally at fault that my inheritance was merely a pittance. "Wait a minute, Son." She wiped her eyes and sat up straighter. "Check the other envelope. Maybe grandpa left you something else."

Slowly, with trembling fingers, I unsealed the second envelope. Nothing but a single sheet of thin onion skin with a few words scrawled in a shaky hand. To mom I read it aloud: "*Sorry, Oliver, I spent the biggest portion of the gold I meant to leave you ... .*"

Mom grabbed the page, ripping the thin paper in two pieces. Silently, she read the remainder to herself before staring at me with tears running down both cheeks.

CHAPTER 27

"**I** guess you're a wealthy man, now, eh," Brad said when I climbed into the passenger seat.

Mom and I had said our good-byes up the street. The bank manager, an old family friend, had scribbled a note of reference, handing it to me as he directed us to a gold merchant. The exchange quickly arranged, we returned to the bank. Now a cashier's check for ninety thousand, eight hundred, and forty-two dollars rested comfortably in my breast pocket. Mom wouldn't take a penny. She and Hernandez were doing just fine, thank you. I promised to call regularly and to be careful.

"Not hardly, Brad. A few thousand, that's all. Plus a boat."

"Huh?"

"Grandpa said he'd invested my inheritance, what he intended leaving me, in a friend's dream. I don't suppose you've got time to make a detour."

"Go where?"

"Lake Hattie, out west of Laramie."

"No problem. We can go over the mountain after leaving Cheyenne. Only fifty or sixty miles out of the way. Why?"

"Grandpa's friend wanted to build a boat, do the whole thing himself. He was already in his sixties when grandpa loaned him the money. That was nearly thirty years ago. Old geezer bound to be dead by now. Anyhow, if he ever finished building the thing, it's mine now. Or soon will be."

"Ah, so. You're a yachtsman."

"More likely the old codger built a canoe."

CHAPTER 28

From Gillette we took that same lonely, narrow road south to Douglas and past Reno Junction where I'd picked up a ride with those two Mormon ladies. Seemed like half a lifetime ago. Beyond Douglas we cut back east to Torrington where Brad picked up another quarter load. He was hauling furniture this trip. Not for people in a rush, but for snowbirds who wanted their belongings delivered to winter quarters down in the Sunbelt.

Then we traveled south through wheat country, catching a glimpse of huge rolls of wheat. Brad said they made him think of golden loaves of bread designed for the giant in *Jack and the Beanstalk.*

In Cheyenne, Wyoming's capital city, I met The Family (capital letters), in-laws, too. "Far as I know there's no party planned, so maybe we won't have to run you by the whole big bunch." He said Beth was an only child and her dad and mom lived next door. "Peter and Lisa will come over before I leave."

Brad was right. His father-in-law, Air Force Colonel Peter Schwartzkopf, with his social butterfly blond wife Lisa popped out their front door as we drew up in Polly Pew. Also Gifford's wife and their four-year-old blond twins. All I could remember about them was their collective nickname, the BBs.

The Colonel at six-foot-something loomed over the tiny petite ladies; Brad, too. But not me. I may be skinny, especially after losing so much weight, but I'm tall. Beth's mom Lisa clapped dainty hands upon meeting me.

"Why, you could be Clint Eastwood! A younger version, of course."

One arm around Beth and both little girls simultaneously clinging to Brad's other hand, he was pretty well occupied. Lisa babbled at me about her plans to travel cross country with her son-in-law soon, while Peter looked on indulgently. Brad had already told me about the *wanderlust* bent for travel in the family. Not shared by Beth, however, who didn't care for her husband's new life on the road.

In the Gifford house Brad unloaded a duffel bag full of dirty clothes into the washer, while Lisa took over the kitchen to brew a pot of tea. The Colonel suggested I might prefer coffee. A man's brew, he added, winking at me. We settled around an antique oak table in the sunlit kitchen, where Brianna and Britanny (I'd remembered their names) clambered onto their daddy's lap. The lovebirds held hands across the corner of the table while we set about the business of getting acquainted.

"Brad said you play a pretty mean game of golf," said Peter.

"Never mind that," interrupted his wife. Brad had alerted me to Lisa's social connections across the state, which precluded her natural desire to uncover my familial background. "Who are your folks?"

Skipping over mom's illegitimacy, I replied that her *father* and stepfather were named Daniel and David, respectively, and my Temple name came from the latter. I also skipped mentioning that I was named for both men, thus producing the *ODD Temple*.

"Temple, Temple," she mused, one small index finger poking her dimpled chin. "I don't recall meeting anybody by that name."

"Give it a rest, Mom," said Beth, a younger version of Lisa. Obviously Lisa meant to determine whether I belonged in the State's social register. According to Brad's description of the Schwartzkopfs, Lisa was descended from a famous frontier family, settlers who had made it big and then helped to make Cheyenne a fancy place during its Golden Gilded era of the late 1800s.

Lisa ignored her daughter's protest. "Your mother's birth name, please."

"Vicente. Full name, Margaret Rose Vicente Temple Hernandez." I was finally willing to admit Luis was mom's current husband.

"Vicente! Oh, my goodness." Mrs. Schwartzkopf practically leaped from her chair to come give me hug." Then you're Family! This is the Vicente Clan you've stumbled into." She took my face into her two small hands to stare at me. "You've even got the look, I'm sure of it." She turned my head to face the others, showing me off like some mad scientist's Frankenstein-style specimen. "Look at him, everybody. He's a Vicente, right? See? Look at that nose. Look at him in profile. Oh, yes."

Laughing, the others didn't seem to put much stock in Lisa's Proclamation. Or care, even if she were right.

"Who cares," mumbled Beth, cuddling into Gifford's comforting embrace. "He's Brad's friend. That's all that matters."

Lisa wanted to haul out old photo albums. "You'll see the resemblance, everybody, when you get another look at Ezekial and Ebekenezer. They were my uncles on the Auld side. Both died during World War One as very young men so of course I never met them. In fact, they were younger than you are now, Oliver, but notice that both, like you, are tall and slender."

Yeah, I thought, so are a lot of people. I was confused. First Lisa tells me I'm a member of the Vicente Clan and then she says I look like a couple of Auld brothers. Then I recalled a bit of Wyoming history. Two young Mormon women had helped settle the territory back in the mid-to-late 1800s.

"Rose DuMauier and Essie Deighton were best friends," Lisa attempted to clarify. "Eventually a few of their progeny married, thus uniting the two great houses of Vicentes and Aulds. Your mother's middle name is even Rose. Get it? She must have been named for my great-great-grandmother Rose."

So what, I mused. A lot of families must have Roses, especially since Rose DuMaurier was practically an icon in this state. Wyoming history tells us she made a fortune in cattle, oil, and gold mining.

Hey, that could be a connection. Rose left Daniel gold nuggets and that's where my grandfather had come by them? Maybe the story of his prospecting in Arizona was a fib. Made no sense to me.

While Lisa babbled, though, I recalled her other ancestor, Essie Deighton, one of Wyoming's most famous and earliest prostitutes, later a brothel madam. Humph. Perhaps my grandma, who had mothered mom out of wedlock, took after Essie. If, in fact, our family had anything at all to do with Brad's family.

Like Beth, I wondered what difference any of this could possibly make to me, here and now in the Twenty-First Century.

"Never mind, Lisa," Peter said, swallowing the last of his coffee in one big gulp. "Another time. The boys have to get going."

Brad's signal sent and received, the Colonel stood to shake my hand. "You come back now, ya hear," he said, his hospitality Southern.

Our good-byes were both cheerful and tearful, as Beth and the BBs clung to Brad. "Hurry home to us," I heard his wife whisper.

Back in Polly Pew, Brad hesitantly admitted that Beth didn't appreciate his new line of work. "She liked it better when I was selling insurance and real estate, wearing suit and tie, and coming home every night."

I wanted to ask him how he had convinced her, but he shared that tale, too. "Lisa and her double cousins, also Vicente-Aulds, are what they call *Wanderlusts*, continuing the traveling tradition established by Rose and Essie a century and a half ago when they came to the territory. Beth and another cousin—third or fourth, I think, namely Ned Fleetfoot, half Arapaho—are the two exceptions. The wanderlusts all descended upon my little Beth to bombard her with reasons why she should not protest my *reaching for my personal star*.That's the Vicente-Auld clan; passionate and overdramatic."

Hauling freight cross country was Brad's star? Hmm, each to his own. "And you took advantage of their support."

"For awhile," Brad said, a mischievous grin playing across his lips.

We fell into a comfortable silence. From Cheyenne over the short forty-five-mile haul into Laramie, the altitude climbs several thousand feet. Polly Pew protested, in fear of stripped gears perhaps, but Brad climbed upward and onward. We passed the Vedavoos, a range of Rocky mountain outcroppings popular with mountain climbers and picnickers. At the highest point on Interstate 80 running east and west from coast to coast is a rest stop with a big, I mean huge, statue, rather a bust, of

Abraham Lincoln. This route was once known as the Old Lincoln Highway, so I guess that's why the famous former President is thus honored here. The altitude is somewhat over nine thousand feet. Often snow lingers beneath the towering evergreens well into early summer.

Window rolled down, my arm resting on the sill and the cool mountain air laced with the scent of fir and pine wafted over us. I was crazy to contemplate returning to the hot desert at this time of year.

We sailed right around Laramie on the Interstate until we reached the Snowy Range exit. Thirty or so miles farther west leered the *Snowies*, nickname for the Snowy Range, another set of mountains, these poking their snowy heads over twelve thousand feet into the clouds. Yup, still plenty of snow up there on the peaks. A favorite tour route of tourists, Wyomingites enjoy taking first-time visitors up there in the mountains to fish the icy lakes and throw snowballs in August.

Were we to continue on this narrow paved road, we would soon be into the Medicine Bow National Forest. We were traveling State Highway 230 to reach Lake Hattie. Had we taken 130, we would pass the airport and then wind up in the small village of Centennial before reaching the local ski slopes.

"Where to?" Brad asked as we approached the lake.

Not large and not very pretty, Lake Hattie sits out on the high plains with few if any trees in sight. The ground alkaline, some residents of the lakeside cottages and trailers must haul in fresh drinking water. Nevertheless, people fished and water skied here, and sailed, rowed, or ran their speedboats. Winter was ice-fishing time, like in *Grumpier Old Men*, with Jack Lemmon and Walter Mathau, where ice huts peppered the frozen lake from shore to shore.

"See what I mean?" I said. "I probably inherited a canoe."

Brad pulled over when we saw a pickup slowly approaching. The driver paused, too, to roll down his window. Brad gave the name we were looking for. The grizzled fellow wearing sweat-stained cowboy hat gave us directions, but not without smirking.

"Yeah, old Samuel P. Jones finally finished building that dad-blamed boat of his. Only now he's too old to sail it, and it's way too big to move. Damn thing ended up three stories high and at least a block long. Hell, it's a yacht! He pointed off round one side of the lake. "See what I mean? Damn thing's big enough to launch fighter planes off of."

We stared, me speechless.

Underway again, Brad grinned. "Canoe, eh?"

CHAPTER 29

"Yeah, sure, a yacht. But what good will that do me?" Damned nuisance.

After reading my letter of introduction from my grandfather, the boat builder gladly turned over to me the title, saying he was way too old to fiddle with this thing any longer. Three decades was enough, he said. He owned the lot and the boat that sat high up on dry land. He was checking into a home for independent living, he said. Calling it quits. Everything.

"Ain't botherin' nobody. You can leave it here forever if you wanna." The black man grinned, showing two missing teeth in front. Then he turned away and on two crutches hobbled off.

"Now what?" Brad said.

"Nothing. We head for Arizona as planned. When the old guy dies, I'll worry about what the hell to do with a yacht that's stuck out in the middle of nowhere."

The rest of that day and night I learned a bit about cross-country hauling. Brad kept lots of records: income and expenses, customer contracts with phone numbers, rules and regs. He used laptop computer, cellphone, and citizens band radio; the latter, he said, sometimes reaching no more than three to five miles, ten to twenty when the weather was clear. On the CB he used the *Gangly Guy* handle he'd given himself.

We talked football. Brad too was a Bronco fan. We agreed that John Elway was our all-time favorite quarterback. He and Tiger Woods had in common the way they could pull a rabbit out of the hat; at the end, when it counted. Elway in the last couple of minutes; Woods on the last few holes.

"That Tiger," Brad said. "Did you see the tournament where he was six holes down on Saturday only to pull out with seven holes ahead at the finish?"

"Yup."

We talked golf, golf courses, golf games, and golfers. We raved about the Tiger.

We talked motorcycles. I told him mine was old, a 1984 Harley, 1000 XLX Sportster, candy apple red. When I bought it off the old guy with a bad back who wanted out, he let me have it for under three grand. Pretty good deal considering the care he'd taken of it. "Only 8,200 miles on it."

I suggested if he wanted to buy into this big-time game, he could add a sidecar. Juan had told me about a Sputnik Sidecar imported from Russia for about thirteen hundred. Beth could ride along, I said. They could take off for Sturgis, South Dakota, for a rally, travel the continent, get in on lots of events. She could get a new wardrobe, all black leather, lots of gear.

"Women like to shop, don't they?"

He shot me a dirty look, then shot a fist into my arm. Man, that hurt.

Brad talked about his family. He and Beth had met at the U when both were majoring in BusAd. A fan of the Bard, he wanted to spend their honeymoon in England at Stratford on Avon. Beth didn't go for foreign travel. So then he recommended Ashland, Oregon—get tickets at the Black Swan or the outdoor Elizabethan theatre, the Allen Pavillion, and book a honeymoon suite at the Mark Antony. That beautiful hotel was refurbished now and renamed the Ashland Springs, Brad said, as if that were relevant.

"Beth didn't want to leave the state, not even for the West Coast."

"Where did you stay?" I asked, to be polite.

"At Little America, a resort hotel with golf course. Right in Cheyenne. Beth didn't want to leave town. So don't talk to me about a cycle and side car."

Again he shared his dream of having Beth at his side, making the occasional cross-country haul. I envied them. Not their conflicts; rather, their obvious closeness, their beautiful healthy children, even their extended family.

At a truck stop out of Rawlins, Wyoming's penitentiary town, I got another glimpse of a trucker's life out of town. It appeared that these days all manner of people were into this business: young, old, fat, skinny, men and women speaking in languages from around the globe. Some oldtimers dressed neatly in clean jeans and a few in white shirts, with short haircuts and shaved faces. We also spotted scruffy beards, long hair and pony tails, faded ragged jeans and cutoffs, sandals with dirty toes, sneakers. Everybody on the phones, records and schedules and atlases spread out on tables in front of them. And, man, the language they used over the phone—words you wouldn't want your grandma to hear. Seemed like most of the truckers had problems—with customers and their company's dispatchers, and shouting at their mates. What struck me was that after yelling and cussing at wives or girlfriends, almost to a man—grizzly like a bear or weak and wimpy like some backroom computer nerd—they invariably signed off with a muttered, "I love you."

The big truck stops, Brad said, provided all the amenities for people living on the road: barbershop and laundry, video games and TV rooms, convenience store, and café proper with a phone at every table and booth. The store offered a cornucopia of items to meet their needs, including paperback books, videos, and music albums; also television sets and stereos, coolers and thermoses, and a wide assortment of items designed to make small repairs enroute. Also clothing.

Outdoors the odors of diesel fuel filled my nose as the truckers refueled hungry gas tanks, checked oil and radiator, sometimes inviting a mechanic's inspection. Elsewhere, Brad said, the occasional truckstop also provided a complete wash job in huge tall sheds. "Think about it, Oliver. One's truck is a traveling billboard. The company logo and perhaps a slogan appear along the sides, maybe on the cab too. Got to keep the advertising piece clean and shiny. Your truck speaks for you."

Brad owned his own cab and trailer, his was a one-man operation. So there was no boss or dispatcher to report to, only his own reputation at stake.

Out on the road these guys had to worry about wind and weather, terrible road conditions and muddy detours, and whether Smoky was creeping up or about to appear coming this way from over yonder hill. Could be hiding in the bushes, ready to pounce. For all these issues, their CBs might prove to make the difference between life and death or provide the answer to one or another nuisance. Truckers checked with each other, with those they trailed or those coming up behind or those bursting from around yonder curve.

Not for me, this life, but I began to appreciate the fascination Brad found with it. The trucker's world, like the astronaut's, could be likened to tackling one of the last few frontiers left on the planet. Face the challenges, conquer them. Very macho. For women? Today's new woman must also enjoy the challenge, or at any rate the money that could be made. If one kept on truckin'.

Seemed it was Brad, not Beth, who had picked up on the wanderlust thread of his in-laws, his adopted clan. Gifford implied I was somehow related, shirt-tail kin, something like that. Could be the travel bug had bit me, too.

Sometimes we talked, mostly we kept quiet. Still tiring easily, I climbed in the back of the cab to catch a few winks on the single pull-down bed next to a refrigerator and TV and a few mesh-fronted shelves for storing gear and small personal items. A huge six-pack of batteries kept things humming even while Polly Pew was stationary.

Up into the mountains, down on the desert floor we traveled. Brad was stopping in Vegas for another quarter load, he said, then we'd backtrack into Flagstaff before heading south through Phoenix for Tucson.

"What's your plan?" he asked later. "You could leave it alone, you know. Turn your back and forget the whole thing. What's driving you to put your life on the line?"

I could have mentioned Vanna, the woman who might (or might not) be waiting for me. Or the loyalty I felt for Brother John, my *surrogate father*. Their lives too could be in danger. I said nothing, a shrug my only reply.

"Can't let it go, eh. Pride, resentment, anger, frustration. One a those."

Didn't sound like questions. "Could be mere curiosity."

"Like walking out in the middle of the movie and you wanna see the ending."

"Could be. Or maybe I think I can help to change it."

"Write your own finis. Before somebody else is

hurt. Somebody close to you."

Speaking of *close*, now he was encroaching on private territory. I fell silent, not glancing at him. I didn't want to see his knowing expression nor risk his reading mine.

More miles slipped away beneath us as Polly Pew rumbled along the ribbon of highway. From studying the big open atlas on my lap, I noticed that the interstates were numbered even, east and west; odd, north and south; low numbers starting in the west, with five, ending with ninety-five back east. Brad said he used another atlas on his laptop. He could pull up any segment he needed to confirm routes, out in the open or in metropolitan neighborhoods.

"The directions customers give aren't always accurate or detailed enough." He'd changed the subject out of sympathy, or was willing to acknowledge my need for privacy.

I closed my eyes. I heard Brad ring up fellow truckers on his CB: "Breaker one-niner, *Gangly Guy* here. What's happenin', man?" Replies came back, with the odd chatter, the boisterous laugh, the bawdy joke.

I sat up. "You asked about my plans down in Arizona. You got any suggestions?"

Tipping back his head Brad drained the last dregs of coffee from his thermal cup. He smiled. "You could use me for a sounding board."

I reached for my cup off the cup holder; held it in both hands, like a prop, without drinking. Then I set it back down. I needed both hands to tick off items and people.

First I told Gifford about my friend Bill, the former football player, now a Gillette cop with contacts in the Drug Enforcement Agency. "The DEA's got something going down. A drug sting, I take it. Down along that southern drug corridor between Tucson and Nogales. What I'm thinkin' is that without realizing it, I'd stumbled onto something. Fess Goodman could be involved and I was getting too close."

"Could be they think you know something you don't."

"Something like that."

"So, what do you know? Start with the little stuff. Fill in whatever details you can. Then we can brainstorm."

"All along I've figured Fess as a small-time thug. Think about it. Golf clubs and tennis rackets, car stereos and a fur jacket stolen from cars outside the church. Green Valley robberies. Vandalism at the Cat Castle—though I don't see how a petty job like that could net anybody any cash, not if the purpose is to fund his, or somebody's, habit. All of that put together doesn't amount to a hill of beans."

"Minor stuff. Like a junkie would heist to cash in quick. Why not survey the pawn shops? If Green Valley has none, Tucson will. Wait," Brad said, holding up his hand as if to halt traffic at a school crossing. "What about the cops? Town or county, they should have been doing something. You or the preachers check with them?"

I slouched in the seat, eyesight barely above the dashboard. "Yup, to pestering the sheriff; no, to his coming up with any concrete answers. As for the vandalism, a high school kid was pinpointed as one among perhaps several of the graffiti artists."

"I can't see any holes in your thinking. Fess looks to be a likely candidate for the perpetrator. 'Course he could have accomplices. Or he's part of a gang. You said Goodman is a known addict, or was." Brad paused while moving into the left-hand lane and passing a slow-moving RV pulling a motorboat. "Here's another idea," he said, while pushing Polly Pew to reach for the speed limit. "What if all those petty crimes were merely a fluke?"

"A red herring?"

"Something like that."

I suggested the collection plate theft was no small thing. "Probably upwards of five thousand bucks, given the take the rest of revival week."

Then I described the cousins' competition and my finding what could be the stolen goods in Dollie's closet. "The poorer cousin can't compete with the wealthy Elise. Except in the music department. Dollie is by far a better soloist than Elise is a pianist."

"Which irks Mrs. Goodman no end, so she plants the stolen items on Mrs. Martinez. Elise couldn't know you would find them, though."

"No, but Juan Garcia might have. As villa manager, he's frequently on the premises, sometimes indoors as well."

"But Juan wasn't poisoned. You were."

"Yeah, right. Which means that's not a reasonable clue. Dollie's closet stuff might not even be stolen. Could be coincidence, or they were legitimate gifts from Elise. Before their falling out. Over what, we don't know."

"What about that photo you found in Mrs. Goodman's wallet?" I'd shared that fact, too, the picture of the two blond teenage boys with some man.

"That reminds me," I said. "One of the first things I'm going to do is find out what happened to Mr. Goodman."

"How will you do that?"

"Approach everybody head on. Come right out and ask Elise or Dollie."

"What's been happening since you left Arizona?"

"Beats me. Time I find out." I fished through my newly purchased backpack for my new cellphone. I'd charged both to plastic before leaving Gillette. I couldn't locate it.

"Here," said Brad, passing over his mobile phone. "Use mine."

Juan didn't answer, at either his office or on his cellphone. Neither did Vanna. I would have tried Derek and Megan or the Derrys, but it was still their busy lunch hour. That left Brother John. He answered on the first ring.

"Thank God you called. Did your mother tell you I was trying to reach you?"

Belatedly I remembered I'd forgotten to call mom about my boat or to check in, period. I was a big boy now. But not a very considerate one. "Why? What's the matter?"

Brother John's voice trembled. "Paul's dead."

CHAPTER 30

"Shot in the back!" Lucas said."I did it. I'm to blame."

A half-dozen thoughts flashed through my mind. Brother John shot Dr. Wallaberra? Not possible. Not that sweet old man, not my father figure.

"He wanted me to go out to the garden with him, but I was too tired. I let him go alone. I'm to blame. If I'd gone, they wouldn't have shot him."

They? Not he or she, but they. That's what he'd said.

"Paul already dug up and destroyed some funny looking plants, he told me. But I didn't think anything about it. That was a week ago. He only got around to asking me to have a look. You know how he is. Was. Paul couldn't tell a plant from a weed."

In the meantime Brad was listening, making faces. He wanted in on the conversation. Pity we didn't have a speakerphone. I'd have to repeat all this.

"So what does the sheriff think? Truman come up with any suspects? Or were there witnesses?"

"I doubt it. Dead of night. Me, I was dead to the world. I don't know why Paul insisted on going out there so late."

"Do you suppose Dr. Wallaberra made an appointment to meet somebody there? Anybody call your house? I mean before the pastor headed out?" I used Paul's last name and title to clue in Brad, who by then was gesturing wildly.

"The sheriff is puzzled. So are the newspapers. No suspects, no motivation anybody can see. No clues at all. Or so go the reports."

When I told Brother John we would be pulling in that night, he said I should come to his house to stay. I wondered whether he would take over the church.

That was his next announcement. "I'll have to take over here for awhile. Until they get somebody else."

I could see it all, now. Twenty years down the road or until he packed it in, Brother John would still be there. With me as sidekick? No way. Nip that notion in the bud before it had a chance to flower.

"I'm not returning so I can resume all those church chores, Lucas. I'm coming back for one reason only. To help solve the crimes and catch the perps."

I heard a long sigh come from the other end. Whether relief at my objective or dismay at my dismissal of church duties, I didn't know and didn't care. Enough was enough. We hung up.

"Hard to believe," Brad said after I filled in the

gaps, "that anybody would kill your pastor over his discovery of a dozen or so marijuana plants." The nature of the plants was our surmise.

"Especially when he'd already dug up and destroyed them a week earlier," I countered. "That's the time frame we're talking about. According to Brother John. Got to be bigger than that. Paul must have interrupted something else. He stumbled onto something deadly and then scheduled a confrontation."

"I thought you said there was an incoming phone call before Dr. Wallaberra left the house. He didn't leave until after that, right?"

"Right. Well, that supports the notion that he knew something about somebody."

"Or they thought he did."

"*They* again," I said. "You notice we keep using the plural."

"Doesn't seem likely that all these petty crimes, followed by your poisoning and the RV getting blown up, also the church theft in between, and culminating with two major murders could be the action of one single person."

I stared at him as we zoomed into Phoenix. "Murders? Plural means more than one. How's that?"

"They tried to kill you, too."

"Gotcha." I sat quietly thinking for a few moments. "Don't forget Elise's husband, the guy who mysteriously vanished some time ago. Supposedly, according to his wife, he's in Europe and South America, *doing business*."

"You say South America, I think Colombia!" Brad said, pounding on the steering wheel. "Say Colombia, right away people think drugs, cocaine in particular."

"Could be things are about to escalate. That's what my pal Bill thinks."

"You want to pin all this stuff on Fess Goodman, right?"

On the southern edge of Phoenix, Brad pulled into a truckstop. Time to feed our faces and Polly Pew, too. Gifford was no fast food or snack guy. He appreciated real food, he said, with green salad and vegetables.

I was anxious to get back on the road. Nervous, too. Would I be next to take a shot in the back? More than likely they'd come on right up front this time, shoot me in the face. I hadn't succumbed to their first prolonged but fumbling attempts, and here I was, back again, like the bad penny returned.

As we pulled up in front of Brother John's house, Brad reached across the cab to sock me on the arm again. "Hey, old buddy. Don't eat anything not bought and prepared by your own hands."

Meanwhile there was Paul's funeral and all that to intervene before I could launch my own investigation. I had every intention of walking right up to Dollie's door. Ask her how she'd come by the stolen goods. After that I would confront Elise, ask her about the missing Mr. Goodman.

The best laid plans of mice and men.

CHAPTER 31

At the funeral I tried to be worshipful, but I couldn't keep my eyes closed. I was busy squinting, taking sneak peaks at the assemblage, hoping to detect a look of guilt on somebody's face. Fess Goodman in particularly, possibly Donny Martinez.

I wasn't asked to play the organ—a new one; used, rather. Elise insisted on playing that. Dollie sang a solo, *Till We Meet Again,* though performed acappella. From behind the pulpit Brother John spoke eloquently. He had also commandeered the Tucson gospel singers to rejoin our choir.

I was surprised that more people didn't show. I had thought Dr. Wallaberra was highly respected in these parts. Perhaps so, but it was Brother John people loved.

Elise and Dollie did double duty. Besides providing the music, they served as lead pallbearers, one on each side of the rolling cart that held the casket. Both wore black, Elise very fashionable with a veiled hat and black leather stiletto heels; Dollie, dowdy, her two-piece black linen wrinkled and shiny in the bottom. Her shoes were flat, broad, and scruffy. Elise glared across the coffin at her cousin. Dollie dropped her head and blushed.

Why the blush? No understanding women. Might just be the fashion comparison between rich and poor, style-conscious and ignorant. Or something far more serious. I couldn't decide whether that issue was worth exploring.

The four men, the Derry brothers and Derek plus one of the ushers, now a deacon, clambered into the black limousine provided for pallbearers after helping to shove Dr. Wallaberra's body into the hearse. In the lead car came Brother John and me, Megan, Juan, and Vanna. I asked Lucas about family. He said there was nobody to contact, none that he'd ever heard Paul mention.

Dick Truman, the Pima County Sheriff, had prevailed upon a half-dozen Tucson cops to provide a motorcycle escort. The sheriff's deputies brought up the rear in their official car. The funeral cortege was headed down Interstate 19 to the tiny art village of Tubac, where Dr. Wallaberra had said he would someday like to be buried. Who could have guessed it would be so soon.

The old Tubac cemetery, a tourist site, is a sight to see. Bodies buried long ago were laid out atop the ground and covered with rocks and colorful stones to hinder the eager pawing of curious animals.

Curious kids playing pranks, too. I don't recall why they weren't buried six feet under. I asked whether these dead heralded from families too poor to dig holes or was this a Mexican custom. Brother John didn't know, either.

Makeshift grave markers peppered the scene, including a lot of wooden crosses leaning into the wind, toppling half over, and commingled with a few large, expensive, marble or granite headstones. Plenty of evidence that these dead people were Catholic, what with statues of Mary, Mother of Jesus, and the variety of folded, praying hands.

Dr. Wallaberra's final resting place sat among all this ancient splendor, only he would be buried below ground. Seemingly a "finished" cemetery, Brother John had got permission to open this one new grave off to the eastern side on a grassy slope beneath the trees. A green canopy covered the grave hole and a collection of chairs for family and chief mourners. Baskets of flowers had been brought from the church by the mortuary staff along with a huge wreath mounted on a stand and bearing on a blue satin ribbon the inscription, "Go in Peace."

All very appropriate and quietly somber. Until all hell broke loose.

For just then three yellow school busses and two Greyhounds roared up. Behind them raced four media vans with antenna poking up like giant bugs.

"What th'hell?" I mumbled, climbing out of the limousine ahead of Brother John. I offered him my hand for support, while he told me to shush.

If the funeral was sparsely attended, the graveside service sure wouldn't be. Who all these people were and why they were so late, I couldn't imagine.

"It was murder, you know," said Brother John quietly at my side.

That explained the media, but not the busloads of people. Unless they were merely *Looky Lous,* Brad's term from his days of selling real estate and running open houses.

I reached into the dim recesses of the car for Vanna's hand, with Juan popping out right afterwards, like a blackhead on an adolescent's cheek. We nudged and nodded at each other, as acknowledgment of the encroaching throng—a long parade of vehicles drawing up. Not a part of the original cortege, the people tumbling out of RVs and SUVs wore the typical tourist clothes, from expensive golf slacks and polo shirts to cutoff jeans, Bermuda shorts, tee shirts with slogans from goofy to incomprehensible, and halters that bared the women's tanned skin. One young redhead showed up in a skimpy bikini. I stared, until Vanna poked me in the side. "Eyes front, soldier," she whispered.

"Yup, tourists out to catch the sights," Brother John said to me and Megan, she with belly bulging.

The mortician paused from directing the pallbearers in proper procedure to stare. Eyebrows raised, he turned to Brother John. Lucas shook his head, No, indicating they should wait for the crowd to finish disembarking from their vehicles and settle into the solemn mood the ritual demanded. All the motion immediately surrounding us had ceased, the pallbearers frozen beside the rolling cart as if in tableau.

The media was well represented. As they burst from their vans like ants whose anthills have been disturbed, their technicians raced to the gravesite armed with equipment. The thick cables uncoiling and slithering across the lawn after them could have been giant cobras let loose from their cages. From the logos on the sides of the vans, I recognized CBS, ABC, NBC, and CNN, but not FOX.

Reporters with microphones and photographers with professional size videocameras rushed to the scene, all but shoving each other aside in their effort to snatch the best positions around the mourners' chairs for capturing tears and moans and wails. I imagined mikes poked in the faces of willing inter-viewees (not me), with the reporters gasping, "How did you feel when you heard your preacher was murdered?"

The newcomers weren't shy, either. Tourists of all ages vied for equally good viewing positions. From the busses piled a more orderly crowd, if only initially. Somebody was apparently in charge, with a couple of big burly guys directing traffic while three pert females distributed placards.

Suddenly the Tucson Gospel Singers burst into song. Alarmed, our choir members gazed at our own music director with but a moment of question in their eyes before he raised his hands to lead them. Not to be outdone, the Tucson conductor frantically waved his baton. The beat picked up, the clapping began, the commingled group of singers swayed back and forth as one body.

Emerging quickly from the busses, that crowd was mixed; mostly black and white, though. They shouted, waving their placards and demanding action. "Lynch the murderers," screamed one old gnarly white woman, grabbing a poster on a pole from a big young black guy, possibly a linebacker.

Dr. Wallaberra would have been appalled had he known that his last rites were to be administered amidst a three-ring circus. I knew Paul well enough to know that much. Just then dark overhead clouds rolled over the sun. Streaks of lightening crackled with electricity, and thunder rumbled from out of the sky like the voice of God. My senses reeled from the sweet scent of roses and lilies.

Brother John had had enough. He nodded at the mortician, as Steven Spielburg might have done with the directing of a great movie extravaganza. Led by the pallbearers, we were on our way, determined as much as could be to ignore the rowdy intruders.

Megan clung to me on one side and Vanna on the other. Both arms thus occupied, I mused that the reporters could take me for a Mormon polygamist, with Wife Number One about ready to pop.

Lucas marched resolutely ahead, glancing neither to left nor to right. He was a great stallion wearing blinders. Puzzled, possibly discombobulated, our regular parishioners stumbled along, closing ranks, steering clear of the advancing mob. Cameras flashed, the crowd mumbled, the combined choirs now singing *We Shall Overcome* raised their voices and increased their swaying. If somebody toppled over, they could turn into a set of dominos with a whole bunch of people tumbling to the ground.

The singers were quickly joined by the bus loads of placard holders, who immediately began clapping hands. Their bodies squashed together and singing off key, they produced, collectively, a natural focus for the media, who fed on the scene with a frenzy. I could see it all, now, the live broadcast repeated for the early evening and late night news and shot around the globe, telling the world this was a demonstration to protest the murder of a black man as a hate crime.

Close at my side, Megan whispered, "I feel sick."

"Don't we all," Vanna replied from my other side.

"No, I mean physically ill."

I might have paid more attention, but just then we were all distracted.

Stumbling along on those ridiculously high heels at the head of the coffin cart, Elise couldn't stop glaring across Dr. Wallaberra's last bed at her cousin. Which was possibly why she missed her footing.

Approaching the open grave, Elise fell straight into the hole, face down.

A collective gasp rose like a cloud from those in the front. Brother John clasped and steepled his hands to stare heavenward.

Fess Goodman shoved through the mourners to stand at the grave side, moaning, "Mama, oh Mama."

Rumors rippled through the assemblage, producing more shoving as the media who had not found a coveted front position struggled to get their cameras and themselves through the solid wall of gawkers. Tourists too hauled their videocams into place.

There was a sudden very brief moment of silence, like that dead spot in the middle of a hurricane. Then a great wave of noise erupted, as if from a volcano. Those of us in the center could have been crushed had it not been for the fast action of Sheriff Dick Truman. Whipping out his six-shooter, an old-fashioned tool straight out of an Old Tombstone movie, he raised it in the air to get off a couple of rounds. His deputies quickly formed a protective circle around the major mourners to hold back the mob. Around the perimeter the Tucson motorcycle squad took up positions.

And the media went wild.

I let go of Megan and Vanna to grab a gravedigger's shovel and jumped into the hole after Elise. She wasn't moving. Could need digging out.

Gently I turned her over and brushed the dirt from her face.

"Where am I? What happened?" she mumbled.

"Oh, Mama. Oh, Mama," Fess moaned from above.

"My water broke!" Megan screamed, swooning into her husband's arms.

CHAPTER 32

L ooked like we were in for a long seige. Yell "Hate Crime!" and every organization and half-baked group on the books wanted in on the action. Great photo ops, demonstrating on behalf of racial prejudice. The local Hispanics and Asians steered clear, but the gays and lesbians showed. What Dr. Wallaberra's murder had to do with gay rights wasn't clear.

"He was living with his lover, right?" shouted a lesbian at me when I had the gall to ask. Egads and little fishes. Reminded me of all that hoopla up in Wyoming when that little guy, Matt Shepard, was robbed, tortured, and hung out to dry, or freeze to death, on a rail fence north of Laramie.

"You think they'll make a movie out of his murder?" I asked the protester standing in front of me. I was half-serious, half-mocking. Several companies or folk had made not one but two movies off Shepard, plus a Broadway play.

"Hey, that's a great idea!" Dragging her placard on the ground, she dashed off.

By this time the private mourners had given up. The deputies had their hands full trying to hold back the crowd, every one of whom pushed forward trying to get a better look. Rumors flew like frantic hummingbirds. Sheriff Truman called for backup, with the highway troopers racing to the ready.

Fess traveled in the ambulance with Elise to the hospital.

Brother John herded the remaining pallbearers and the rest of us into the limos, where we raced back to the church. "The mortuary staff can lower Paul's coffin into the ground," he said. "They don't need us standing there gawking down into that hole."

Inside the church I took my place at the organ, with Vanna beside me holding open the hymnbook. Dollie led the mourners in singing *Whispering Hope* and *Amazing Grace.* By then the gospel singers from Tucson had pushed their way into the sanctuary and they, too, lifted their rollicking voices to the rafters.

I didn't know what was happening outside. Apparently the whole crowd had followed us. I kept right on playing. The combined choirs and the legitimate congregation kept on singing, to the accompaniment of busses revving their motors, highway patrol sirens soaring, feet shuffling, and many dozens of vehicles drawing up outdoors.

Dick Truman, the Dick Tracy look-alike, was the sheriff, but you could have fooled me. He appeared perpetually confused. Country bumpkin or an act? He made me think of Sheriff Andy Taylor on the Mayberry TV sitcom. I promised myself to keep on his tail, see if Truman would finally welcome my offer to help look for the crooks, and now, especially, for the pastor's killer. One thing might lead to another, from petty crimes to attempts on my life to this grand but horrible finale of Paul Wallaberra's murder.

CHAPTER 33

I met with Sheriff Dick Truman. This time to report that my various illnesses were due to poisoning, from one or more unknown perpetrators. He said Yeah, I could press charges, but who was I charging? Without the papers signed, his hands were tied, he said. He did agree to keep his eyes open, his ears to the ground, whatever these vague half-promises meant. I reminded him that it seemed they'd increased their efforts to kill me.

"How's that, son?"

"When I didn't die from poisoning, they blew up my home, the RV."

"Oh, yeah. Well, you come up with some names, I'll get busy."

Sounded pretty vague. Not what you'd call a promise. Taking another tack, I insisted that somebody ought to check into Mr. Goodman's disappearance. Dick ridiculed the idea that he might have been done away with. Mrs. Goodman said her husband was in Europe and South America on business. That was enough for Truman.

"Solving crimes and catching bad guys is best left to the professionals, son," he said. Which didn't mean I had any intention of backing off.

Again I dropped by the sheriff's office, and then again. I was eager to share clues with him, if he were of a mind to share. What was happening about Dr. Wallaberra's murder? About that, Dick shrugged. Out of his hands, he said. The FBI had stepped in, what with all the rigmarole about a hate crime that the protesters and media hype had made the killing out to be. Of course, if he just happened to solve the crime, it would be a feather in his hat. He looked at me shrewdly, before coming right out and saying it.

"You scratch my back, I'll scratch yours."

Apparently he was eager for me to pass on my news, when and if I produced some real dirt from my digging. Whether he was willing to do the same was up for grabs.

When I repeated our various exchanges at the Cat Castle, Mike said the sheriff was understaffed and that his jurisdiction was limited to the county, anyhow. I looked at him, deadpan, without speaking. Like, what else is new. I changed subjects.

"Did anybody hear Fess when Elise fell into that grave hole?" Nobody else had. "He said, 'Forgive me, Mama. I'll be a good boy, Mama. If you just don't die on me.'"

Leaning forward eagerly over his mug of coffee

now grown cold, Matt said: "Sounds like a confession. He'll 'be good,' he's 'sorry'."

Following that fiasco, Fess had rushed Elise away, presumably to the ER up at St. Mary's, for that's what he'd muttered upon clasping his dirt-covered mama in his arms. I wondered then, for the first time, why I'd never tried to get close to either boy, Fess or Donny; maybe invited them for a game of golf, or to go for beers. Too young for me, not my type, some reason I hadn't made their acquaintance. Now it was too late to cozy up to the college boy and the drug addict in the red Jaguar. My intentions would be immediately suspect. Rightfully so.

I couldn't play detective all the time. I made time to enjoy fun and games with friends. Their house finished, I would rather have moved in with the Cat Castle bunch, been a part of the family ready to raise a youngster, one Matthew Michael Derry. But that would mean Brother John was left all alone. So I stayed put with him.

The Dolan baby was a few weeks premature, which meant they would keep him awhile at St. Mary's Hospital.

"Overstressed." That was the doctor's statement of cause and effect. Matt called it an understatement.

When Derek and Megan weren't lingering in their baby's nursery, holding hands and staring at their collection of baby equipment or at the window sill piled with stuffed animals, we put our heads together. Or the Derrys and I went into a huddle when the Dolans zipped up to the city to be with the baby, which was often. Their son, they reported, was gaining weight rapidly and it wouldn't be long before he could join us.

"Sorry to mention how happy we are, Oliver," Megan said. "How can we be this ecstatic, with Dr. Wallaberra murdered? Besides, it could have been you."

"Never mind me. It's natural to feel joyful when a newborn comes into the world. Almost at the same time the pastor left."

Hugo barked from the front porch, but I didn't let him in. I went outside instead to play with him, rub his head behind the ears, and give him a doggy snack. No pets allowed in Brother John's housing development, so Hugo was still parked with Juan. Except when I picked him up to come with me. He had grown attached to Penny and now rode in the basket I'd mounted behind the seat of my cycle. Wind blowing in his face, ears lying flat, he rewarded me with the occasional yap as we traveled from Juan's place out to the Cat Castle and back. I ate breakfast with Brother John. Otherwise, Hugo and I showed up daily at the café for lunch and dinner, lingering through the afternoon with my dog romping in the fenced back yard next door.

Man, that Vanna, she's something else! I could admit it, now. I'd fallen hard, head over heels, as they say. Seemed like we had everything except religion in common: classical and country western music, both; football and golf—she had recently taken up the game; favorite foods—made from scratch, not processed or junk stuff; movies—adventure and comedies. A whole lot more I couldn't remember.

The Derrys introduced us to *Texas 42*, a domino game played with two sets of partners, four people total. Something like bridge, they said, though I'm not familiar with the latter. In the comparative quiet of mid-afternoon or late into the night after the Cat closed, we kept a game going at a back table. Vanna and I changed off with Derek and Megan, or whichever pair needed to hop up to serve the few diners who showed, mostly for coffee after the busy lunch hour.

Then Juan got wind of our enthusiasm for dominos and, when he could get away from his busy job, he started dropping in, too. Glad to see him, I nevertheless felt uncomfortable. I still didn't like the looks he and Vanna exchanged or their cozy talk and flirtatious laughter. I hadn't asked either, and neither had ever shared with me the nature of their relationship. Had they been lovers? I didn't think I wanted to know. Those elk bull feelings of jealousy and possession kicked in every time the three of us were together; memories of Arlo, Patsy, and me.

Everybody laughed at my boat story, the thirtieth birthday present that was supposed to be my inheritance. "Dry-docked at present," I said. "It's sure not going anywhere under its own steam."

Before leaving Wyoming, I'd had a batch of new tee shirts inscribed. Since mom was with me, I succumbed to her preferences for Shakespeare. But only on a few. The remainder were mine. As a tongue-in-cheek reminder of my silly birthday present, I now wore a sky-blue tee, emblazoned with the slogan, *My bus has sailed.*

"What a card," Matt said, almost but not quite giggling.

"Yeah, well, my boat will sail about as easily as any bus."

Vanna told me in private she'd like to see the yacht, even if it wouldn't sail. And meet my mom. My heart fluttered.

Nights, well, she and I started hanging out at her apartment, first on the couch, then in the bedroom. We were compatible there, too. She's one passionate little lady. Enough said.

Meanwhile, there was all the business I'd set for myself. Which gave the seven of us, in any combination of twos, threes, or the whole bunch, plenty to talk about.

Immediately following the funeral, none of us knew what exactly had happened. The true mourners had stayed cloistered inside the church. Only later, on the ten o'clock news, did we hear that with no specific targets left to interview by the press or protest to by the mob of demonstrators, the whole she-bang quickly fell apart and everybody soon dispersed. Like desert nomads, they *folded their tents* to slip away.

Next, I was headed for Dollie's. Although Vanna, nearly in tears, wanted to come with me, I insisted she stay behind. She had afternoon clean-up chores at the Cat, I said. She was afraid for my life, she said.

I couldn't help smiling. "At the hands of sweet little Dollie?"

In repetition of our first encounter, Mrs. Martinez welcomed me onto her patio and into her home. Over two dainty cups of Raspberry Zinger, her favorite herbal tea, we sat in the cool air-conditioned comfort of her living room.

"I'm going to ask you a question, Dollie. Please give me an honest answer." I looked right at her. She dropped her head, but said nothing. "How did you come by those expensive golf clubs, the tennis rackets, and that fur jacket I saw in your open closet?"

She gulped, splashing tea down the front of her blue and gray striped sundress. She gripped the lightweight, crocheted shawl thrown over bare shoulders. "You looked? You pried into my private things?"

"The closet door was open, Dollie."

She sighed. "No big deal, Oliver. Those were all gifts from Elise. Back when we were still bosom buddies." Another sigh, louder and longer this time. "Back when she was my best friend in all the world."

"Why was that?"

"Why did she give me presents? She was always doing that. Pitied my poverty, I guess." Now her voice turned bitter, as if reconsidering the motive behind her cousin's generosity. "Looking down on me, no doubt. Feeling sorry for me. Laughing behind my back. She never did care much for my husband. Told me way back then I was out of my mind marrying some Mexican. She'd turn up her nose, like Martinez was dirt to her."

"Wait a minute. Don't try to distract me with all this stuff. I asked you a question. Are you going to tell me the truth?"

She appeared genuinely surprised, her face an open question. "What? Just ask. I'll tell you whatever I know. Oliver, believe me, I've nothing to hide."

Whenever anybody says that, my hackles shoot straight up. Seems like they're trying too hard to pass off fiction for fact. Dollie sat perfectly still in her needlepoint covered chair, while I rocked back and forth in the matching rocker that was way too dainty and short for my long legs and big body.

"I asked what your fight was about. Why are you mad at each other?"

"Oh, I'm not mad at her. Or I wasn't at first. Now, after her wretched attitude and stupid competitive shenanigans, I'm not sure but what I hate her!"

"All right, I'll buy that. But, why? How did it start?"

"She thinks her husband was unfaithful." Dollie shrugged, flipping her hand over nonchalantly, as if it were an insignificant matter. "Elise insists that it was her husband who fathered my Donny with me."

CHAPTER 34

Brother John interrupted my mopping to walk across the wet kitchen. He commenced unloading the dishwasher. Was this an early sign of the Alzheimer's absenteeism, or was he just inconsiderate? He's hard to figure sometimes.

He too was concerned with my welfare and safety. "You're not so far out of your sickbed, Oliver. You could have a relapse." He paused between shelving plates and poking sharp knives in the spoon compartment. "Whoever tried to kill you must be thoroughly disgusted at his failure. He'll come back at you now with a vengeance. Mark my words." He shook one of the knives at me. "Mark my words, Son. Leave this whole mess to Sheriff Truman."

I wondered whether he included the attempt on my life along with Dr. Wallaberra's murder. Was everybody determined to keep me out of the investigation? Obviously somebody had secrets that he or she didn't want uncovered. Couldn't be my *family* down at the Cat. Nor Brother John either.

Finished with the mopping, I said I had errands, and left.

Sometimes I dropped by Juan's office, more often at his home, where Hugo regularly expressed an oh-hum disdain at my arrival. Bringing treats wasn't the best training, Juan said, but it was the only way for me to get Hugo's attention. An orphan, Garcia called himself. Must be lonesome. I could hardly begrudge him Hugo's affection. Just so Vanna didn't succumb to Juan's charms.

When I told Juan about my confrontation with Dollie and her revelation, he said: "Sounds like she was pretty blasé over bearing Mr. Goodman's baby." Then he thought a moment. "Long time to keep such a secret."

"Let me finish. I don't think she knew. Not until recently. Even now, it's only a wild guess."

"What? How is that possible?"

"Artificial insemination. Martinez was sterile from a case of adult mumps. Neither he nor Dollie had any idea who the donor was. That's what Dollie claimed. In the meantime, all these years, they kept silent, letting Elise and the world think Donald was conceived the natural way."

I paused to pat Hugo. We sat in the shade in Juan's back yard. Finally, my dog was ready to make up. I reached down for a stick, gave it a toss with my pitcher's hand. From sandlot softball back home in my middle-school days. Hugo barked happily, leaping high to make a half-turn before dashing across the yard bent on a fast retrieval.

"Ahh," Juan mused, smoothing his mustache. He could have been the villain in an old-fashioned melodrama. "Then, as adolescents, the boys had their picture taken with Goodman."

"Probably. Dollie said when she got the photos developed, she spotted the resemblance immediately. Who wouldn't? We did. She hid the tell-tale evidence."

"Then how did the picture wind up in Elise's wallet?"

"Dollie doesn't know. She didn't even miss it, which was why she was so hurt and puzzled for so long over Elise's sudden anger; her turn-about face, from the cousin Dollie had known and loved all her life to a hateful shrew."

"A real witch."

"Yeah, looks like it. Dollie rarely opened her souvenir cache, an old shoebox tied with blue ribbon and tucked high up on the back of the closet shelf. She took down the box one day to savor her keepsakes. Like a fifty-year-old soda cracker with a single bite missing, a thing she'd copped from her prom date with a guy she'd had a crush on all through high school. Nothing came of the date, she couldn't stand the BGOC after all, too superior acting."

"BGOC?"

"Big man on campus."

Juan reached down into the cooler beside his lawn chair for another couple of icy Coors. "So how did Elise come by the photo?"

"Dollie doesn't have any idea. She only discovered it missing after I returned from Wyoming. When she confronted Elise, Mrs. Goodman admitted to prying. There was a big row, a lot of screaming back and forth, Dollie said. Elise refuses to believe her cousin's artificial insemination story. Too much coincidence and she insists she never heard anything about her husband serving as an anonymous donor at the sperm bank."

"You're right. Rather, Elise is. That's a pretty big mouthful of a story Dollie expects her cousin to swallow." The first beer Juan gulped, this one he sipped. "What's your next move?"

"Confront Elise."

I threw the stick a few more times for Hugo to fetch, patted him, fed him, and said goodbye. Juan was leaving with me. Hugo came bouncing after us.

"Heel!" Juan commanded. "Sit!" he said then. Reluctantly Hugo obeyed.

Suggesting we could ride together if he too had a cycle, we headed for Tucson. Juan was attracted to the Blast, a top of the line machine by Buell, starting at over five thousand, plus taxes, title and licensing. Shiny, with red and silver chrome trim, its 492 cubic centimeter, single-cylinder motor made it a blast, all right. I wondered how much money he earned in his villa management job. Of course he had no mother to share his salary with.

I had no salary, period. And my mom insisted that Hernandez was bringing home a good paycheck these days, what with the regular construction job he'd landed with Ashbery Homes. No need to send money home nowadays.

Without searching further, Juan put the price on his credit card, completed the paper work in record time, and we took off. Riding side by side now or single file when the traffic along I-19 demanded it, we returned to Green Valley. Just a couple of carefree guys, the wind blowing against goggled eyes and helmeted heads. With an apparent appetite for acceleration, Juan pulled on ahead of me to zoom down the highway. He had to get back to work.

We agreed to meet on the weekend to give his bike another type of run out in the desert. Man, he'd have me eating his dirt.

I left him at the maintenance sheds behind the shopping center, where he asked about my next step. I said I was ready to take on Elise, with or without Fess. I didn't mention I planned to stop by the Cat first. Juan needn't know the full nature of my relationship with Vanna, though he'd probably guessed.

"Wish me luck," I called, mounting Penny. "I'm off to beard the lion in her den."

CHAPTER 35

At the Cat Castle I repeated the Dollie-Elise tale, contributing to Megan's "Ongoing Saga of the Cousins' Squabbles." The young mother squealed whenever she used the phrase, making it sound like the title of a soap opera.

This time I wore a cheery, bright yellow tee shirt carrying the inscription that mom used on me all my growing up days: *Happiness isn't suggested, it's required.* She didn't like no grumpy boy around the house.

At the back table, our habitual haunt, Vanna poured coffee all around before taking her place beside me. Under cover of the white linen table-cloth in preparation for the dinner crowd, Vanna placed a hand on my leg. A sideways glance at her and she smiled back, her left cheek dimpling. With the other hand she brushed back her long, thick brunette hair.

"I worry about you poking your nose into all this business," she said, adding to her statement with a pinch to my knee.

"Oh, yes," said Megan. "Oliver, you must be ever so careful."

"Sounds like he's already decided to throw caution out the door along with the bath water," Matt muttered, referring to Fess Goodman's semi-confession at the gravesite.

"I think you're mixing metaphors," Vanna said, this time with a stroke to my upper thigh. Like my mom, my sweetheart was into the beauty of language.

It was one thing for me to shadow the sheriff, try to pry news from him about Dr. Wallaberra's murder investigation. Quite another for me to hit on the people we all believed were behind the attempt to murder me. Sighing, I agreed to *watch my Ps and Qs*, as Megan put it. I said goodbye in preparation for heading on down to the estate-size development north of Tubac.

Matt and Megan got up to handle a customer and Mike went back to his ceramic cats that he was painting in a rainbow of colors. He said they were his idea for table decorations.

This wasn't my first trip down to Tubac in search of Elise, nor had I been able to waylay her at church. Neither Mrs. Goodman nor her son was to be found anywhere. What, they were holing up until Dr. Wallaberra's murder investigation cooled, or somebody else was accused? I had plenty of suspicions about cause and effect here, especially after hearing Fess's statement to his mom when she fell into the grave hole.

My supposition included that Elise had told her son about his half-brother, Donny Martinez. Fess committed the petty crimes to support his drug habit and Elise planted some of the goods on Dollie. Fess went along.

So what? Nobody but me had made the connection between Dollie's closet cache and the church thefts. No point in implicating Dollie if the authorities didn't know.

The competition between the cousins. Initiated by Elise as a means of showing up Dollie, or merely her unthinking response to her own wedding of anger and frustration? Could be, though I could see no other point to it.

Waves of heat shimmered along the ribbon of highway on that super hot August day. With the wind blowing my hair, the scent of truckers' diesel and desert sagebrush commingling in my nose, I pulled off the Interstate at the Tubac exit. I had some questions to ask of the bartender there; namely, had Fess or Elise been spotted recently in the village saloon? If so, were they alone, one or the other, perhaps dining in the adjacent restaurant or meeting with one or more strangers? I recalled the exchange I'd spotted in this very bar that shouted loudly of a possible drug deal.

I don't know why, perhaps I was influenced by the movies, but it seemed that bartenders are often privy to secrets. Confessions from disgruntled, half-drunk drinkers, or a bored barkeep's observations. Could be the sources of their knowledge.

Joe Joseph, that's his handle, scratched his beard and rubbed his bald head. "Naw, ain't seen nobody."

After no more than a single swallow of Coors, I stood to leave. Not much use of this side trip.

"Hey, you didn't drink your beer."

"Yeah, well." Back in the sweltering heat, I climbed on Penny to start and rev the engine. On to the estates.

No sign of anybody at the Goodmans' house. The drapes were closed against the heat, the double-car garage doors shut. I beat on the front door anyhow, then pressed a finger against the doorbell, leaving it there. I could hear the chimes, over and over again, playing London's Westminster Abbey bell tune. If anybody was home, her or his head should be ringing, as if from bedding down in the bell tower of Mission San Xavier del Bac, off to the north.

The door opened a crack. From the dim interior, Elise's tousled head appeared. Dressed in a pale pink negligee, she tightened the belt, smoothed the ruffles around the neck and running down the front of the flimsy garment.

"What do you want?"

My foot in the door, like a salesman at Blondie and Dagwood's house, I pushed my way inside.

"What th'hell!"

"Talk to me, Elise," I said, with no other preamble. "Now."

She stumbled backwards, one hand covering her mouth, fear appearing in her eyes. "About what?"

"Did you really think I wasn't on to you, with all that poisoning?"

This time she moved backwards, as if on roller blades. She banged into a hassock and stumbled, going plop on her bottom. Staring up at me, a hand again covering her mouth, she sputtered, "Why ever would you think such a thing? Me? Why, I never."

She didn't ask about the poisoning, didn't seem surprised at that. Only that I was accusing her. Pretty revealing, sometimes, what people <u>don't</u> say. Leaving that topic, I immediately socked her with another. "Why are you mad at Dollie?"

"Oh, that." She sighed, visibly relieved. The folds and pleats of her long garment curled over her feet. She gazed downward, as if seeing her lower appendages for the first time. "Sh-she's so damn uppity. Dollie doesn't have a pot to pee in or a window to throw it out of, but she invariably acts like she's just as good as me."

Ah, another red herring. Okay, I'd keep switching back and forth between topics. "Why'd you and Fess rub my pajamas with poison ivy leaves so the doctors would quarantine me with a case of the shingles?"

There was no sensible cause and effect in that conclusion, as any other doctor other than the dim-eyed old Green Valley coot might have diagnosed my rash correctly. I simply meant to throw off Elise, toss her disconnected questions and note her reactions.

In her eyes I spied caution, and what I perceived as guilt. Covering herself—literally, by blanketing her face with both hands—she quickly recouped.

Stared straight at me, while returning both hands to the act of nervously re-smoothing the pink negligee across her lap. "Don't be silly. I don't know what you're talking about."

"When all else fails, simply claim ignorance. Is that your strategy, Elise?"

"When did I ever give you permission to call me by my first name? Its Mrs. Goodman to the handyman."

The once elegant lady wouldn't admit I was her competition on the piano and organ benches. Back to *general factotum*, right when I'd quit the church altogether.

Ignoring the insulting tone of her voice, I again switched tactics. This time I meant to hit her and hit her hard.

"What happened to Mr. Goodman? You bury him in your back yard?"

She gasped and tried to stand. Tripping on the long, pink pleated skirt, Elise fell backwards over the hassock and crashed to the floor.

CHAPTER 36

I was back on the organ while Elise recuperated from a bad back and twisted knee. *Air for the G String,* as a prelude, introduced the congregation to a bit of Bach, though I would need a lot more practice before I could spring his *Fugue in D Minor* on them. People are more comfortable with the familiar, though, which soon returned me to the old gospel songs straight from the hymnbook. Elise's notes alerted me to her choices, which I followed for the interlude between early worship and the eleven o'clock sermon service. Smiles replaced frowns on parishioner faces with my renditions of *Precious Lord* and *In the Garden.*

Outdoors, little remained of the garden. The demonstrators' shuffling feet had trampled it to death. Now, in the place of tomato and carrot and okra plants, there ranged in a quarter-block square an array of plastic flower wreaths and bouquets and wooden crosses. A great variety of sympathy cards and handwritten poems were poked into the holes along the chicken-wire fence. In response to demands, Brother John had invited grief counselors to visit with the assemblage and members of the congregation made their own appointments. The media, mostly out of Tucson, continued with the periodic account. Thus our garden fence with its memorials gained its share of press attention; a micro-mini aftermath version of Princess Di's death, the Oklahoma City bombing, or the Columbine High School mass murders, and nine-eleven.

Dollie was missing at church that morning and so was her son, but then Donny seldom came to services. Elise was resting at home and, as to be expected, there was no sign of Fess.

Sheriff Truman had said Yeah, I was welcome to stop by his office from time to time. He admitted, each and every time, that the pickings were slim. This time, right after church, he called me. He thought we could pick brains. The way he said it, the metaphor sounded gross, but an up-front exchange of ideas was what I'd been after all along, so I agreed to meet him at his office.

I changed clothes into light blue tee shirt with the slogan, *Fight til the last gasp,* from Shakespeare's King Henry the Sixth. Another among what my mom called her variety of special gifts.

Determined to solve Dr. Wallaberra's murder, if not the explosion of Brother John's RV (and my home!), Dick Truman asked where I was coming from. "What have you discovered? Who do you suspect? Level with me, son."

The Sheriff leaned back in his wooden swivel chair with the arms, a captain's chair on wheels, clasped hands behind his head and squinted at me. I felt scrutinized like a foreign virus under a microscope. I knew he wanted to get the jump on the Federal Bureau of Investigation. The Tucson FBI agents assigned to the pastor's case totally ignored Dick. Early on, he said, before I returned to Arizona, they had prowled the church grounds. "Haven't been back, since. I ain't seen hide nor hair of 'em." The chair plopped back into position, he stood and commenced to pace. "Too much media attention for them to have forgotten Dr. W." (It came out sounding like Dubya, a familiar nickname.) "I thought you might have heard somethin', all your runnin' back and forth."

Putting our heads together, picking each other's brains, we didn't come up with much. I wondered what he was holding back. Me, I was of two minds: reveal all, versus share a few things while keeping a bit in reserve. I opted for the latter; tell him about Dollie's stolen cache but not about Donny's father's identity. Standing up to leave, I promised to get back to him again soon.

Just then, however, the door burst open and in marched a pair of federal agents, easily identifiable by the big FBI letters on the back of their jackets. I would have thought they'd be in plain clothes. Why advertise, unless they meant to intimidate the sheriff. And possibly me.

The latter proved to be fact, because the big

blonde shook his finger in my face, while the smaller guy, a redhead, warned me to mind my own business. When they had questioned Mrs. Martinez, said the blonde, she complained that I'd been harassing her.

"We're making the rounds, interviewing key players in Dr. Wallaberra's congregation," said the redhead. "You stay out of it, ya hear."

Mr. Blonde, who had yet to identify himself by name, whipped around to face Truman. "The Drug Enforcement Agency is in on this, too. You local yokels messing around will only screw up the caper we think is comin' up."

"A DEA sting operation?" I said, while sticking out my chin in defiance.

Redhead jerked around. "Where'd you hear that?"

Hah. I had my sources—Bill back home, Brad, and hearsay from the Cat.

"Never mind," he said, turning toward the door and jerking a thumb at the blonde. "This is a warning. Steer clear. This is an FBI-DEA investigation."

"In a pig's ear," said Dick after they left, slamming the door behind them. "Pima County's my jurisdiction. No matter what they think they're doing, I'll do as I please." He said no more, neither complaining about the FBI nor issuing a personal warning for me to back off. That could mean he counted on my help.

At Vanna's I built a tuna and green salad, adding raisins, walnuts, shredded cheddar, cottage cheese, and a few slices of banana, while she set the table and poured us each a glass of dry white wine by Inglenook. Later, much later (if you get my meaning), we went shopping in Tucson. She was dragging me to the mall to buy a decent suit. She said she was tired of staring at my old thing with the shiny bottom. She knew I'd picked that up at the Salvation Army on my return to Arizona. I could see no reason for two suits hanging in the closet all week between services. It wasn't like I had an executive position in some corporate cubbyhole, like Scott Adam's *Dilbert.*

Couldn't be for a wedding. That requires a tuxedo, if Vanna and I were to take the fancy route. Not that she had said Yes, and not that I had popped the question as yet. Not because I didn't want to. I already knew she was the one for me, the lady I wanted to spend the rest of my life with. Granted, I'd been stalling, possibly because I was afraid of another rejection.

Taking my hand as if I were a seven-year-old resisting mama's determination to deck me out for the new school year, pert and pretty Vanna led me to the men's department at Goldwater's. My sweetheart pawed and poked and prodded me into trying on one jacket after another until we settled on a fine set of threads by Burberry of London. Fine, muted stripes, barely discernible, on a dark charcoal background. I maintained position, like Hugo's response to Juan's "Stay" command, while the in-house tailor pinned up cuffs to the proper length. Not much on my long legs.

Next, Vanna took me on a quick tour of the campus where she would be a sophomore next term.

She was more interested in pointing out the academic buildings and the library than the athletic fields or the student union, though she did condescend to taking tiny bites of plain yogurt at a shop in the union. I opted for a hearty subway piled high with turkey, cheese, lettuce, tomato, and thick slices of Bermuda onion.

I took a few peeks at the pretty coeds in their short, tight mini skirts and low-necked, revealing tops. To those wearing loose tee shirts and faded jeans, I gave no more than a passing glance. Over the blare of a loud rock band playing next door and the magpie chatter all around us, Vanna said, "Eyes front and center, private."

"Yessir. Yes Ma'am, Captain." I saluted, smirking.

She grinned back, and fed me a French fry, not bothering to dip it in catsup, the way I like them. She wanted my opinion of the campus.

I didn't ask, but I mused over the point of this tour. Vanna wanted to share with me her "other" world, her preferred image? Not merely was she a Cat waitress, but more importantly she was a serious scholar. Hell's bells, I knew that. Or was this side trip a subtle hint she would prefer an educated man? Juan's handsome face immediately swimming before my eyes, I too turned serious. "Okay, I guess. Glad you're a happy camper around here."

I didn't want her trying to change me, if that was her aim. What you see is what you get, babe. That's what I was thinking. In point of fact, I'd already tried college. A half-dozen courses was enough.

I turned up my nose at the string quartet she recommended next. Not that I don't appreciate classical music, of course I do. I can play it, some of it, sometimes. Vanna might not know that. She was absent the times I tried introducing our congregation to more variety in their musical fare.

Guess I just felt cantankerous. Little doubt I was sounding like a pouty kid or an old maid resisting change. First the new suit, then the campus tour, and now a quartet of strings? No thanks. At that point I longed for the company of Brad and the macho truckers we'd met on the road.

"Let's go to a baseball game," I suggested, not knowing who was in town or whether any game was scheduled. In the burning heat of August, possibly nothing. Spring training was more like it, when several ball clubs took advantage of the comparatively good weather down here in the southwest's winter clime.

"I've never cared much for baseball," she said, not looking at me.

I decided to give her the full whammy, let her know that sports are important to me. "You've heard of the fall of the Roman Empire? Of the 1929 crash of the New York Stock Exchange? How about Pearl Harbor or the D-Day invasion or Hiroshima! You should have been into baseball during the 2001 season with the Seattle Mariners. Man, what a season. We'd have to go back to the 1907 Chicago White Socks and the 1939 New York Yankees to find such an astonishing, extraordinary historic start in Major League Baseball! Why, by June, the Mariners had already won forty-five and only lost twelve of their first sixty-seven games. That's nearly eighty percent. Besides that, the number of new, all-time records they had set would fill a page. You've gotta like baseball, Hon."

Vanna pushed away her unfinished carton of yogurt and stood up. "Okay, then," she said, with a flounce of bare-shouldered sundress. "Let's get you back to Hugo. Or to your on-going investigation. Sorry I took up so much of your precious time." Over her shoulder, she mumbled an epithet, "I imagined you might go for a little culture."

She made my quest sound like a kid's search for lost marbles. Neither of us said another word, not even when my head turned to stare at another pretty girl. Nor when she climbed on the back of Penny and tucked her full skirt beneath her.

At her place, I asked what she wanted to do that evening.

"Nothing with you. I'll call Juan."

Revving Penny's motor in anger, I zoomed down the road. I was steamed. Then, for the first time in a long time I thought about Patsy Parsons. After the row with Vanna, for that was certainly what it was, I asked myself if I still wanted to locate Patsy.

Yup.

CHAPTER 37

"Could be anybody," said the sheriff, hedging. Anybody? Santa Claus or the Tooth Fairy? Truman was reaching. "You agree with the FBI, then, that it was a hate crime?"

"Naw, probably not." Dick shuffled papers on his desk, his eyes on them.

I leaned forward. "If we're to believe the media, it was."

He flipped a hand in a throw-away gesture. "They gotta hype it, give the ten o'clock news a sensational twist. Catering the special interest groups gets them all riled up. Any excuse to purport their cause."

I wasn't naïve. Determined to squeeze blood from this turnip, I egged him on. "Which cause is that?"

He glanced up to gaze at me, scratching his scalp as if trying to figure me out. "Any cause.

The gay life style. The pity party song blacks keep singing."

"I didn't see Jesse Jackson or Al Sharpton at the demonstration."

Again Truman stared at me, this time like he expected to see I'd grown an extra head. "Too small time for the great men." He shuffled more papers in the open file on his desk. Found a paper and waved it in my face.

I tried another topic. "What about the FBI's claim that Dr. Wallaberra's murder had something to do with an upcoming DEA sting? You think that's possible?"

"Anything's possible." Standing, he abruptly changed tactics from putting me off to inviting me in. "You wanna come with me? Deputies all out on patrol. I got me an idee."

Eager to find out more, I trailed along. In the sheriff's car we headed into the foothills. Dick said there was a trailer up there he wanted to visit. "I'm thinkin' it could have been those kids, one or more," he said, both freckled hands gripping the wheel as the car trod and dodged the bigger rocks in the graveled road. "You know, the ones Dr. Wallaberra hired when you was under quarantine. To jack up and paint that shed out back a the church. While goofing off, they could a planted MaryJane plants. Preacher caught 'em. Kapowee. End of story."

"Dr. Wallaberra or maybe Brother John had already dug 'em up," I said, playing Devil's Advocate. "Before or shortly after I left town."

He looked surprised; that I knew, possibly. Unless he'd forgotten the sequence of events, or didn't realize that Brother John and I were in contact while I was home recuperating in Wyoming.

"Okay, try this on for size," he said. "The kids returned to check on their crop, found the plants gone, and Preacher came out to confront 'em. Same thing. Kapowee!"

The sheriff pulled up in front of the old trailer, stirring up a cloud of dust and braking in front of a green and white striped awning hanging lopsided on one end. Beneath it a card table with dirty dishes and half-eaten food attracted insects. A swarm of flies ignored our approach until Dick righted a couple of chairs lying on their sides to shove them under the table. The insects took off, much like the mob outside the church after we mourners refused to emerge.

"Place looks deserted," he said. Understatement. Next, he'd instruct me that the sun comes up in the east, sets in the west. "Something sent them scurrying off in a hurry."

"They could have seen us approaching." I was staring back down the hill at the dirt trail we'd navigated coming up. "We raised a huge cloud of dust."

"Where to?"

"Up in the hills?" Amidst the scrub grass and cacti, from tall bulky saguaro and ocotillo to the shorter ones, the prickly pear and la cholla, the area was crowded with pinion trees, Palo Verdi, and a few drooping weeping willow. "Plenty of places to hide, if they ran off on foot. Who lives here, anyhow?"

"The twins, George and Jack Manson. With their old man, a wino. No mama that I ever heard tell."

I stepped up to the door, the screen off one hinge and slipping to the side, to rap my knuckles on the aluminum siding. A portable air conditioner hummed in the front window.

"'Bout time you boys came back," said a voice through the crack that opened behind the screen. "Where's my whiskey?"

"Not your boys, old-timer," said Sheriff Truman. "Looks like they brung pizza and then left before eating it." Dick held up his wallet, open to reveal his shield. "Open up. We come to talk."

"Got a warrant?"

"Uh, no. Thought you might cooperate. Tell us where the twins are, how to find 'em. Them and their buddies."

"Got no warrant, you got no right." The door slammed shut in our faces.

"Got any guns you keep in there?" the sheriff yelled.

"Go 'way."

We went, Dick cussing all the way down the trail and complaining that he should have thought of that. A search warrant. "Bet we're on the right track, though. Whaddya think, Oliver?"

"Speak of track, look ahead. Here they come," I yelled, pointing down the one-way graveled road. "That's their old pickup."

Dirt flew as the driver braked, flipped a brodie, and gunned it back down the mountainside.

"Hey, there, younguns," the sheriff shouted, accelerating.

Both vehicles careened down the road and around corners, the dense foliage up here occasionally putting the boys beyond our view. Onto the highway they shot, our car right behind them.

Dick took one hand off the wheel to grab his mobile phone. He screamed for backup. Then he yelled at me to get hold of the dispatcher. "Report our position and tell 'em what's happenin'." He sounded gleeful, a kid in the middle of his own car chase. "They're heading for Mexico!" he gasped, this time reaching for his bottled water. "We'll never catch 'em," he shouted next, as the green pickup pulled away from us. "They must have that thing all souped up."

We hit ninety and then passed a hundred miles an hour. Just then we heard sirens, from both fore and aft.

"Ah, just in time. The troopers. Better than the FBI or DEA."

A shot rang out from the passenger side ahead. I saw a long rifle poking out at us.

"Ohmigosh, they're shooting at us. Duck!" he shouted, pounding the steering wheel with one hand while clinging to it with the other.

From behind us a state patrol car came zooming past.

Ahead, another cop car heading our way leaped across the center grassy area dividing the four-lane highway, bounced over and through the natural flora growing in the middle to head straight for the pickup on a collision course.

At last the Manson boys gave way. Braking hard and veering sharply to the right, the green pickup hit a culvert and flipped over. Dust, dirt, steam from their radiator, all ascended in a dirty white cloud. The troopers, Sheriff Truman, and I all piled out of our vehicles. Curious travelers, truckers and tourists, and commuters into and out of Mexico and Tucson gawked out their windows as a couple of highway patrol officers set up orange cones signifying caution.

Truman and I were the first to reach the truck. On the driver's side one boy hung upside down from his fastened seat belt. His twin, Jack or George, held his head in both hands, splinters of glass poking out from where he'd been stabbed on cheeks and forehead.

Both boys blubbered, while clambering out of their overturned truck.

"We were only go-going after b-booze," the driver stuttered.

"For Pa," cried the other.

"Yeah, so why'd you shoot at us?"

We got more wailing, but no further explanation.

CHAPTER 38

W hen I shared that story with the bunch at the Cat Castle, Mike doubled over laughing and Matt pulled on his ear. Across the table Vanna stared somberly at them as if she couldn't see the joke.

"Oliver could have been killed, Mike," she said quietly.

"Yeah, but he wasn't," Juan said. Turning to me, he asked, "So what happened?"

"When the kid said they were only going after booze, Sheriff Truman replied, 'To Mexico?' Then the boy, the driver, still hanging upside down and bleeding from all the broken glass, gasped 'Into Tubac.' So Dick says, 'Ain't no liquor store in Tubac.' Then he stalked off.

"He didn't even cut the kid loose? Pry him out of the busted car?"

"No. He said the troopers could do that, and book 'em, too. For reckless driving and running from the cops. As for buying liquor under age, there was no evidence of that."

Matt leaned forward over his coffee mug. "Why didn't the sheriff book the Mansons for murder? I thought that was the point of the whole chase."

"Truman hates paper work. That could be the reason."

# # # # # # #

That night I proposed to Vana. The love of my life not only refused, she backed off completely and utterly. She broke up with me!

I didn't know why. I wasn't about to believe her flimsy excuse about wanting to finish college. This wasn't the old days when a wife was expected to stay home tending the hearth fire and serving her husband's every need. Naturally I expected her to stick out her degree program at the U. Or for that matter up in Wyoming. Whyever not. What did that have to do with anything?

All I could think was that Juan had beat me out. The competitive moose bull had a bigger rack of horns. Or he was beating my time all along.

I saw red.

CHAPTER 39

I didn't call Vanna or stop by at the Cat when she was on duty. Call it pride or stubbornness. Whatever.

Back to Patsy and my search for her. She must be up around Tucson somewhere. I would have asked Juan to help me dig, but he was my enemy now. I'd convinced myself that he had won the heart of my true love.

This morning I wore a white tee with another quote from Shakespeare: *The smallest worm will turn, being trodden on.* From King Henry the Sixth. If I ran into Garcia, let him think what he pleased. On the contrary, if I ran into the people who'd poisoned me, I wanted them to get the message, too. I was not only back, but I wasn't giving up. I poured myself coffee, got out a sack of leftover donuts, and sat down at Brother John's kitchen table.

Lucas was up early. Gulping a cup of coffee, he said he'd get breakfast in town. He had an appointment with a couple whose marriage was in trouble. Married fifty-five years and they're talking divorce? Brother John reported the facts: she said he was inconsiderate and had a roving eye. He said he'd met a cute young thing (of 72!) at the pool who actually listened to him.

Alone, I dipped a stale donut in the hot coffee and read the comics. I wasn't about to consider the nature of long-married people seeking separation.

When Brad called from Phoenix, enroute once more to Mexico to deliver and pick up more loads, I asked him whether he was game to dig, not for Patsy Parsons, but for dead bodies.

"You got to be kidding, right?"

"I guess. But I'd sure like an excuse to turn over all that sod in Elise's back yard. Bet we'd find Mr. Goodman." I dipped another donut in the coffee.

Gifford guffawed, without further comment right then. He wanted to play golf at Tubac, he said. I agreed and we talked about the weather, and then again about the Seattle Mariners. Brad too was an enthusiastic baseball fan. Before signing off, he asked whether I'd run my idea by Brother John.

"Does he also suspect Elise of murdering her husband?"

In the background I could hear the roar of Polly Pew and the rumbling of traffic along the interstate out of Phoenix. With my mouth full of donut, I had to excuse myself and swallow before replying.

"Naw. He believes her. She told him weeks ago that Goodman was in Europe or South America on business."

"What does her husband do?"

"Beats me," I yelled across the crackling in the airwaves. "Imports, exports, something like that."

"What I don't understand," Brad said in the cab, after picking me up outside the church where I'd gone to practice while awaiting his arrival, " is why nobody has again tried to kill you." His tee read *Truckers Drive America!*

"How's that?" I said, only half listening while glancing around the interior of Polly Pew. I'd tossed my golf clubs behind the seat.

"Don't act nonchalant with me. At least one person was out to poison you. I take it you suspect the Goodmans."

"Who else? You don't think sweet Dollie could be the culprit, do you? Or pretty Megan, while she was preparing my food dishes."

Brad mashed the accelerator, roaring right past Tubac, Rio Rico, and the old Spanish mission, now a tourist site just off the Interstate. He pushed up his glasses. The horn-rimmed frames had a tendency to slip down his nose.

"Sounds pretty far-fetched, huh, suspecting those dear little ladies of anything. Still, one of them, Dollie more than Megan, I'd say, could be hiding something and you were getting too close."

I hadn't told him about me and Vanna; neither my proposal nor her rejection. Happily married people, I've observed, seldom notice the heartache of the singles, nor our frantic actions in pursuit of the mating game. He didn't ask and I didn't share. So I was surprised when he mentioned Patsy.

"You give up on finding her again?"

"Not at all. But my search takes second place to catching the killers."

Brad fell silent while concentrating on his driving. We had crossed the border, again with minimal hassle, and he had to navigate Polly Pew through the busy Nogales traffic, both vehicular and pedestrian.

Between delivering fabric to a Mexico-based American firm engaged in sewing clothes, mostly for the American market, and picking up electronic parts from another corporation to deliver in Silicon Valley, Brad returned to one among several of our recurring topics: drugs.

"On both sides of the border people are growing marijuana plants. Up in the hills off Interstate 19 is one good place—obscure, isolated, hard to reach." He made a comparison with the Prohibition days and the moonshiners dotted about the Appalachians. "Same thing. Easy to hide operations off in the hills."

He had told me before, so I knew that truckers picked up plenty of gossip while traveling America's highways and byways. They pass it along by CB, to help alleviate the boredom, I supposed, when they weren't listening to music or stories on their CDs.

"The artsy-craftsy people, you mean?" I said, thinking about that a moment. "Come to think of it, that's a good cover for anything illegal."

"Also a good excuse as an income. Anybody could pay any prices they claim to be getting for any fool craft thing."

I took it Brad wasn't into art. "Rumor or fact?"

He shrugged. By then we were sitting in a long line awaiting our turn to re-cross the border. "Both, probably. It's about harvest time. DEA agents, or so I hear, have been busy searching for pot plants. The idea is to locate and destroy mature plants and catch the planters."

"Seems like penny-ante stuff."

"Not when multiplied by hundreds of growers."

"What about cocaine, heroin?"

"Those, too, though not as prevalent in these parts. You're thinking Colombia, Southeast Asia." He paused, pushing up his glasses and glancing in my direction. "Still, you're right. There could be a big shipment coming through Mexico." In Polly Pew we moved up a few spaces, closer to the inspection center. "Taking longer, this time," he said.

Both of us peered through the bug-splattered windshield. "Appears as if they're doing a more thorough search this morning." We watched as vehicles were searched, pickups were pulled over, and big semi-trailer rigs were directed to one side.

"Oh, hum," he muttered, adding an exaggerated sigh. "If we have to go through all this, I wish they'd stopped us when I had the load of fabric. Nothing suspicious in that." I wondered how electronic parts could be suspect. "I'll have to open crates for them to paw through," he replied to my unspoken query.

Despite the indoor cooling and the outside heat, waves of which shimmered on the hot asphalt, we rolled down our windows. We could hear babies crying, kids screaming, drivers cussing. Hot, disheveled people squirmed in their cars or got out to stare forward, and then back along the long line. Their expressions spoke for them; they were angry at being held up, glad they weren't any farther back.

"What's up?" Brad asked a fellow trucker who approached us.

"Big drug deal going down," said the middle-aged, clean-shaven cross-country hauler. "That's the rumor. "Nobody, neither the DEA nor the border inspectors on either side know exactly what. Or when."

"Marijuana or the hard stuff?"

Our informant shrugged. "Nobody knows, for sure. Probably the latter. In the meantime DEA agents are searching abandoned buildings and truck trailers parked semi-permanently off in the boonies. Up north, as in upstate New York, it's old barns the authorities search. I hear tell that's where the contraband coming down from Canada is temporarily stored. Heroin and designer drugs from Canada, also cocaine from Colombia via Florida."

"Also into Mexico, then over border crossings at Tijuana and Juarez," said Brad.

"Yeah, and now Nogales." The trucker bid us adieu, or the equivalent thereof, before passing on down the line. Then he turned back to Brad. "You guys watch your step. Don't pick up no hitchhikers.

Never know who's dealing, or who's addicted." He glanced my way, his comments assuming I too was a driver. "Local people serve as warehousemen and contacts, between local distributors and out-of-town couriers." Then he was off to spread more gossip, like manure on a garden patch.

Twisting in my seat, I watched the big fat guy's passage. His belly beneath a thin tee shirt had rolled, not like a bowl of Jell-O, more like a series of ripples after tossing pebble to pond. On the back of his shirt, I read *Road Rebel.*

We closed the windows and turned up the air conditioning. Brad moved Polly Pew up one more space. "Hungry?" he asked at last. When I nodded, he told me to climb in the back and build us a couple of man-size sandwiches from the mini-fridge. I did, passing over a couple of thick ones resembling Subways. No beer while on the road, I settled for iced tea, replenishing the thermos that sat in the divider and holding station between us. By the time I had resettled, Brad was allowed to move up one more space. We sat back to enjoy lunch. Though slender and fit, short and compact, Gifford could eat like a horse.

"I been thinkin'," I said, after swallowing my last bite and refilling my thermal cup. "Up near the Sahuarita schools there's an abandoned building. Used to belong to the pecan orchard, now it's half falling down from neglect."

"Oh, brother," Brad said between bites. He was a slow eater. I'd noticed his expletives were invariably mild. "Near a school. I hate that. Curious kids could break in, discover a cache of drugs … ."

"Get high. Get addicted."

"Get an overdose. Die."

"Start dealing. Want in on the morbid scene. Get in over their heads."

"Get shot at. Killed."

This time we got to move up two places. Getting closer. Might still have time to get in a golf game at Rio Rico or Tubac. Brad's record was stuck on the kids not only getting high, but dead.

He snapped finger and thumb. "Hey! Maybe your country sheriff was right after all. Might be those teenagers you guys chased are into drugs and dealing."

"Or warehousing," I added, thinking the scatter-brained kids Brother John had hired while I was sick didn't know their elbow from Page Twelve. They could get caught up in something bigger than they'd ever imagined. Get shot and killed.

CHAPTER 40

That night at the Cat there was me with the Derrys and Dolans, minus Vanna and Juan. We talked over coffee. I'd pitched in to help clean up following the last diners' departure and now it was relaxing and recap time.

Matt as usual was counting the take and subtracting expenses. He could make the calculations in his head. Mike showed off his painted ceramic cats now lining a long shelf on the far end of the big room. Spanking new booths marked the edges and green and white checkered tablecloths covered the tables crouched in the center.

"Tell us more about your yacht, Oliver," Megan said.

"You go first. When does little Matthew Michael come home?"

"Day after tomorrow! Oh, Oliver, we're so excited!"

"What does Brother John think?" Matt said, looking up from behind a stack of greenbacks. "About your yacht."

"He wants to see it. Says he's coming with me when I return home."

Megan stared at me, tears quickly gathering. "Oh, Oliver, we'll miss you, so. When are you leaving?"

"Not before cradling MM in my arms. And not before these crimes are solved." I didn't add, *Not before I find Patsy Parsons.* Nobody but Juan and Brad knew about her.

This was Vanna's night off. None of them asked me where she was, so I didn't have to admit I had no idea. My friends probably sensed, if they didn't actually know, that we'd broken up, and out of loyalty (to me or to her?), they made no mention of their star waitress.

"You could come, too," I suggested.

"You kiddin'?" burst out Matt. "Close down this gold mine? Shoot the goose that lays the golden eggs?"

"I meant for a visit, Matt." Then I stared around the table. "But of course you could. Sell out here, open up in Wyoming."

"No, we can't," said Megan matter-of-factly. She pushed away her mug, leaned back, and crossed her arms over her perky chest beneath a flowered blouse. "Mom's coming."

"What? Why didn't you guys tell me first off? When? How?"

Megan gleamed. Mike's sly grin could have been taken off his painted cat's face.

Matt scowled, saying, "I'll believe it when I see it."

"She raised enough money from waitress tips and carrying bedpans for a flight home," Megan replied. "She wants to hug her grandson."

I smiled round the table. "Bet she and my mom will get along great."

"What?" squealed Megan. "Talk about keeping secrets! When's she coming?"

"She and Hernandez, her husband, are driving down. Should pull in tomorrow or the next day."

"Wow, sounds like old home week," said Mike. I thought it sounded like nothing of the kind, but I kept mum.

Before I left the Cat, Megan took me aside. "Look, Macho Man," she said, grabbing my arm and turning her face up toward mine. "I know you must be hurting. Awhile ago Vanna showed up with Juan, him looking all goo-goo eyes at her; her avoiding my sharp look. Now you appear, without either of them. What's going on?"

"We broke up."

"That's what I suspected."

At home Brother John was waiting up for me. You'd think I was an adolescent who had to be checked on. Nothing like that, he said. He had news that couldn't wait until morning. He wore blue and white striped cotton pajamas, but no robe. Pulling out a chair, he motioned me into another.

"Sheriff Truman captured and arrested Paul's murderer."

Startled, I plopped down on the kitchen chair

opposite him, my legs stretched out beneath the table. "Who? How?"

My host grinned. "First things first. You've got to play the organ on Sunday. Better practice." He leaned back, clasping his two big paws behind his head. I waited. This was his idea of humor. Drop a bombshell and then change the subject, speak of the mundane.

"Donny Martinez."

"Ah, come on, Lucas. That makes no sense at all."

"It does when you hear the whole story." Lucas grinned at my dismay. Obviously Donny wasn't my first choice. "He was caught returning to the scene of the crime."

"The church garden? So what? How many times you been there since Paul died?"

"None, to my knowledge. Donny was digging in that empty space where Paul discovered the poppy plants."

"Maybe he dropped something, thought he'd lost it there."

"Right. Where he shot Paul."

"I don't think so. What other evidence did the sheriff turn up?"

"Donny has no alibi."

"Do you?"

"Now, Son. Donny could have been your poisoner, too. Ever think of that? Why are you defending him?"

"Because both Donny and his mom are, uh, nice." It sounded lame when I said it.

"So are a lot of people. Just because Elise and Fess are nasty, you want it to be one of them?"

"Dick Tracy, uh, Truman, must have something else to go on."

Brother John shrugged. "He might, but if so he didn't say."

"Maybe he'll tell me," I said, pushing back my chair. I stormed off to bed, but not to sleep. I had a lot to think about.

CHAPTER 41

The next morning it was all over the news: *Sheriff Arrests Pastor's Killer!*

"Now maybe the protesters will shut up," Brother John said complacently over breakfast preparations. He was wearing another of my tee shirts that came from mom. This one read: *Thou shalt not kill.* Biblical and appropriate. Wherever he wore it, I hoped the killer read the message.

While I fried bacon and eggs, Lucas made pancakes. When we're both at home for meals, we eat hearty.

"I've been meaning to ask you," I said, before shoveling in the first bite. "Uh, was Paul gay?"

Lucas gulped, spewing coffee all over his food. "Implying I am, too?" he sputtered. Grabbing a napkin, he tried sopping up the mess. Failed, and arose to dump his plate and start over. With his back to me at the stove, where he helped himself to breakfast number two, he mumbled, "'Course not. Neither of us. Why do people think such things just because two men live together? Next thing, they'll be saying that about you for having moved in with me." He replenished his coffee.

"Okay, but the gays and lesbians kickin' up a fuss around here don't know that. They're still protesting."

"So are the African-Americans. At least Truman didn't arrest a black guy."

"Nor a white man, either. Will the Mexicans also rise up in arms, do you think?"

"Why ask me? Go see what Juan says."

Without responding, telling Brother John that Juan and I were on the outs, I excused myself and left the house. I couldn't take comfort in Hugo's company. Might as well admit it. My dog's allegiance was to Juan, the guy who fed him, gave him a home, had trained him to heel, sit up, roll over, and fetch.

Of course I could stop by Garcia's place during the day. He would be at work. On a whim I grabbed my new black zippered windbreaker out of the closet. Hugo would like that. A lure to win back his affection. I poked the jacket in Penny's right-hand saddlebag and climbed aboard the cycle.

First, though, a stopover at the county jail. I was ready to take on the sheriff, challenge him about his decision to arrest Donny.

I found Truman rushing out the door of his office. Reluctantly or otherwise, he invited me to join him. Fast as a squirrel after an acorn, I leaped into the passenger side of the county's best cop car.

"Where're we off to this time?" I shouted over the roar of the engine and the shrill scream of the siren.

"Back to those kids. Donald Martinez confessed!"

"To murder?" I couldn't believe it.

"Naw. Can't expect the game to play out that fast and easy. He confessed to knowledge of an upcoming drug deal. A big one."

"Donny's involved?"

"Prob'ly. He didn't admit that. But knowledge of, that makes him suspect in my book."

"I don't get it, Sheriff," I yelled. "Why are you taking charge? Arresting Donny, giving statements to the press. I was there when the FBI told you hands off." Hunched over the wheel, he ignored me.

We flew across the bridge and passed the pecan orchard, braked to take the corner, and sped past the church, loose gravel flying when the car lurched off the paved road. Tires spinning, Dick turned left toward the Sahuarita junction. Beyond, up in the foothills, squatted the Mansons' trailer, where we'd visited earlier. From the narrow winding road, I spotted other dwellings: more ramshackle trailers, shacks, a few livable cottages. Homes to pecan workers, I supposed, along with some of the hippy, artsy folk. The latter included painters, sculptors, leather and stained glass workers, and potters

"Potters!" I yelled, pointing toward the scrubby trees and cacti growing in abundance up here. "Those arts people could be into pot. Growing and selling the stuff. Why Donny? Why the Mansons? We already chased them, Dick."

"Cuz Donald claims the kids are acting as couriers. I know we found nothing when we searched their wrecked car. Unlucky that time."

He turned off the siren as we turned up a narrow dirt trail. "To answer your question, Oliver, I intend to beat both the FBI <u>and</u> the DEA at solving the pastor's murder <u>and</u> some of this dadgummed drug dealin'. This here county's <u>my</u> patch, not theirs!"

He drove slower now, coming to a halt not outside the family's trailer, but a quarter-mile beyond, in front of an abandoned building. Once a warehouse of sorts, I figured it belonged to the pecan people. Condemned now, Dick said that bums, derelicts, some homeless people sometimes squatted in there.

He reached back inside the car to grab his bullhorn to accompany the rifle in his other hand. He yelled for me to stay put, but I was already out and running up behind him.

"Shouldn't you call for backup?" I shouted.

"Quiet!" he hissed. Crouched, on tiptoe, he crept forward, bending low to avoid a sighting through the dusty, grime-encrusted windows on this side. In case anybody was in there. Dick scooted along the wall toward the front door with me poking my head above the nearest windowsill. Couldn't see zilch.

"Down, boy!" he whispered at me. I could have been Hugo.

Not a sound emanated from indoors. Outside I heard the coo-coo of quail, the rustle of small creatures through the bushes, and an Air Force jet breaking the sound barrier high above the drifting clouds. A trio of vultures circled low, not far off. Awaiting lunch—an injured animal about to die.

The two of us could hardly surround the whole building, but that's what Dick yelled through the bullhorn. "You're surrounded! Come out with your hands up or we'll start shooting." He got off a round to prove he meant business.

Nothing. Nobody. Again I peered through the murky glass. Returning to Truman I said the place looked deserted. The doors were locked, too.

"You see any boxes or trunks or storage bins for stashing drugs?"

Nope, I replied. Nor could I see any evidence roosting in there.

With neither key nor warrant, the sheriff broke in. Using the butt end of his rifle, he smashed the glass and knocked out the splintering shards. "You climb in and then unlock the front door for me."

Dirt, broken bottles, empty half-crushed cartons and other rubble. This stuff didn't look fresh, though. Couldn't be from recent invaders. Some shingles were missing, I could see holes in the roof, and water puddling from a recent mini flood—a fast gully washer rushing in and washing right back out again. Nobody and nothing else. Not even a derelict. No drug dealers or junkies, no cache, hidden or otherwise.

"What in the name of all that's holy!" Dick yelled, his voice echoing in that big barn-like structure. Clearly disappointed, he made ready to leave.

On the road back to town, Dick was quiet awhile until he started beating on the steering wheel. "What'd Martinez do? Blow me off with his cock-and-bull story?" Disconsolate, Truman was disinclined to talk as we drove into town. No siren this time. Just the sheriff making his rounds, a passenger eager to get at the truth sitting by his side.

"Tell me, Sheriff. What led you to think Donald Martinez, of all people, was Dr. Wallaberra's murderer?"

Truman hemmed and hawed. Finally he admitted to receiving a tip over the phone from an anonymous caller. He held up a hand, as if to turn off the faucet of my protests. "Then the mayor called me on the carpet, demanding I make an arrest. Did no good tellin' him the FBI and DEA said hands off. More important that we get the collar. Quiet the dadgummed press. Get shut of the last of these pesky protesters."

"I understand all that, Dick. But why Donny? I can't believe you'd pick him up on the basis of one unverifiable phone call."

"'Course not. But the caller directed me to search the Martinez villa. I got a search warrant and me and that Mexican manager guy, what's his name, beat it over there."

"Juan. His name's Juan Garcia." Why hadn't he told me? Yeah, sure, feeling guilty about stealing my girl, why would he say anything at all to me?

"We found it all right. A 10-shot Glock, Model 26, poked down in a golf bag, back of the closet. Ballistics matched. That's the murder weapon, all right," he said smugly.

"Why didn't you arrest Donny's mom?"

"You kiddin' me? Get real."

I said I wished he'd solve the other crimes, too. Months ago, I reminded the sheriff, Dr. Wallaberra had invited Brother John down here to help out with a "church in trouble." Lucas hadn't managed to stop the cousins' bickering, and so far the vandals and thieves hadn't been identified, either.

"Dick, I had hoped to help, get the church's money back to them, at least. You won't like my saying so, but I don't see Donny as a killer."

Pulling up in front of Brother John's house, he ignored my objections.

"Look here, son. The record shows if you don't solve a crime, especially murder, within the first twenty-four to forty-eight hours, chances are the trail will grow cold and the perps'll go free. Look at the Jon Benet case up in Boulder."

I unfastened my seat belt and opened the door to get out.

He patted my arm. "Just you remember, it was me who caught the murderer. Not those interfering FBI. Me!" His chest swelled with pride.

About the attempts on my life, he made no mention. Looked like if I was going to get anybody to move on my behalf, I'd have to organize a protest group. Get organized attention, lotsa media hooplah. Hah, fat chance.

CHAPTER 42

"I hear tell," said Matt at the Cat, "that you're not supposed to make up your mind about who's guilty and who's not, until all the evidence is in."

It wasn't quiet and we weren't gathered around our usual back table. I had dropped in hoping to see Vanna. No such luck, she was off that night. I stuck around to help out in the kitchen because the salad chef didn't show.

I plucked leaves off a head of lettuce and then began to chop onions. Matt put away clean dishes. Periodically he held up a glass to the light, inspecting it carefully. His hair, cropped short as defense against the hot desert and the hot kitchen, was bleached blond from the sun. No need for him to wear a chef's hat, as Mike did. Megan tucked my thick locks beneath a baseball cap. She habitually pulled her own blond hair back into a pony tale,

333

adding a variety of pretty ribbons. Covered in a big white apron, she stirred a bubbling cauldron of soup. She could have been the golden witch of the west.

Busy night coming up, as usual. They anticipated a lot of calls for the chef's special. Tonight that was Granny's Chicken and Homemade Noodles; Granny Derry, that is, from whom Megan admitted to having copped a number of choice recipes.

"I'm trying to avoid prejudging, Matt," I replied, with a vicious hack to a big Bermuda onion. "But if Donny's a murderer, I'm a monkey's uncle."

Megan set down her ladle and moved to check the noodles. Mike mashed potatoes, grumbling that the cafe needed more equipment; too much hand labor. "We know where you stand," he said. "You're convinced Fess Goodman is the perp, right?"

I shrugged and gave the onion another whack.

"Hey," Megan said, with a quick little laugh to temper her words. "Don't take out your frustration on our vegetables."

"Makes more sense, doesn't it?" I settled down to chop steadily and carefully. "Fess steals petty stuff from the retirees and the church, Elise uncovers his cache, and plants a few choice items on Dollie, who she now hates for having slept with her man and having a baby with him. Fess grows illegal plants in the church garden, Dr. Wallaberra catches the kid at it and Powee! Fess blows Paul away. Then the young Goodman, following his mom's model, plants his shooter on Donny Martinez."

Matt poked his head into our huddle. "Then our country bumpkin of a sheriff, who can't see beyond the end of his nose, finds the gun and Donny at the scene of the crime. And that's all she wrote, right? I can follow your train of thought, Oliver. Just don't jump to conclusions. This whole business may not be that simple."

"No? Then where's Mr. Goodman?"

The minute hand on the big wall clock clicked over to six o'clock and soon we were all too busy to think about anything beyond dishing up food, serving hungry diners and cleaning up. We slipped down that slide and into the tunnel of Time, not quite like *Alice in Wonderland*, but close. Could have been a few minutes or a day and a half had passed. Time sometimes seems liquid, sloshing around and completely out of control.

Eventually we emerged at the end of the tunnel when Time slowed and seemed to stop completely. Would the last table of people ever leave so we could mop and scrub? We busied ourselves cleaning the kitchen. Megan dropped a bowl of Jell-O, smack, all over the floor. Two little hands flew up to cover her face.

"I'll clean up, Megan," I said, gently taking one hand and leading her away. "Tomorrow's a big day. Getting your baby home. Your mom arriving." I offered to pick up Mrs. Derry at the airport. By then the Dolans would be home with young Michael Matthew. And her brothers up to their eyeballs at the Cat.

"Oh, would you? Thanks ever so much, Oliver.

Mom will be disappointed that we're not there to meet her, but … ."

"But you'll have your hands full." The new chef was hired to take up the slack while Megan and Derek were getting used to parenthood.

Soon, I suspected, the new baby with all the equipment and all the stuff he required would be right there in the middle of the Cat Castle with the rest of them. Might even be an attraction. People oohing and aahing over baby along with Mike's newly painted cats, now decorated in bright stripes and polka dots. Certainly there was no comparison—live cooing baby versus silent ceramic cats.

I'd agreed to pitch in. The Cat bunch felt like family now. What they didn't realize was that I was serious when I suggested they sell out here and move to Wyoming with me. Not right away, but eventually. So what if they were burdened with property. Sell it, café and house. Probably make a mint. Mom and Hernandez, when they arrived, would fit right in, fall in love with these people; what's not to like.

As I mopped and chuckled, I wondered how I could be so blasé. Here we were, eating well at the café, enjoying our freedom. And there poor Donny was, incarcerated. Dollie couldn't raise bail. Elise sure hadn't offered to help.

Matt asked if I was headed home. I admitted I was determined to prowl.

"Let us come," said Matt.

I shrugged. We climbed into the Derrys' car, with Mike at the wheel, and headed for the

Goodmans. I meant to sneak around the back yard to search for evidence of disturbance in the lawn or garden. With three of us, we could cover more ground faster.

"After all this time," said Mike, reminding me it had been months since anyone around here had seen the man. "If Elise buried her husband in the back yard, wouldn't grass or plants have grown over his grave by now?"

We didn't get a chance to even reach the back yard, for as we slowly inched forward after parking the car a half-block away, up came the garage door and out shot the red Jaguar. We waited until the car was turning the corner, its taillight fading, and then we raced for the Derrys' car.

"It's Fess," I hollered from the back seat. "Out prowling the midnight hour, with us right on his tail!"

Mike switched on the ignition and right afterwards the lights, only to quickly douse them. "Damn! Sorry about that, Oliver. I forgot. We better drive in the dark until we reach the highway and can mingle with other vehicles."

The Jaguar took the frontage road, not the Interstate, straight down to Tubac, a mere couple of miles south.

"Just out for a late drink," Matt grumbled.

"Maybe not," I countered, as we paused to watch from the corner. The Goodman car sailed right past the only bar still open.

"What in the world?" said Mike, edging our car forward.

"Got a late-night liaison," Matt said, amending his first assumption. "Gonna have that drink in some lass's bedroom."

Hanging back along the dirt road under over-hanging shade trees, we watched the Jaguar pull into the old Mexican cemetery. The one with bodies buried in mounds atop the ground beneath a thin layer of soil and covered by piles of rocks.

Quickly we stepped out of the car, barely latching the doors to avoid the noise that might alert Goodman to our presence. In the night air, still steaming with heat, we could hear cicadas clacking, an owl hoot. A coyote's lonely howl echoed off the walls of the canyon yonder, with an answering chorus singing from his or her buddies across the way.

"They got themselves a regular choir going," whispered Mike.

"Hush," shushed Matt. "You'll wake the dead." Appropriate, that, since by then all three of us were hunched over, entering the graveyard.

"Hey!" I said, startled. I grabbed the arms of both Derrys to halt their forward progress. "That's Elise, not Fess."

She wore a long sheath, some kind of gown or dress. We watched, amazed, as Mrs. Goodman marched directly to Dr. Wallaberra's grave.

Mike shoved away my hand to plunge ahead. Stubbing his toe on a rock, he cursed. Not loudly, but loud enough.

Kneeling by Paul's gravestone, Elise reared back. "Who's there?" she called out sharply. We three stood paralyzed, as still as Lot's wife turned to a pillar of salt. "I said, who's there? What do you want of me?" This time her voice trembled.

Might as well cease with the charade. Resolutely I stepped into the pool of light shining down from the street lamp. "Just us, Ma'am. What are you doing out here, all by your lonesome in the middle of the night?"

"What are <u>you</u> doing?" she countered, getting up off her knees to stand and smooth her long skirt.

"Frankly, my dear, we were following you. I repeat, what are you up to?"

"None of your damn business. But if you must know, I was paying my respects to our pastor. I miss Dr. Wallaberra."

"Oh, sure, and if you expect me to believe that, perhaps you'd like me to also think you've got a Picasso to sell me, cheap."

CHAPTER 43

Mom and Luis showed at first light. They had spent the night at a Phoenix motel and couldn't wait to get here, she said, following a hug and exchange of big smiles and a handshake with Hernandez. Since mom demands that everybody be identified by the celebrity they look most like, in her case I would suggest Estelle Getty. Not the old lady Sophie she played in *The Golden Girls*. More like Sylvester Stallone's mother in *Don't Move or My Mom Will Shoot.*

As for Luis Hernandez, with a similar hairstyle he could have passed for Mexican-born Carlos Santana, who won a Grammy for his record, *Corazon Espinado*. It wasn't tough to guess who mom was eager to meet. First, Brother John, followed by Juan. Same name, different languages. I hadn't properly described Juan, mom complained while we were still standing outside by the car.

"Is Juan a young Luis Lopez-Fitzgerald, who played in the soap opera *Passions?"* my cute mommy asked. "Or does he look more like that older guy, Antonio Barderas?" Seemed she was embarrassing Hernandez, or he was eager to get a move on instead of standing there holding a suitcase in each hand.

I told mom I really couldn't say, seein' as how I'm not into the soaps or the Grammies, MTV, all that. I suggested we go indoors. My boss awaited us.

Brother John poured coffee from a fresh-brewed pot while I scrambled eggs and fried bacon. Mom manned the toaster, talking all the while.

"I thought you said he looked like Gary Cooper. Cryin' out loud, Son. He's *Eric*, for sure. John McCook, I mean, from *The Bold & the Beautiful*."

Lucas wasn't a bit embarrassed. He grinned at her, winked at me. As if all that weren't bad enough, mom proceeded to tell Brother John about Patsy Parsons (her other son's fiancee!), claiming the country music star Faith Hill could have passed for Patsy (not the other way around) when she was younger.

I went off to show Hernandez my room, which he and mom would share. "No problem, I'll sleep on the couch," I said, cutting off his protests by leaving.

Mom cornered Brother John to tell him about my youth. "Oliver was playing the piano for the children's Sunday service since he was ten and the organ for the grownups from the age of eighteen." Without waiting for his response to that revelation, she went on to seek his evaluation of my church music, these days, demanding to know, with arched eyebrow, whether I was a regular church goer even when not assigned to play.

Lucas hedged. He escaped her interrogation by excusing himself to get dressed. Mom took the hint, adding that she and Luis would freshen up. That meant switching from pink pantsuit to pink flowered dress. In her spectacles, she surely could be Ms. Getty.

The four of us piled into their car to head for the airport to pick up the Derrys' mom. Enroute, we heard honking behind us. Matt, Mike, Derek and Megan with their baby in a blue blanket, waved. Pulling up alongside, and rolling down the back window, Derek's message was obvious; the whole bunch of Derrys and Dolans were coming, too.

Now I'd have to describe them. No need, mom checked her notebook and then squinted at them and back at me. "Megan could be Drew Barrymore, right? Or Heather Tom in her role as Victoria, from *The Young & the Restless.*"

Brother John knew who mom meant. From the back seat he knocked on her shoulder. "Which means Megan's husband Derek is a Scott Reeves look-alike?"

Mom took him seriously. "I'm not sure."

Hernandez kept his eyes on the road, his face expressionless. He'd been through my mother's game plenty, I'd bet, and learned how to tolerate it. Then he surprised me.

As the other car passed us, Luis furrowed his brow. "Let me guess, Margaret Rose," he said.

"If we're talking *The Young & the Restless,* how about those guys up front? Would you say they remind you of David Lago and Thad Luckinbill?

"Hmm, maybe. I'll have to study on that."

She's really something, all religious one minute, praying and singing hymns, and the next switching to the soaps. Then I remembered that she and Hernandez had agreed on a few compromises—he would listen to classical music if she would sample country western. What had she exchanged to get him hooked on the soap operas with her? Marriage is sometimes funny.

Now we had a whole bunch of people traveling to Tucson to meet Merry Derry: four in our car; four, no, five counting the baby, in theirs—a proper entourage to greet the wanderlust returning from Europe.

We were late. Finding parking slots, cooing and petting the newest Dolan, and making introductions when we'd all tumbled out of our cars took time. More hugs, squeals, greetings, and introductions when Merry Derry burst onto our cozy multi-family scene, Mrs. Derry's arms full of souvenirs and brightly wrapped gifts from her over-long sojourn on the Continent. That's what the perky blond actually said: *On the Continent.* As if this were the 1890s and she was disembarking from the Queen Mary along with royalty, instead of as the waitress and chambermaid, so-called, that she really was.

Mom nudged me, then pulled me down so she could whisper in my ear. "She reminds me of Lea Thompson. You know, Oliver, she played in that series, *Caroline in the City*." She didn't ask whether I agreed. I knew from zilch.

With all the hubbub I was totally oblivious to the madhouse of arriving and departing travelers. Until mom tugged again on my arm. "Look over there, Oliver, quick. Before she gets out of sight. Isn't that Patsy Parsons? You remember her, surely. She was engaged to Arlo."

This time I didn't faint.

I forgot everything and everybody else to run after my sweetheart. My former sweet thing. I grabbed her from behind as if snatching my beloved Patsy from the jaws of death. Belatedly, I wondered whether she was somebody else, a stranger.

Slowly the pretty lady wearing a tight mini skirt in blue with matching skimpy halter turned around. I thought she might raise a hand to slap this arrogant stranger. But, no. She did a quick double take before falling into my arms.

"Oh, Oliver. I thought you'd never get here."

CHAPTER 44

Naturally everybody rushed up for another introduction. Mom already knew Patsy, so right off she began talking about Arlo. She, not me, did the honors, gathering my newly adopted family around her like a mama bird tucking babies beneath her wings. Patsy and mom grabbed each other, hugging and kissing and tearing up, just as if she had never dumped my brother. Then my once-upon-a-time darling oohed and cooed over the baby. Our crowd stood there in a clump tight as concord grapes passing Michael Matthew back and forth like a sack of cantaloupe they meant to squeeze to check for ripeness.

He was ripe, all right. At both ends. Megan excused herself for the ladies to make a diaper change. Mrs. Derry naturally dashed off behind her daughter, dumping her presents in Matt's and Mike's arms and snatching the diaper bag out of Derek's.

Patsy and I just stood there, silent as ghosts, staring into each other's eyes.

"Where have you … .?"

"What have you been … ."

We spoke simultaneously, shutting up the same way. Then we broke into laughter, hers a trilling giggle, mine a nervous guffaw.

"Hey, you two. Let me in on the joke," said mom. "What's so funny?"

"All this time," I began, "I've been searching for her … ."

"And all this time I've been waiting for him to come after me."

"But you never said. You never wrote or called," I protested.

"Neither did you." She said she'd left her number with her mom.

She didn't explain that her family had moved from Gillette, leaving no forwarding address. Perhaps they'd had a one-time-only contact. Patsy clung to my arm, bending her full body into the length of mine so that it felt like an intimate, possessive cuddle.

Mom looked puzzled. Then her face lost its question mark to be replaced with a smile of understanding. "That's right. You two were a couple before Arlo, uh, intervened."

"You bet we were," Patsy said.

"Well, my dears." Mom paused to reach out and pat our joined hands. "What does it matter, now that you're back together."

Bent on kissing those once familiar lips, I leaned

down. But just then, over Patsy's shoulder, I spied a huge hulk, a frown covering his face like carpet over the Taj Mahal. Pausing in the act of joining my mouth to hers, possibly for all time, I stared.

The powerful pug snatched my new-found love right out of my arms. "What you think you're doin' with my wife?" he demanded.

Drawing away from me and looking embarrassed and sheepish, Patsy said, "Oliver, this is my husband. We got married yesterday."

Stunned, I backed off.

My mom murmured, "The Lord giveth and the Lord taketh away."

CHAPTER 45

No Patsy, no Vanna, no brother Arlo, no buddy Juan. Even Hugo had deserted me. My dog, once a little puppy happy to snooze inside my zippered jacket, now gave his allegiance to the two-timer who was feeding him.

"Now, what?" Matt demanded in a whisper that afternoon.

I shrugged, not trusting my voice, now grown husky from unshed tears. Then I pulled him away to reply in private.

We were at the Cat, since mom was eager to visit the establishment. Hernandez, silent and taciturn, nonetheless appeared willing to follow her wherever she led him.

"Oliver and I have errands," Matt said nonchalantly, shoving me ahead of him out the back door. "We'll take my car. Leave your motorcycle here."

"Where are we going? I'm supposed to be at the

church. Practicing. My mom expects to hear me play the organ on Sunday and I'd better not make any mistakes. She'll hang me out to dry."

Wearing a white tee with a cat advertising the Cat, Matt motioned me into the passenger seat. Out on the highway, he confessed. "I'll drop you off at the church later. Your mom said she and her husband will meet you there. But first I thought we'd go into Green Valley and swing by Dollie's villa."

I couldn't even begin to guess why. He'd tell me when he was ready.

Enroute, I had a sudden thought. "Hey, Matt. Last night when we were out at the Tubac cemetery, did you notice anything strange about Dr. Wallaberra's grave?"

"Huh? Pretty dark out there and Elise was all in a flap trying to make us believe she was sincere in 'paying her respects,' as she called that visit. Shoot fire, Oliver, she didn't even bring flowers with her. Some respect."

I waved a hand in dismissal of the obvious. "Think about it, Matt. You were a pallbearer and so was Elise when she stumbled and teetered on those spike heels ... ."

"Yeah, that was pretty funny. Her falling head first into that hole."

"That's what I mean. A hole, Matt. Brother John had the gravediggers dig a deep hole, the usual size and depth, for burying Paul in."

"So what. SOP. Standard procedure."

"Right. But last night, didn't it look like Dr. Wallaberra was buried <u>above</u> ground? Like everybody else in that old graveyard. Above ground, with rocks piled all over him."

"You're right. What gives?"

"Your guess is as good as mine. But I aim to find out."

Both of us deep in thought, we continued on up the Interstate. After taking the exit into Green Valley, Matt turned into the parking area of the shopping center. This wasn't the way to Dollie's, not even a shortcut. Matt parked in front of the villa maintenance shed. "Time you and Juan made up," he said grimly. He could have been my fourth-grade teacher determined to force two schoolyard bullies to kiss and make up.

"Not very likely." I too could be stoical, dig in my heels, refuse to budge.

I could see Hugo in Juan's pickup, the windows cracked for air. Garcia came through the open bay doors, a clipboard in hand and a pen stuck behind his ear. Not clad in a suit today, he wore clean white coveralls. Grinning, he approached the car and leaned both arms on the open windowsill. "Hey, good buddy. See your dog? He's been trailin' me everywhere lately. What's cookin'?"

"Nuthin' much," I said, feeling a pout creeping up, pausing, deciding whether to linger. "Steal my girl and then call me 'buddy'? I don't think so."

Juan jerked back as if slapped. "That's what you thought? Hey, man, I been busy; hearing complaints from the villa people, trying to help settle their squabbles. As for Vanna, no way. We're just friends, that's all." He was talking fast, like I might roll up the window any second and cut him off. "She broke up with you because … . Hey, you really don't know why?"

"'Figured she preferred you. Why else?"

"You're not serious enough." He reached in and slapped my shoulder. "About either religion or finding steady work. That's what she told me."

Goll-eee, could have knocked me over with a feather duster. I felt like Jim Nabors in his Gomer role on reruns of the old *Andy Taylor Show*.

"If you're as smart as I think you are, Oliver, you'll figure out how to bring Vanna around. Never mind that, now, though. I called Matt at the Cat to get hold of you, and tell you to run up here to join me." Without further ado, Juan fetched Hugo, returned, and jerked open the back door. He and my dog got in.

I couldn't take all this in so fast. Could try to be half-civil, though, change the subject. I stared back and forth between the two of them. "What now?"

Juan leaned forward. "Those villa squabbles I mentioned? They're over Donny's arrest. The Owners' Association is up in arms. At the insistence of a bunch of old biddies, there was a special meeting called this morning. They want Dollie out of here. She and her son 'give the place a bad reputation,' to quote the association president. Even as we speak, a delegation is possibly already storming Dollie's door. What we don't want is for this ruckus to turn into a mob, vigilantes taking things into their own hands. Could get worse than the demonstrations out at the church over Dr. Wallaberra."

It was a long speech for the laconic guy. Then, thinking of something else, Juan excused himself. This time he returned from the office clutching a brown paper bag. He handed it to me. "I should have thought of it sooner, Oliver. You need protection."

"Jeez, Juan. I don't have a license for this thing." Though small, the snub-nosed Smith & Wesson .32 caliber revolver looked deadly.

"I do. And I suggest you carry it with you from now on." Juan ran again to his car. After something else, possibly.

Withdrawing the gun from the sack, I slipped it into the right-hand pocket of my windbreaker, zipped up, and tossed it back on the floor. I might carry the jacket with me, but I seldom wore it. Too hot.

With Juan back in the car, Matt stepped on the gas, sailed out of the parking lot and past the Christian Church on the corner. Brakes screeching, the car leaned on two wheels as we took the next corner, this one leading onto Dollie's street. A line of cars was parked along both sides of the private road. Strictly verboten, Juan said, but the guest spaces were full. Matt drove right up on the grass in the center of a park-like circle, very nicely landscaped. Now we were as near Dollie's villa as we could get without squashing a half-block of carefully planted cacti and flower beds. Juan, in charge of maintenance and the keeping of the Villa Association's Rules & Regs, didn't make one peep of protest.

From his coverall pocket Juan drew a fierce looking Colt .45. I didn't even know he owned a shooter. Man, this could be bad. Releasing Hugo to follow us, we set off.

We ran into an angry crowd, already shouting and shoving for front-row position. A shout went up for Dollie to come outdoors. "Face the music!" squealed a trio of neatly dressed ladies at the top of their tiny squeaky voices.

Two old codgers, both bald, one waving his cane and the other a golf club, took up the cry to make it a chant: "Come out, come out. Face the music! Face the music!"

On the other side another cluster of women, some still carrying cards from their bridge game, wanted in on the act. They started screaming their own slogan: "Get out, get out. Get clear outta town!"

Over and over these two choruses from the competing choirs sang out. Hugo barked, then howled, adding his voice to the throng. Juan snapped at him, "Heel! Quiet, or it's back to the car." My dog immediately obeyed. Before setting out, Juan told me to keep Hugo with me.

While Juan and Matt pushed their way through the crowd, I lingered in the rear, assessing where the best vantage point was in order to lend some assistance. Planting myself, I commanded Hugo to stay. He obeyed me, too. Could be I'd act as heckler, to issue arguments to the contrary. Something like a carnival shill. From the rear of the crowd I caught the first glimpse of the arriving media. Merely a reporter with a camera woman from the local bi-weekly paper. Oh, man, this confrontation would soon hit the news. Thus reminded, I stared around the crowd searching for some of the same demonstrators who'd claimed Dr. Wallaberra's murder was a hate crime. Maybe they were also the instigators of this mad cry for vengeance.

With his voice alone, Juan tried to quiet the crowd. To no avail. Then he got off a couple of shots. I thought he might blow a hole in Dollie's porch roof. Instead, a pigeon fell at his feet. Jeez, next thing we'd have the animal rights people jumping all over us. Hugo yapped twice. At my stare, he ceased.

Momentary silence. Stunned, people began to murmur among themselves, while the reporter raced about poking his microphone in faces and the camera woman clicked away. Somebody picked up the dead bird by its claws to hold it aloft. Hugo howled. Jeez.

Just then the villa door opened and out stepped Donny Martinez with Dollie hovering in back of him as if taking cover behind a saguaro. He's big, she's tiny. Not as short as my mom, but in that age group and size range.

The crowd went wild.

Again Juan pulled the trigger, this time glancing skyward to be sure he wouldn't hit anything else. "Shut up," he said, using his normal speaking voice.

Like Hugo, they obeyed. Seemingly mesmerized, they promptly shut their faces.

"What happened to common decency?" he proposed, still speaking quietly. "What happened to 'Innocent until proven guilty'?"

Once more the mob roared like a lion before settling down to a kitten's mew. From the back of the crowd and with Hugo getting restless, I decided it was time for the carnival shill to speak his piece. I shouted, "Let Donny talk!"

Martinez, at Garcia's side, gazed grimly around at the assemblage. Spotting me, he nodded; briefly, barely perceptible.

"I'm out on bail as of an hour ago. Forbidden from leaving town. Against the law. So we aren't going anywhere." With that he disappeared back inside, leaving his mom to follow or linger, as she chose. Hesitating but a brief moment, the little lady dressed neatly in a lavender linen two-piece with her brunette hair perfectly coifed, stepped forward. Holding up both arms, fingers spread on palms facing outward, she smiled gently.

"I'd offer you lemonade and cookies, but I didn't know we'd have so much company to greet Donny's return home to us."

That cracked the ice. And broke the dark mood. Titters here, laughter there, nervous embarrassed glances between and among. Again I took up the gauntlet, to shout, "Way t'go, Dollie!"

Peculiar, how little it takes sometimes to change the tide, from outgoing to incoming; or, in this case, from dark to light mood. The crowd broke up. No longer one determined body, they were now separated into very human, and weak, and anxious individuals, some of whom obviously recognized they'd made fools of themselves. They departed as quickly as they had assembled.

Juan, Matt, and I, with Hugo trailing, entered Dollie's humble home to check on her welfare, see if she needed anything, and, incidentally, to hear Donny's story. Dollie did in fact serve us lemonade and cookies, homemade raisin oatmeal with pecans, warm and fragrant from her oven. We moved back outside to the patio. Our hostess tossed Hugo a couple of cookies. He sniffed, gulped the first and disdained the second. He left my side to explore the patio. I expected to see him cozying up to Juan, but he had his own goal, Dollie's small but nice garden that fringed the inside walls of her patio.

"Of course I'm innocent," Donny said. While Juan lounged on the chaise, the rest of us sat at the patio table, with Martinez leaning forward tensely. "I couldn't hurt Dr. Wallaberra, much less shoot him dead." He said he went to visit the church garden later, not to "return to the scene of the crime," as the sheriff supposed; rather, to search for his mom's wedding ring. "Yeah, she still wears it. Mom thought she might have lost it while weeding the garden. Just my luck I started with that empty patch first."

At my arched eyebrow in her direction, Dollie said defensively: "Yes, I still love Donny's dad." Now that could be taken two ways: did she mean Mr. Goodman, who'd supposedly sired the lad, or Mr. Martinez, her former husband?

Donny resumed his tale. He didn't know where the gun had come from, how it got in their closet, or who it belonged to. A plant, I suggested, looking at Dollie. Correctly reading my expression, she said she'd turned over to Brother John the items that Elise had given her. I already knew that, for he'd told me that morning, saying he in turn had called the parishioners, the proper owners, even before alerting the sheriff. Dick Truman now had in his possession, as evidence, the golf clubs, tennis rackets, and fur jacket. Obviously the sheriff had even more evidence to use against Donny. If the boy was a thief, he could easily have turned killer, Truman would reason. I could guess that much.

Dollie couldn't have chosen a worse time to confess or to turn over Elise's gifts, hidden for so many weeks in her closet. How she came by them would certainly sound lame to any jury when Donny came to trial. I could well imagine the prosecutor. He'd likely portray Dollie as the lioness defending her cub.

It occurred to me that Brother John could have held on to the stolen goods and kept mum, at least for awhile. No, I guessed not. The innocent often make poor judgments, often trusting that Truth will out and that Innocence speaks for itself. Hah, think again, Mr. Preacher Man.

"Hey," I said, interrupting Dollie who was babbling on with a long account about how much she still loved Martinez and had made a mistake divorcing him and wanted him home with her, only she worried now whether he'd ever come round and take her back. While waiting for her to wind up this sad love story, I glanced idly at Hugo. Still digging, he'd found a stick. Or bone, perhaps. Doggies love bones.

"Hey," I said, repeating myself. "How'd Donny make bail? I can't see you going begging to Elise, Dollie."

She smiled sadly. "Brother John came up with the ante when I handed over the stolen goods."

Just then Hugo's pawing turned frenetic. "What th'hey? Hugo, leave Dollie's garden alone."

"That's not the way to do it, Oliver," said Juan calmly, quick with his instructions in how I should speak to my dog.

I jumped up, knocking over the folding chair. "Ohmigod! What have you got, Hugo? That's a human bone!"

Donny blanched.

Dollie fainted.

CHAPTER 46

Dollie was hospitalized with concussion from hitting her head on the cement patio. She had toppled out of her chair and fallen over sideways like a paper doll. Donny was back in jail.

Sheriff Truman gloated. Hugo's treasure, the bones, had gone off to the state lab, but I was positive it would turn out to be Mr. Goodman.

"Hard to identify, work the DNA bit. These things take time," Dick said. "Should a listened to you first off, though, son. You wanted me out searching for Fess's daddy's remains. Donny poisoned you, too, probably. Him with his botany. Dollie with her plants."

The sheriff had his theory, I had mine.

The Derrys had a point, though. I should have waited for more evidence before insisting the Goodmans were the bad guys. The way things were shaping up, Truman was making a damn good case against the Martinez pair.

Eventually I made it to the church, but not until the next day. I wanted to practice before mom, Hernandez in tow, arrived to sit with arms crossed ready to critique my every note. I had worked my way through a couple of Bach's best when Juan poked in his head. *"Que pasa?"* What's happening? I shrugged.

His tee shirt read: *Hero today and gone tomorrow.* He had errands in Sahuarita, he said, and thought I might like to have my dog with me. Juan was about to pen up Hugo in the dog run when I said he could stay with me. "Seein' as how he's so well trained now."

Juan grinned and departed. Clinging to the leash while Hugo dragged me about, I wondered if the commands only worked when coming from Juan.

"Stay!" I barked. Stay, he did. Amazing. "That deserves a reward." So saying, I retrieved the windbreaker, this one in black, and patted the pocket. Cocking his head to one side as if trying to remember something, Hugo suddenly yapped. Yup, he yapped, just like the puppy I'd found abandoned last winter on the blizzardy Wyoming road.

I tossed the jacket on the floor at my feet. He approached eagerly, sniffing. Then it was my turn to remember. From the left-hand pocket I withdrew a couple of Dollie's delicious cookies. Hugo leaped and said Yap. I said "Sit!" And he sat. On my jacket, scarfing cookies.

I hadn't slept well the night before. Shakespeare

wrote that *Love comforteth like sunshine after rain.* I could use some of that love and comfort, that was a given. Dreams and then nightmares, all mixed up, all about Vanna. Juan had said she broke up with me because I wasn't serious, about life or work or religion. Heck, what was so great about serious? It wasn't all that much fun.

Back at the organ and immersed in the music, all else vanished from consciousness. From Bach I switched to Gospel. Following Dr. Wallaberra's murder Brother John had reconvened the choir, with most of the same singers from the group organized for his first revival. Now the good brother was putting together more of the same.

"A Grand Finale," he called it, "before my departure, and on to our next church in trouble." He didn't bother asking whether I would accompany him on another mission. He assumed I would, since he was booked into my home territory. "In Laramie," he'd said, his back to me while making gravy for the pot roast. That was a couple of days earlier.

He no longer depended on me to do all the cooking, having discovered and experimented with mom's recipes that she'd faxed to us. At the time, with the aroma of cooked meat and vegetables filling the small kitchen and my stomach growling, he was trying to convince me to go with him. "I'll get to see your yacht," he added, winking, as if that were a big joke. It is.

Brother John was calling it quits here. The church deacons had organized themselves and found a new pastor. Managing things and people and staying put, taking responsibility for a single congregation, none of that was Brother John's style.

No, Elise wouldn't be playing the organ for the revival. "I just flat out told her No," Lucas said, as he dished up mashed potatoes for the two of us. "Elise is no good, and unless and until she takes formal lessons for a couple of years and practices for another five, she's never again going to play for one of my churches. Should have told her that right off the bat."

I had noticed lately that he was becoming more aggressive, an unfamiliar and uncomfortable garment for him to wear. Comes with the territory, I guess. All that management and control, hurting feelings when it can't be helped, not if he wanted to protect the common good. Can't mess up the many to shelter one person's sensibilities.

"Stand by your convictions!" he preached from the pulpit, and from the sink and stove when I was the only member of his kitchen congregation. Tough call, trying on his own advice. Which might not fit well for awhile.

Now I was winding up my organ practicing. At my feet Hugo yapped. Cookies finished, he wanted action. I stopped playing to pat him and give him a rub behind the ears. Only temporarily satisfied, he mewed, almost like a kitten. Sniffing at the zippered zipper, his message finally came through. He liked either the jacket or the zipper. I unzipped the windbreaker, tossed it over, and moved across the podium. The next medley of hymns, including *Follow the Gleam, Holy Holy,* and *When They*

Ring the Golden Bells, was better rendered on the piano.

Hugo followed me, gripping my jacket between his teeth and dragging it along behind him. He resettled himself at my feet.

I knew the gist of Brother John's opening sermon for the revival. He'd told me he would use Psalm 27—David waiting for the Lord to let him be King; also Luke 13, verses 31 through 35—Jesus's fear of going to Jerusalem to die, but trusting in the Lord's plan for him. The point was, Lucas said, to let God lead you. I knew what came next: read the Bible, pray. Sounded like mom's admonitions echoing in my head. Vanna might have repeated this advice.

From my account of the confrontation at the Martinez villa, Brother John knew that some of the congregation members were present among the mob. I had spotted them chanting and shouting for Dollie and Donny to get out of town. Sunday service ought to humble them, bring out some guilt, get them to make promises; to God, if not to Brother John or Sheriff Truman or me. I couldn't see the point of church if it didn't make you feel better. Or encourage you to make vows; get on with and try to improve your life. Had to be something, some reason for making such a big commitment.

Kinda like marriage. A life sentence.

Glancing up from hymnbook and keyboard, I noticed mom slip in the side door to quietly take a seat way over on the edge. So she wanted to be unobtrusive, eh. Sometimes mothers sit front and center, cheering on their kids, whether at Little League or piano recitals. Other times they seem to prefer blending in with the background; assuming anonymity, as if watching their children through the eyes of a stranger.

My role in this game was to pretend I hadn't seen her. Fussing about finding the right page, propping open the book, adjusting the piano bench, I remained silent, avoiding a glance in her direction. Alone, she must have left Hernandez out in the car. He had air conditioning and invariably a book to read. He was a Dick Francis fan, I'd noticed. Also, these days, Luis was reading Charles Dickens. Margaret Rose's influence again.

Mom hunched low on the third row from the back, taking cover behind and between the pews. Yes, we had cushioned benches by then. The contributions and pledges were pouring in regularly.

It had crossed my mind to wonder whether turning over bail money for the bondsman in order to gain Donny's release from jail was an appropriate use of church funds. Also, said the sheriff, the Martinez boy could be Mr. Goodman's killer. Which was why Donny was back in jail. Truman had arrested him all over again, for this new murder. Old murder, rather, since Goodman, to my knowledge, had been missing for months.

I belted out one verse and then repeated it for extra practice, still avoiding mom's reaction. Funny about mothers. Everybody's mom had shown up: mine, for me; The Derrys' mom to squeeze and smooch her first grandbaby. Of course Donny's and

Fess's mothers were already present. No dads. Divorced, dead, missing. I still wasn't convinced the bone Hugo had turned up in Dollie's tiny garden came from Goodman. If not, this would be a good time for him to turn up. Like a carrot or turnip, like a bad penny. If he were still among the living.

I couldn't believe Dollie would still sing the solo parts, not after getting concussed, not after suffering the sight of her son returned to jail. Especially if it were she, not he, who had done in Mr. Goodman. If the bones were, in fact, Mr. Goodman's.

Still no reaction from mom. Arms crossed over her bosom, head tipped downward, she could have been studying her shoes. Or she'd nodded off.

Yeah, that's how provocative and earth shattering my piano playing was. Put my own mama to sleep. Oh, well. I thought about the choir members and who could take Dollie's place on the high descants. She was supposed to have practiced with me that morning; not from her hospital bed, obviously. The doctor said she should be out, soon, when they were sure she'd be okay.

Before Hugo had hauled out that first bone, Dollie admitted to Juan and me that Yes, she'd tried talking sense into Elise. "She wouldn't listen when I said Donny was the result of artificial insemination. You'll recall, Oliver, that I told you that before. Anyway, Elise called me a liar when I said my son's physical likeness to her husband was pure coincidence." Those two statements were contradictory, but I didn't realize it at the time.

Not easy turning up the truth this long after the fact. Laboratory records from that long ago were private, sealed. Even those might not convince Elise. Get a bee in your bonnet and the buzzing drowns out every other sound. I agreed with Elise, though. Did seem peculiar. Moreover, why hadn't Elise noticed anything back then? During adolescence when the similarity was more pronounced? Why now, with nothing to go on but one old photo?

Right then Vanna tiptoed in the side door. She took a seat on the opposite side of the church from mom. I doubted that either noticed the other. A glance at Vanna, a tentative wobbly smile, and she smiled back. And winked. Oh, man, when I introduced her to mom, and vice versa, mom would go ape. At mom's insistence, I'd sent her a photo of my sweetheart. Back when she was still my sweetheart. Mom wrote back that Vanna Solano could have passed for Jessica Jimenez, who played Catalina on the soap opera *Guiding Light*. On the phone mom said Vanna was lovely, with that long black hair, olive complexion, dark flashing eyes, and slender but lush body. I countered that she was drop dead gorgeous. Now I could hardly keep my eyes off her. I hoped she'd come to make up, give me another chance. At the piano I started making mistakes.

With mom staring at me as if shamed, and me with my mind drifting, neither of us, nor Vanna, noticed the stealthy figure crouched and sneaking along a back pew. Not until it was almost too late.

A shuffle, some sense of a foreign presence, and Hugo's sharp bark alerted me in the nick of time.

Glancing up, I stared at the gun pointed straight at me. Without conscious thought I bent and grabbed, snatching up the .38 Hugo had dragged out of my unzippered pocket.

In one smooth motion, I clutched the gun, clicked off the safety, and shot without properly aiming. Hugo barked and ran down the aisle. Mom screamed and slid down in her seat, her hands flying to cover her face. Vanna stood, turned, stared, gasped, and ducked low. Good girl. I didn't have time to rescue her on one side of the church and mom on the other and still chase the shooter.

He yowled, dropping his gun and grabbing his hand. Then he turned and raced out the door, with me leaping over the front rail of the podium to give chase. I was vaguely aware of sobbing coming from behind me in the church.

CHAPTER 47

Mom and Vanna came running fast out of the church, right on the heels of Hugo and me. I jammed the little revolver under my belt in the back. I couldn't get my cycle going. On the cellphone I jerked out of my breast pocket, I called Juan for backup. "Fess tried to shoot me," I yelled at him. "Meet me at the Sahuarita Junction. I saw the Jaguar head that way."

"Should I call the Sheriff?" he hollered. I said No before cutting the connection.

Mom wailed. Hugo barked. Vanna clutched her hands and wobbled.

"Mom, meet Vanna. Vanna, this is my mother," I shouted, as my motorcycle fired and caught. Thinking fast, I told Vanna to call Lucas, and to get hold of the Cat people.

"The 'Cat people'?" Mom straddled the front wheel, clinging to my handlebars as if to keep me at her side by putting her body up as shield.

I revved the motor. "Gotta go, Mom. Get outta the way," I hollered over the roar of Penny. "Tell you more later. Or Vanna will explain."

"Should I, uh, we wait here for you?"

"Go back to the Cat," I shouted over my shoulder. Then I waved and took off up north, leaving the two little ladies to make their own acquaintance.

"Lost him," I said to Juan, who pulled up at the Sahuarita bar shortly after I did. We parked our cycles out front, strapped helmets on seats, and made our way into the dim saloon. The place reeked of stale beer and bodies sweaty from a day in the mines or working the pecans. The sheriff with one of his deputies sat in a back booth. Fondling a coffee mug Dick motioned for us to join them.

I waved while Juan ordered us a couple of Coors at the bar. We took our frosty mugs, foam on the top, over to their booth. I gulped mine half down. "Man, I needed that," I said to the table.

Tom the deputy turned toward me. "What's up with you guys?" he asked while sipping a Saisparillo, its foam and color reminding me of a Pink Lady.

"I take it you fellas are on duty," I said, pulling up a straight chair to straddle it backwards. Juan took a seat on the bench beside Tom. Now we had a good view of both their faces. I described the scene at the church and Fess's fast get-away in the Jag. I expected Truman to demand that I turn over the gun, or arrest me for carrying without a license.

The snub-nosed, blue steel Smith and Wesson .32 was a beauty, all right.

The sheriff ignored both me and my shooter. He was having trouble hiding his glee. Why not, he'd arrested Donny, not once but twice. My news could wait, he had a fast-breaking bulletin of his own. He'd share it only when he got damn good and ready, though; that's par, for him. Better prod him, play along. Or I never would get a chance to report the shoot-out in the church.

I asked if there was any word back from the lab about whose arm those bones might belong to. I was thinking Goodman. I was also thinking that Dollie couldn't have buried Elise's husband in her patio, the garden was too narrow, probably too shallow.

Here's the plot I'd described earlier to Juan: Elise murders her husband, dismembers him, buries his pieces and parts only God knows where. She saves her husband's lower arm, the ulna and radius, to plant on her cousin's property. If Hugo hadn't dug up one of them, Elise would have found some other way to draw the attention of the authorities to the burial plot.

What a shabby thing to do to her once beloved cousin. That's what I'd said to Juan. He'd replied with a cliché: *Hell hath no fury like a woman scorned.*

Yeah, I said, but I thought that meant getting revenge against a guy that dumps you. He smirked, as if to say, *No understanding women*, scorned or not.

The sheriff enjoyed building suspense, I guess, because he looked from me to Juan and back again, his glee turning to gloating. "The FBI demanded a rush job, so they flew in their own forensic pathologist. The woman and team worked all night. You guys ain't gonna believe this."

"Yeah, okay. Give." I expected my plot would play out.

"Dr. Wallaberra." At our wide-eyed stare, he elaborated. "The bones your dog uncovered at the Martinez house belong to Dr. Wallaberra."

" How could that be?"

Another smirk. "The FBI are on it. Have to wait til they're ready to report. You guys can just keep your pants on."

"Us, too. We gotta keep our pants on, too, ya' know," mumbled Tom.

Changing the subject, I described the episode in the church. I might have shot Fess. I suggested to the sheriff that he check with the hospitals.

Dick leaned back, then forward. Slowly he sipped his coffee, and then, finally, like doing one of those double-takes in the movies, he noticed the gun.

We were both watching him. "Figured Oliver needed protection," Juan explained. No doubt we'd both get a lot of flak.

Waving a hand in dismissal, he backtracked. "You get a look at the Jaguar's driver? You swear it was Fess?"

"Hey, Dick, he shot at me."

"From the back of a dim church. Could a been anybody."

"Yeah, anybody," repeated Tom.

The sheriff ignored his deputy. "You hit the guy when you shot back?"

"Probably. He yelled and grabbed his shooting hand before whirling around to run back out the door."

"But you can't identify him as Fess for sure, can you?"

Truman scowled and gnawed on a pink toothpick. I'd anticipated plenty of questions, but not these, "Why? You think it was somebody else?"

Now he grinned again, as if to tell me he'd been painting me into a corner. "Couldn't a been Fess. We were trailing him at the same time, him coming the other way, out of Green Valley."

"Lost him down the road apiece. Minutes ago," Tom said.

"Maybe he doubled back," suggested Juan, holding up two fingers to the bartender, who presently brought us a couple more Coors.

"Don't think so. Me and Tom think there's a meth lab opening up here in the neighborhood somewheres. We figured to catch 'em at it. That's why we trailed Fess."

"He involved? You know that for a fact?" Juan asked. He wiped foam off his mustache.

"Not for sure, no."

"Then why do you suspect Goodman?" My turn to beckon the barkeep.

"You always have. Right, Oliver?" said Truman. "You suspected him all along of poisoning you."

Tom lifted an eyebrow and held up an index finger for attention. "I didn't get in on that. Will somebody tell me something?"

I dropped my glance to the table. Dick shook his head. "Later, Tom."

"What about the boys?"Juan asked. "You give up on the Mason twins?"

"Not quite. Fess or somebody could be using the kids as couriers." Dick didn't look at any of us, embarrassed maybe at his previous mistakes. He sighed, got up, and said they were hitting the road. He didn't say where to and we didn't ask.

Delay him another minute, even though we were both eager to talk about the bones that were now supposed to have come from Dr. Wallaberra, and the sheriff would remember to do his duty: confiscate Juan's gun; insist that I follow them to his office to give my statement about the church shooting.

Apparently he forgot all that. He hated filling out forms.

Left alone to finish our beers, I said it had been a crazy day. Sheriff not interested in the shooting out at the church, him wanting to surprise us with the bone news. Then he won't talk about that either.

"Instead of doing anything significant, our sheriff ran off looking for a meth lab."

Juan grinned. "Could be important."

"Priorities, Juan. One-two-three, I'd give the *possibility,* the pretty vague possibility of a drug manufacturing hideout third place. If that."

I replaced the chair I'd been straddling to scoot

into the scarred booth with its taped-up maroon vinyl cushions. We stared at each other a few moments until he made the first move. "Whadda ya think, Oliver?" He ordered another round, though he never touched his fourth.

What I was thinking had nothing to do with murder and mayhem. Or drugs. I clutched the mug of beer, trying to hide my trembling hands. Shooting somebody, even if I hadn't killed him, shook me up. I needed comfort. Preferably from Vanna. Here she'd shown up at the church and I didn't even get a chance to hug her. What did she want? To make up, I hoped.

When I looked at Juan, all I could see was the two of them together. My glance dropped back to my hands. He repeated his question. "What you think?"

"About what?" Neither of us mentioned Vanna, the girl I'd supposed had come between us. We were simply trying to pick up where we were before. I didn't tell him about running into Patsy, either, her nearly stopping my heart action when she threw her arms around me. And then to discover she'd been waiting for me to come rescue her (I never did discover from what I was supposed to have saved her). Only to learn I'd arrived the day after she married another man. It didn't bear thinking about; I wasn't keen on sharing my pain.

Juan drew me back to the moment. "What Dick said. Oliver, you think there could be a meth lab in the vicinity? Me thinks there could be a whole drug factory producing everything from tablets of ecstasy to cutting heroin for sale on the streets up Tucson way. What I hate to see is them hitting the schools, especially our own Sahuarita High School."

Juan could have friends enrolled there. I stared at him while corralling my thoughts from my broken heart. I'd have to tame this wild horse within me all by my lonesome.

"Could be, though it hardly seems likely."

"Why not?"

"Why are we talking about this anyhow? We're as bad as Dick and Tom. I could have shot somebody, but nobody, apparently, thinks anything about that. The sheriff tells us that it was Dr. Wallaberra's arm bones Hugo dug up at Dollie's, and we don't talk about that, either."

"I can't take it in, Oliver. The pastor hasn't been dead that long. How could his bones be free of flesh already?"

"Some wild thing gnawed it clean?" I leaned forward, smacking the table with my fist. "Gotta be a mistake. That pathologist got it wrong."

"I think you're right. Can't be Wallaberra. Might not even be human."

"Except that forensic pathology is pretty sophisticated these days."

I leaned back and closed my eyes. Three beers and I was mellowing out, my memory of the shooting gently disappearing into the ozone along with what might have been. Between Patsy and me.

As for Vanna, she might not be in my future, either. Not if Juan was right. She wanted to change my stripes, eh. Turn me from tiger to pussy cat.

Vanna and mom would make some pair, both of them eager to push me into the vat of conversion. I continued to view all that religious dogma as gooey, sappy, sticky stuff. So long as I'm breathing, I would keep right on resisting.

Better to forget Vanna, too, than have to watch her join forces with mom in setting about to change my whole life. Women, humph.

Juan was talking about something. "Where would you look, Oliver?"

"Uh, for what?"

"Cripes, you weren't even listening. For a drug factory, a meth lab."

"Try the school," I said, tossing out the idea like a pebble in a pond. Then sit back and watch the ripples grow.

Eyes opened wide, he fingered and stroked his mustache, in deepest thought. Could have been *The Thinker*. He shoved his gun across the table at me and stood.

"Keep that. I've got another. Let's go."

"Where?" As if I cared. I was still thinking about Vanna and Patsy. For all the pain, it was easier than wondering whether the guy I'd shot was dead.

"To the school, of course." His look told me he thought I'd gone daft. It dawned on me I had no idea if he'd ever lost a sweetheart. What'd he know.

"Who cares? Why do we wanna follow up on the sheriff? Don't you think we should be looking for Fess? Or prowling around Dollie's patio searching for more bones?"

He stood over me, shaking his head like I'd

turned into a purple frog. It didn't occur to me until later that my lethargy could be post-traumatic stress from the shooting. Macho guys don't think like that, not until or unless the notion gets shoved down your gullet. I stared back, awaiting a reply.

"The sheriff already said it wasn't Goodman who shot at you. Pretty good alibi, I'd say, what with the sheriff himself chasing him. And we can't prowl Dollie's villa, anyhow. Not even me, no matter the number of legitimate excuses I could come up with. Police tape marks the Martinez property as off limits. For now. So, Oliver, since we're stymied in both those directions, I thought we might as well follow Dick's lead."

"Can't. The school's all locked up. It's still summer, you know."

"If those teenage boys broke into the chemistry lab, we sure can."

Resistance low, it was easier to go along than resist. Besides, I needed my strength to keep my back up against mom's proselytizing. If it wasn't church-going and praying she wanted out of me, it was marriage and babies. She wanted to be a grandmother. Now that she'd met Vanna, mom would turn over every stone to get us back together, especially if by doing so she could kill two birds with but a single missile—those two little ladies might soon be working in joint harness.

Juan didn't wait for me to reply. Nothing to do but follow along.

We parked our cycles near the tennis courts. The high school campus with its various structures and covered porches as walkways stretched all over the place. Have to hoof it in the heat around all of them until we found the right wing. And then what?

I forgot this was home ground to Juan, his alma mater. Blocky and short-legged compared to me, it should have been easy keeping up with him. But he'd had three beers to my four and he wasn't recuperating from a shooting while simultaneously suffering a broken heart twice over. Counting when Patsy left me for Arlo, that made three times. Jeez, my pity party was starting to sound like a broken record.

Yellow crime tape crossed the outside door that opened directly into the chemistry lab. "What's happening?" Juan shouted.

We peered through the window at the disarray: a jumble of half-destroyed equipment, chairs knocked over, trash littering the floor.

What a mess. "Guess the cops or the DEA beat us to it, Oliver."

"Not the sheriff, though. Or he wouldn't have been wandering off half-cocked. Wonder where he and Tom got off to?" They weren't at the school.

"So you were right," Juan said. "You and Truman. It <u>was</u> those teenagers into drugs. And they were working out of the school while it was closed for the summer."

I nearly said *So what*, but caught myself. Time I sobered up. We returned to our bikes and got underway.

Garcia and Truman and the DEA might be interested in drugs and meth labs. Not me. I wondered how many more bones might be buried at Dollie's.

CHAPTER 48

Maybe nobody else was interested, but I certainly was. If not Fess, then who? And why take a shot at me in the church? Right in front of my mom.

I had a hunch. Before returning to the Cat Café I turned off at the church. Nobody around. I used my key to the side door to make my way down to the back pew on the left-hand side. There had to be some reason, some clue, perhaps, to why the killer set up his shooting position between these two pews.

I was off by one row. In the next-to-last section, I found it, what looked like an ordinary hymnbook lying on the floor, half-hidden beneath a pew.

Opening it, I discovered the book had been mutilated. This was the gun's hiding place, all ready for some special time when it was needed. Inside the book a cutout exactly fit the shape of a gun.

The one used to shoot at me might not have been the same that took Dr. Wallaberra's life, but I guessed this hiding place had been used before. Carry your own Bible. Bring your own hymnbook. Innocent enough. Then jerk it open and whip out the gun whenever desperate. That was the way I saw it.Then I had another hunch and wanted to check it out before I forgot.

I'd swing by the Cat Castle first, see how Vanna and mom were getting on, before I set off to follow my new clue. When I roared up, they burst out the front door of the restaurant to surround me. That's what it felt like. Yeah, two women can surround one man. I hoped that Vanna would talk to me.

Talk! Well, I guess. Both of them babbled, cackled, cried, carried on. Where was I? Was I all right? Did I catch the shooter? They sang a duet of worries, fretting over what I'd been up to. They imagined me shot at again and this time killed. Did I have no consideration? This from mom.

I apologized. Profusely. The reward—hugs and kisses, from the both of those pretty little ladies. They wanted me off the cycle, safe. I was still mounted, the engine continuing to hum.

A grin splitting his face, Hernandez too came out of the café to stand on the front steps. An audience of one. If anybody indoors had heard me arrive, they were pretending not to notice.

"Where are you off to, now?" Vanna demanded.

"It's obvious you're itching to go somewhere else," said mom. I could imagine how much she'd shared with Vanna of the stories from my childhood and youth. Tough for a guy to keep anything private when women are bound and determined to unravel your personal history.

Mom didn't wait for an explanation. She insisted I get off the bike and come inside. "Everyone is eager to hear your account of the shooting."

"Forget it, mom. Let's talk about something else."

"You didn't catch him, then."

"Nope. Ran into the sheriff, who said <u>he'd</u> been trailing Fess. At the same time. So there goes my suspect. I thought it was Goodman. Guess not."

"Leave the chasing of killers to the sheriff, Oliver." She started to drag me into the Cat before I'd had a chance to speak with Vanna.

Vanna winked, tucked her hand inside my arm and squeezed. Her touch was warm and tender. Jeez, talk about *Died and gone to heaven*

Nowadays the Cat closed its doors in mid-afternoon. I knew I must smell like a brewery, especially when Vanna handed me a tic tac along with a grin.

We gathered at our usual table; two tables, shoved together. The moms, mine and the Derrys, played with the baby, while Megan, the brand new mommy, sat between them holding the tiny new Dolan.

I thought they weren't listening to the rest of us, but it was Megan who heard the news and turned up the television set housed high in the corner on a shelf. Dick, with sidekick Tom next to him, was all smiles.

"We caught 'em," he gloated on the screen. "I figured all along it was them teenage boys what was into drugs in these parts, and sure enough it was."

"Sure enough," said his echo.

The reporter out of Tucson, Lydia Somebody, asked about the kids' parents. She wanted to interview them, she said. See how they'd felt when they discovered their kids were into the growing and marketing of marijuana. She had rosy cheeks and blond hair, brushed every which way with no precise part on her head. She could have been a messy peach, ripe for plucking. She made what the kids had been doing sound exciting, worthy of respect, like it was a new computer game product all ready for national distribution.

Distributing and selling, right. Get more kids hooked.

Then I remembered something. When Juan and I had run into the sheriff and Tom at the bar, they were on their way to find a meth lab, not a marijuana patch. Either one, they didn't seem to have any idea how to locate it. Something must have happened since, because they'd sure moved fast.

In the background behind the reporter we could hear a roar. The photographer immediately turned his lens to focus on the crowd rapidly gathering. On TV we could read the placards: "Free the kids," on one side of the street; "Down with Drugs," across the way. Again two opposing sides had burst onto the scene. Anything for a little excitement.

"Where do all these people come from?" asked my mom in amazement.

"Outta the woodwork," mumbled Matt.

"Through the cracks in the sidewalk," muttered Mike.

"They don't have much to do," Brother John suggested.

"You should have seen the crowds when Dr. Wallaberra was murdered," I told mom and Hernandez. He and mom held hands. Sweet love, humph.

Sheriff Truman held up both hands, as if his gesture, backed by uniform, gun, billy club, and big Stetson could stun the crowd into silence. The camera switched from sheriff and deputy to the crowd, and then to the reporters, and back around again, all the while maintaining focus.

"How do I feel?" shouted Dick over the racket, while pushing back his hat to rub his forehead. "Vindicated! That's how. People laughed when I said those kids were guilty of selling drugs, but I showed 'em."

"Right on," chimed in Deputy Tom.

"Anything else, Sir? Did they also kill Dr. Wallaberra? Is that what you mean? These boys are guilty of murder?"

"Innocent until proved otherwise!" shouted a scruffy pair, man and woman, with their long, straggly hair, both of them, with gold earrings spouting from ears, nose, and eyebrows, she in a long print cotton shirt and he in cut-off denim shorts. Both barefooted, I took them for craftsy folk. The rest of their crowd, dressed similarly or worse, took up the chant.

On the other side, a few neatly clothed old-timers startled the television audience by yelling back, "Boo, Boo!"

When baby Dolan heard that he started to cry, a soft little whimper. Grandma Derry handed him back to Daddy Derek.

"My word," said mom, motioning to the chanting crowd.

"I've seen worse. In Europe," said Merry Derry.

Mike held a rattle out to MM, as we'd taken to calling the newest Dolan, and Matt stuck a pacifier in his mouth. Derek shook his head and passed it back

"Coo coo," baby MM responded.

"Howl!" yelped Hugo through the window open to the back yard.

The adult M-n-M-n-Ms raised eyebrows, while Derek laughed outright.

"Crazy world," said Hernandez, excusing himself for the facilities.

"I can't help but agree," said Merry Derry.

"Let us pray for their immortal souls," said Brother John. It wasn't clear to me exactly whose souls he meant.

"Oh, yes. I couldn't agree more," said mom, who obviously knew what the good brother was talking about. She promptly bowed her head and everybody followed. Yup, even me, though I was thinking my own set of tortured thoughts.

First off, I didn't think I understood much of anything any longer. At the bar that very afternoon the sheriff was beside himself, couldn't wait to talk about the bones' identity. Now, at a press conference, or whatever it was, he made no mention of bones or the Martinez patio. He was off on the kids and drugs again.

Dr. Wallaberra's bones, the fact that they weren't Goodman's, was the biggest news of the day, surely; news that apparently hadn't reached the media yet. Why not? It was Dick Truman who'd gleefully told Juan and me. So excited about telling us the identity of those arm bones, he couldn't be bothered with relieving me of Juan's gun. This was the same sheriff I was watching on the tube bragging about a junior-sized drug bust? Something amiss here.

. I stood to leave. Most of them took little notice, except Vanna and mom.

"Now, what?" Vanna demanded, skipping along behind me.

"I want to get over to the villa development. Check out something."

"Me, too," she said. Not waiting for permission, she followed me out of the Cat to clamber onto the seat behind me.

Right behind her trotted mom with Hernandez lumbering behind.

"Can we help?" offered Luis.

I started to say No to all of them, except I didn't see much chance of dissuading Vanna. Then, too, I recalled mom's knowledge of herbs and poison plants. "Good idea." I turned to Luis. "You and mom follow us in your car."

We took off, Vanna's soft warm body pressing into mine, her tender hug an excuse to keep from falling off. As if she would. I didn't mind. On the contrary, it was hard to keep my mind on business. I'd rather have detoured to Vanna's place for a sweet cuddle.

I was headed for the west side, beyond the villas, to the rear of another housing development; different architectural style, larger dwellings, all in almond or white stucco with Spanish tile roofs. The area I was thinking of belonged to nobody; the town, maybe. Lots of undergrowth, weeds, a couple of narrow paths. Nearby residents walked their dogs out here, Juan had said.

Great place to plant herbs and poisonous plants; scattered out, mixed in with the natural foliage. With mom along she could pinpoint specifics, foreign plants, especially those not indigenous to the region.

We had to park a block away. This was wild country back here, undeveloped, unclaimed. When I told mom what to look for, she and Luis returned to the car after her reference books. Hernandez, I'd noticed, willingly obeys mom like Hugo obeys Juan.

Vanna reached for my hand. Mine clammy, I was embarrassed. I removed it long enough for a swipe along my jeans.

She laughed. "Your mom likes your choice of tee-shirt slogan, Oliver." It read: *Ill deeds are doubled with an evil word.* From Shakespeare's *Comedy of Errors.* "Me thinks you're very involved in solving the crimes around here. Too busy to find time for me?"

She breaks up with me and then backs up? "I'll always have time for you, Vanna."

She didn't explain what she meant. I might have time for her, but, more importantly, was she still interested in making time for me?

"Your mom's a wonderful person. I just love her to pieces."

Soon my mom and Luis rejoined us. We four spread out to search, in the fashion of hunting for a lost jewel—one step at a time, eyes pinned to the ground. My hunch panned out. Within ten minutes and without recourse to her book of herbs and poisons, mom spotted larkspur and vox.

"What's this tell you, Oliver?" Vanna asked, coming up to again clasp my hand. "This plot of tangled, unclaimed land is so close to the villas. Donny had a degree in botany. Are you beginning to think he really is the guilty one?"

I didn't get a chance to reply, because just then shots rang out.

Luis yelled, "Duck!" Pushing mom to the ground, he threw his body over hers.

I should have moved faster. Maybe I could have saved Vanna like Luis did mom.

Too late. My beloved took a hit to the head.

CHAPTER 49

Dollie confessed! To Dr. Wallaberra's murder, to poisoning me; from the poisonous plants near her villa. Even to shooting at me in the church. Nobody told me though. Not right off. I was too focused on Vanna.

My sweet Vanna lingered in a coma, hovering between life and death, me holding her hand, crying; mind in a fog and life in limbo. Juan came by St. Mary's hospital to tell me the news. That's when I heard it, from my pal. Not on the TV set, which stayed turned on and tuned low, day and night.

"Humph," I said, head bowed, tears gathering.

"Dollie's protecting her son," mom concluded. Trust a mother's intuition.

The sheriff came by to say he'd booked Dollie, too. For attempted murder, with me as the intended victim. I didn't see how I could possibly care.

I had yet to pray, though of course mom and Brother John made up for my reluctance. I hoped Vanna would come around before I had to reach this last resort—prayer and all that that implied; for me, that meant total commitment.

The doctors had said Vanna should be okay, given time. The bullet had passed along the inside of her scalp, into her head and right back out again. Close to her brain but not directly striking critical tissue. The medical people couldn't say why she remained comatose; burdened with this utter silence that had captured her mind and soul.

"Could be trauma," mom said. "Pray, Oliver!" she commanded me over Vanna's bed. "You've got to pray with all your heart and soul. And mean it."

Brother John called a special prayer service. The whole congregation turned out. Everybody loved Vanna Solano.

It was at that point Juan appeared with the news of Dollie's confession.

Again the media appeared, Juan said. They covered the protesters.

Because with the news that Vanna had been shot, another demonstration, though small and half-hearted, had formulated itself outside the church. This time on behalf of Hispanics. Hernandez seemed mildly surprised. Mom questioned whether these people—protesters, she meant—had enough to do; perhaps they needed jobs, or, better yet, God.

In Vanna's hospital room in Tucson, I noticed mom's prayers included me. She sensed my love and devastation. Along with the guilt. Because I should never have allowed my loved ones to come with me. Out of the mists of my foggy mind, a couple of lines by Elizabeth George came to me. They surely describe my own mother: *I have a mother who prays for me And pleads with the Lord every day for me.*

At last I prayed. Sincerely, I hoped, if mood and intent were registered in some book or computer record on high. I don't remember what I said; made some promises, probably. I do recall how I felt. After surrendering my soul. To use a cliché, a great peace fell upon me, like a dove, a whole flock of cooing turtle doves.

I talked to Vanna and read to her from the Bible and Shakespeare, and sang from the gospel hymnbook. Sometimes, though, I was too tired to do or say anything beyond holding her hand and bowing my head in prayer.

Still, I couldn't sit there beside her forever. I needed food, sleep, a shower. Excusing myself for the latter, I continued pushing aside the sustenance offered by family, friends, and the hospital staff. Mom worried that I'd waste away to nothing. Occasionally I napped in an easy chair.

"Oliver?" a tiny, sweet voice said. "You look awful. Where are we?"

Vanna was back! From wherever her conscious mind had disappeared, she was back. She'd returned to me. To us.

Word got around fast. If Paul Revere's declarations of the the shot heard 'round the world amazed people back then, the news of Vanna's recovery and the speed of it passing through the community was, to me, equally surprising.

Soon she was up on her feet, checked over and checked out. "That's the end of that, Oliver. Back to normal. Now you can get back to your sleuthing."

Sarcasm, huh? What I wanted to resume was a whole lot of lovin'. What she didn't realize was that by praying and getting back the best answer on the face of the globe, I was now in debt. I must make good on my promise to the Lord that if He'd let us have Vanna back, He could have my soul.

If I could change my life for the Lord, surely I could make a few changes for my beloved. "What do you want, Vanna?"

"You. I want you, Oliver. I missed you so much. I had no idea how much I could miss you. I, uh, guess what I want most is for us to be together."

I couldn't believe my ears. The shot to the head must have stabbed her brain, after all. It wasn't possible she could capitulate this easily. Or I didn't understand. Determined to go through whatever rebirth Vanna demanded before she'd be mine, I begged of her, "What do you want me to do, Hon? Go to school? You want me to enroll in college all over again? I can do that." I was pleading for my life.

She grinned. "You'd do that for me, Oliver?"

"I'd move heaven and earth. Climb mountains. Swim oceans."

"Silly boy. Let's get out of here. We'll talk later."

Of course we called everybody. To let them

know she was okay and that we'd return soon to the Cat Castle.

The next day after breakfast, while I washed up and Vanna sipped tea, she demanded that I talk to her about my suspicions. "Talk it out, Oliver. You might know more than you think you know."

Reluctantly I agreed, speaking as the ideas tumbled out of me in a jumble. A lot of things made little sense, but a few things did, I said. Dr. Wallaberra's grave wasn't right. Whatever Elise had done with her husband's body in the interim—assuming she'd done away with him—I didn't know and couldn't guess. But I'd be willing to bet a hundred bucks he now lay in Paul's grave. Which meant Elise or Fess, one or both, had stashed the pastor somewhere else.

"That's what poisoning you was all about, you think? Which means Fess suspected you of getting too close to the truth."

"Silly boy jumped the gun. Back then I didn't have Clue One to anything. Still, Elise could be covering for her son. After I left town, Dr. Wallaberra caught on to the two Goodmans. So he had to go. Then Fess planted his gun on Donny. Which still might come off as believable. The Martinez trial is coming up in a few weeks."

Then I had another thought. "We all assumed it was marijuana plants Fess had planted in the church garden. When Dr. Wallaberra dug them up, they must have hoped that was the end of it. Had he and Brother John dug down deeper, they might have found Goodman's body."

"Okay, you've run that idea up the flagpole. You expect me to salute?" Her grin tempered the implied criticism.

"You don't buy that, eh?"

She said she'd have to think on it. We made ready to leave. I wanted to pamper her, carry her around in my arms like a baby. She said that was silly. She was fine. The doctors had agreed no damage was done. "Sore head, maybe, sentencing me to sleep for awhile in YonderWorld. I'm back now, Oliver, so stop treating me like I'm wrapped in cotton batting."

She hopped on the back of my cycle and we took off, stopping first at Juan's to pick up Hugo. Too big now to ride inside my windbreaker, he sat in Vanna's lap. "Yap, yap," he barked happily. It felt like we were a family.

At the Cat, Vanna was greeted like a long lost explorer from the North Pole. Nobody said anything about our overnight detour. I started to mumble about needing a shower, shave, and shampoo, but Vanna nudged me into silence. I guessed they could figure out what we'd both needed most.

Around our table in mid-morning, it might have been Old Home Week. Derek was holding his baby, while Matt made faces at the infant and Mike laughed. Mom was especially considerate, of my feelings and of Vanna's. She and Hernandez held hands. I gave the baby my finger, which he promptly stuck in his mouth. Then he looked at me with big round bright blue eyes and said "Coo." Or some such. I'm not exactly familiar with that language.

It was then I noticed who was missing. "Where's Megan and her mom?"

"They went shopping in Tubac," said Derek. "Merry was eager to see that cemetery where we buried Dr. Wallaberra. Brother John went along."

My Adam's apple rose in my throat. "Alone?"

"If you call three people *alone*, yeah."

Just then a bunch of bikers pulled into the parking lot. We could see them dismounting through the big plate glass window. With the roar of their motorcycles, I couldn't hear the rest of Derek's comments.

Matt and Mike jumped up to do the duty. With their new kitchen chef, Megan wasn't putting in as many hours as she once had done. My mom took baby MM and Derek too joined the parade of Cat servers. Vanna warmed a bottle but she didn't return to waitressing. It was too soon, everybody agreed.

My cellphone buzzed. It was Brad Gifford. He'd just left Tucson, once more headed for Nogales. He couldn't make time for golf, but would stop by the Cat Castle for coffee. Just checking to see if I was around, and had any news.

I had news all right. "Too much to tell over the phone. I'll wait until you get here."

"That hostage situation have anything to do with you guys?" Brad said.

"Hostages? What are you talking about?" I yelled at my end.

"Down at Tubac. It just came over the radio. Some people at the cemetery were taken hostage by a crazy man."

"Megan and Merry went down there! Hold it!" I hollered at Hernandez to turn up the television set in the corner. I forgot all about Brad on the other end.

The television reporter said she was speaking from the Tubac cemetery, where a trio of people were being held at gun point by a mad man. "The sheriff and deputies are on the way. Even as I speak, some FBI guys are pulling up." Lots of noise and background babble. We couldn't see anything beyond the reporter, her image filling the screen. "Oh, yes, and the DEA."

At our end, everybody was gathered around the set. That whole bunch of bikers shut up and paused, as if paralyzed, to watch and listen, too.

Somehow, slowly, and then more rapidly, like a rush of water released to spill over a dam, things started coming together for me. I don't know how or from where my revelations appeared—during the quiet time spent with the comatose Vanna, in the back of my mind, while half-asleep, while praying, or from the television news filtering around the edges—I simply could not say how it happened. But a lot of small, seemingly unrelated clues started making sense.

.As the sheriff had said once: "Remember *KISS*—Keep it simple, son."

So that's what I did now—played it simple, even if that meant it was coming out stupid. Because another piece of Truman's advice surfaced: "If things look a certain way, chances are, that's the way they are." At the time it seemed a garbled message, and his caboose didn't help much: "Don't sweat the small stuff."

Small stuff, meaning clues. How could I not sweat those? Dick had said he meant they could fog up my main perspective.

Now it all came together, who was guilty and who was not, and why. Not all the pieces, but enough for me to know the danger that Megan and her mom faced at the hands of the discombobulated cousins and their misguided sons.

The cellphone still dangled from my hand while I'd disappeared into this fog of new-found perception. Vanna gave me a sharp poke.

"You still there, Brad?" I said, getting back to him. "Sorry about that. Yes, we're getting the news this very minute. Megan and her mom are down there! And Brother John. Could be all three of them are among the hostages. Brad, I'm afraid for their lives!"

Gifford yelled in my ear. "What are you going to do?"

Obviously I had to do something. "Pray," I said. This set of prayers should come easier, begging for Megan's safe return along with the others. "I sure can't do anything from here. Gotta run, Brad, get myself down there."

"Me, too," said Brad. "Meet you there."

What I didn't know was that my trucker pal would pass on the personal side of this bad news by getting on the CB. Plenty of other truckers heard him.

At my feet Hugo argued with the zipper. He wasn't satisfied with having his own zippered windbreaker, he had to manage it. He had learned how to bite the tiny handle between his teeth and zip it up and down. Now it wouldn't work. Guess it had jammed from all that doggy saliva clogging the catches. I grabbed Hugo, jacket and all, on my way to the Cat's front door.

CHAPTER 50

On the way to Tubac the wheels of my mind were spinning as fast as the wheels on my cycle. The DEA, if not Sheriff Truman, must have made the connections: between the hippies in the hills growing pot and the buyers, ready with big bucks; between the Manson twins and their crude meth lab at the school and their buyers. Then there was the cocaine coming up from down south. Would the DEA, by now, have traced its path from Colombia through Mexico and into Tubac? Doesn't take much of a stash to make a buck. A mere ten pounds can run a half-million on the street.

Didn't need a warehouse to stash the cache on its route to city streets and school playgrounds. Meanwhile, wouldn't do to stick it under the bed or shelve it in the garage. Use a half-abandoned ceme- tery, instead, stick the stuff in a hole.

Agents from the DEA along with the FBI could

have set up their sting operation in the belief that Tubac was the focal point. I wondered whether they were onto the suppliers or the buyers. The latter, representing big time Underworld bosses, could be arriving from Tucson, Vegas, L.A., or the East Coast. That part didn't matter. Not to me.

A drug deal gone sour, that's what this hostage situation was all about, I'd bet a bundle on it. The DEA was getting too close. Me, too, back then, when both me and the local suppliers were still fumbling around in a fog. Murder, accidental or otherwise, had intervened along the way. Not surprising, to me at least, when the recipe for crime includes the ignorant and naïve trying to make a killing from dealing.

If the DEA was honing in, as my Gillette buddy Bill had predicted, so was the FBI. The FBI, poking out a paw for a handout. Regain their reputation.

As I pulled up a block before reaching the Tubac cemetery, Hugo barked. "Quiet!" I barked right back. He obeyed. Hey, I was getting good with the doggy commands. He had the last word, though. He snapped at his windbreaker, clutching it between his teeth to drag it along.

I spotted the SpyCam helicopter down from Tucson. So that's how the TV reporter had gotten on screen so fast. Possibly the station's road conditions and weather reporter got wind of the news, figured to make it big in crime reporting.

I stared at license plates. If the DEA and FBI had already arrived, they were in unmarked cars. Or, unlike my first surmise, they might not as yet have made the connection—between suppliers and buyers, between their own sting and this hostage caper

State troopers had cordoned off the area, using their vehicles as barriers, with yellow tape strung between the cars. A few uniformed cops stood around, not sure I guess whether to spit or go blind. While fingering holsters or billy clubs, they smoked, leaned on car fenders, muttered among themselves, or glanced nervously up ahead, toward a blue-striped tent, its flaps down, usually erected to protect gravesite mourners—from the elements, from Looky-Lous.

This time the tent housed the hostages and their captors. That wasn't hard to figure, with the sheriff shouting at them through his bullhorn.

Peering at the scene from the rear, I wondered at first why the group of sightseers wasn't larger. Hah! This was no formal demonstration, organized by experienced black or gay protestors on behalf of one of their own. This was no small bunch of senior citizens mimicking an old-timey vigilante committee. This was merely a trio of white hostages whose lives were on the line.

Juan pulled up behind me, climbed off his motorcycle, doffed his helmet, and quickly caught up. He grabbed my arm. "I don't get it, Oliver. What's this business got to do with the bones in Dollie's yard?"

I was eager to get up front, past the state police if they'd let me through. Join the sheriff, assess the situation. Or, maybe not. Might be better to sneak around back. Juan's questions right now were a nuisance.

"Truman told us they belong to Dr. Wallaberra," he said, "not to Mr. Goodman. I don't get it. Why didn't he arrest Dollie? She confessed."

I figured to answer him quick, get him off my back. At the hospital before Vanna's return to consciousness, the sheriff had dropped by to share a few of his thoughts. Shoved to the back of my mind until later, I pulled them out now.

"Because, Juan, he didn't believe Dollie's confession. Like my mom, Dick thinks she's the mama bear protecting her cub. Also, the sheriff won't accept the pathologist's report that those bones came from Dr. Wallaberra."

"Why not?"

"Because, Dick told me, *'them bones ain't black'*."

Juan's mouth dropped open. Then: "What are we doing now?"

"I'm going this way. You circle around the other side." We parted ways.

From the action out in front of the mourners' tent, I surmised that was where Megan, her mom, and Brother John were being held. Not that anybody had as yet identified the hostages, on or off the media. I just knew.

I took up a position behind the striped tent, back aways, where I could hide among the cacti. Avoiding an anthill and the stickers of prickly pear, I crouched. I needed time to get my bearings. Get the lay of the land.

Some of the artsy people from up in the hills arrived, along with a handful of Tubac shopkeepers and their customers, plus a bunch of senior citizens, a few Mexicans and a whole lot of tourists. Some of the gawkers hauled lawn chairs and coolers from their vans and SUVS. Others dragged out video-cams. Hah, and I'd imagined this was going to be a small gathering.

Then I saw my friends appear. I sighed. Hard to protect your women folk when they insist on grabbing a front-row spot. Derek and baby and the Derrys, I could understand. It was their wife, sister, and mom inside that tent; also, Brother John. I knew that for sure by then, from peering through the back tent flap, opened now for air. As for Vanna, my mom, and Hernandez, I wished they'd stayed home. Hadn't Vanna been through enough?

The bikers from the Cat roared in next. They dismounted their cycles, grabbed or propped up helmets, and joined the throng.

While the sheriff yelled at the tent, the captors responded only by note. A child, a small boy of no more than eight, ran back and forth. I continued to assess the situation before deciding how to make my move.

Through the flap I could see Megan and her mom, huddling together and sitting on the ground. Brother John clasped his hands in prayer. Of their captors I could see only slight movement, a pistol waving back and forth, a rifle over a shoulder, probably Fess's.

I had lost track of Juan's whereabouts. No doubt steering clear. Hugo must have followed him, because I couldn't see my dog anywhere, either.

Truman called for surrender. Then he paused and turned around to confer with Tom and a state trooper. More yelling. Yeah, he'd ordered a van. Yeah, it would be gassed up, ready for their get-away. To Mexico, I assumed.

Beyond the sheriff's party the hawkers were arriving. Shortly they passed among the crowd, shouting their wares—popcorn, peanuts, candy, hotdogs. "Get your cold drinks!" "Keep cool with a snow cone!" "Frosty beers!"

"Step right up, get a souvenir!"

I stared. What kind of souvenir? Looked like rocks. Who'd want to buy a rock?

Over all this hubbub the TV reporter continued to report, joined now by a flock of other birds—reporters from Tucson and Green Valley and Nogales.

I was sick of this scene, seemed like any excuse was good enough for a gathering, a reporting, for commercial enterprise. The misery of others a freak show for the curious.

I tried getting Megan's attention. The young mother was bent on comforting her mother. Brother John's eyes remained closed, and I could hear him blessing the captors; the bad guys, for cryin' out loud. Made no sense, until it flashed before my mind that the preacher's prayers might calm the savage beasts.

Down on hands and knees I vacated the security of prickly pear and barrel cactus to creep up a few feet to take a new position behind a cluster of Palo Verde trees. From inside the tent one of the captors, a woman, spied me!

Backing out through the tent flap, Dollie stumbled across the intervening distance to my side. "Oliver! I thought that was you. Oh, Oliver, you've got to do something. Quick." She knelt on the ground beside me, the skirt of her long sundress wadded into a ball to use as kerchief. "Fess is totally hyped! I think he's going to shoot somebody."

"Make him wait," I whispered. "The sheriff promised a van. It'll be along soon. Meanwhile, get back in there and try to keep Fess calm."

"How about the money? Fess is demanding a million!"

That was a surprise to me. "No way. Pima County can't come up with that kind of dough. What's with Fess?"

"He's high. I told you. Elise is no help. She's a mess, too."

"And you?"

Dollie dropped her glance. "I already confessed. You must know that."

"Silly girl. Sheriff Truman doesn't believe you." I was trying to placate her, lull her into thinking she was innocent in my eyes, too. Hah.

At that moment Hugo came trotting over to us. No barks, just a friendly yap from a dog awaiting play time. "Not now, Hugo," I yapped back.

Too loud! Inside the tent, Elise, alerted, lifted her eyes and gasped.

Fess dropped the rifle and spun around to point the pistol straight at Megan's head. I came unwound. No time to think, I rushed the tent and my friends' captors. Threw a tackle straight at Fess. Smacked him in the belly. He went down.

Elise sobbed and covered her face. Megan screamed. Brother John ceased praying to scramble for the downed rifle.

Above the open grave Elise slipped. Fell in. Atop the cache of plastic wrapped bags. Mrs. Derry squawked. Ignoring her mom, Megan yelled at me, "Help, Oliver! She's getting away!"

I turned to see Dollie creeping off. "Stop her!" I hollered at Hugo.

Well-trained by now, my dog leaped to knock down our church's best solist. Dollie fell, screaming. Immediately she commenced to crawl on hands and knees. Reaching down for his unzippered *Linus blanket*, Hugo quickly dragged it over to Dollie. Covered her with it. With his two front legs, he rested forepaws atop the pile of downed Dollie. Her head covered, I wondered, briefly, whether she could breathe beneath my jacket.

While I was thus occupied, turned away from the action in the tent, Fess grabbed Brother John, snatching the rifle out of his hand to sock him up the side of the head with it. Moaning, Lucas John fell to the ground beside the grave.

Quick as a blink, Fess turned the pistol back on Megan, poking it into an ear. Now he yelled at me to forget Dollie and come rescue his mother.

Man, I could have used Juan's help right about then. Still no sign of him.

Just then the cavalry arrived. Not on horseback but in a big rig. Make that plural. Behind Brad

Gifford's huge truck roared a whole fleet of other semis.

With Hugo holding Dollie captive and Megan under the gun, literally; with Brother John rolling on the ground, alternatively praying and nursing his sore ear and head where Fess had bopped him, and me momentarily mesmerized, Brad hopped out of Polly Pew bent on rescue.

The sheriff's deep voice boomed through the bullhorn. The hawkers ceased their hawking. Colored rocks from the old graves forgotten, the souvenir sellers aimed to back off, forget it.

Sirens screamed. More highway patrol cars pulled in, and a fleet of cops on motorcycles escorted a parade of FBI and DEA cars into the area beyond.

Apparently Brad hooked up with Juan, as I spotted the two of them join the sheriff. I could see them shuffling out front, meanwhile ignoring yellow tape, consumers eating and drinking and buying rocks, the bikers and truckers commingled with senior citizens, Mexicans, artsy folk, tourists, and church parishioners.

Brad, spying me, yelled, "What you want us to do, Oliver?" I supposed he included all the other truckers along with Garcia.

"I want you all to shut up out there, afore I shoot somebody!" Fess roared, or tried to. In his drugged condition, it came out a wavering squeak.

I nodded at Brad and Juan. As they rushed the tent, I slammed into Fess, knocking him into the grave hole atop his mom. Then I turned, ran out, and threw my weight with Hugo's over the struggling Mrs. Martinez. Holding on tight at first, I then let her up.

Gasping for air, sobbing, Dollie threw herself at me and wrapped her arms around my neck. "Oh, Oliver, I can't stand it a minute longer. You've got to hear my side of things before they come for me."

Sitting there on the ground, cross-legged, facing each other, she spilled the beans. I interrupted only twice.

Soon it was time to go. Deputy Tom came to get her.

Based on Megan's clear description of what had happened, and at whose hands, the sheriff arrested both Goodmans, along with Dollie. Dick sent Tom to cart them away. All this hubbub amidst a chorus of protesting FBI and DEA agents, whose big drug sting was *foiled by ignorant, bumbling civilians*, or so they yelled at the rest of us, including the sheriff, me, Juan, and Brad.

"Not so," I replied. With nothing but my nod and pointing finger, Brad with his truckers tackled and downed the other bad guys—the three men hawking souvenirs. "Here's your drug buyers," I said to the pair of agents, Mr. Blonde and Mr. Redhead.

Offering to sell colored rocks, supposedly from the old Mexican graves, was absurd. Gave themselves away.

The sheriff got the collar and the credit. That's all he wanted, to show up the professionals. Hedging with me, seeing I'd give him no argument, he turned to the reporters, including those who'd recently arrived. Dick Truman, puffing out his chest, a wide grin splitting his face, stepped front and center with his very own press conference.

# # # # # # #

"How'd you know it was Dollie?" Megan asked later at the Cat.

"Tell all," Juan demanded.

Among the missing was Brother John. We aimed to head into town soon to visit him at the hospital, where he was suffering from concussion. First, however, we needed a respite, for food and talk. Matt and Mike set out cold cuts and bread for sandwiches and Vanna poured iced tea around the table. Mom and Hernandez held hands. Derek cradled the baby while Megan and her mom Merry leaned against one another; like if they didn't prop, they'd fall down.

Next to me, Vanna's soft hand rested on my leg. Juan sat opposite, way over there on the other side of the table. Hugo got a bone; T-bone, that is.

Gone were the truckers and the bikers, Brad Gifford too. The Cat Castle was closed for the rest of the afternoon.

"I can't believe you'd suspect that sweet, dear lady," said Vanna.

"That's the thing. She was too sweet . All gooey, sticky, goody-two-shoes sweet." I deferred to Megan and the others. After all, they were the ones held captive.

Megan and Merry Derry picked up the story. When Megan and Brother John wanted to show her mom Dr. Wallaberra's grave, they'd interrupted the Goodmans from uncovering their drug cache.

Which, I inserted into the tale, was garnered from all over the place, from the potters up in the hills growing marijuana, from the boys' meth lab, and from a number of recently recruited but naïve couriers who'd smuggled cocaine over the border. Elise was awaiting the big city buyers.

"Fess borrowed the tent from a nearby grave," said Megan. "He needed a place to hole up and to hold us hostage."

"He alerted the sheriff by cellphone," said Merry Derry. "To state their demands—for a van and a million dollars in unmarked bills."

"I guess it was Dick who called the TV station," I said. "He wanted an audience."

Tell us about Dollie and her cousin, Oliver," said Juan.

"Some of their story is pretty bizarre," I commenced, settling back. My audience including mom knew about the look-alike second cousins, Fess and Donny. "No artificial insemination involved. Dollie and Hal Goodman had an affair, just as Elise suspected." Megan and Vanna looked pleased with themselves, as if vindicated. They had insisted all along that coincidences are all too rare. "That was after Elise and Hal were married but before Martinez came along. Already pregnant when she married, she never told her husband. Elise got suspicious when she saw the photo and threatened to tell Dollie's husband if Dollie didn't go along with her schemes. Elise also confronted Hal.

He in turn tried to get back together with Dollie the minute Martinez took off. Dollie was so furious, she says, she gave him a big shove. He fell, cracked his head on the cement of her patio, and died on the spot."

"Wait a minute," Matt said, leaning forward. "So it was Dollie who killed Goodman? Where'd she bury him?"

Mike paused in the act of spreading mustard on his whole wheat bread. "Let me guess. Dollie buried Hal Goodman in her patio."

"Wasn't his bones Hugo dug up," Vanna objected.

Everybody again facing me with keen expectation written across their faces, I continued. "In the plot at the church, before the garden went in."

"Ahah. Then Dr. Wallaberra found Goodman's body, so he had t'go."

I nodded at Juan. "After the pastor's burial, Elise got the bright idea of using his grave to cache the drugs. All the other graves were on top of the ground, why not Dr. Wallaberra's. She didn't think anybody would notice the difference. The old deserted cemetery with hardly any visitors any more seemed like a good place to meet the buyers."

"I don't get it," Juan said. "How did Elise get into drugs? I would have thought it would be Fess."

"Drug smuggling and dealing, that was Hal Goodman's business. With his death, she had to live. Fess confessed—told mommy what daddy was up to. But Fess didn't know the business details and, besides, he was too spaced out. Elise, the little social butterfly and good church lady, hardly knew where to start. Every decision she made was fraught with fumbling, naïve innocence."

"And Dollie?" Megan prompted. Baby Dolan had finished his bottle and the little mother passed him over to Daddy Dolan to burp. Michael Matthew then spit up, dribbling over Derek's shoulder onto the top of Hugo's head. Hugo yapped and ran across the room, for once deserting my windbreaker.

"Elise was blackmailing her. When Hal died on her patio, Dollie went to her cousin, the formerly trusted and trustworthy Mrs. Goodman, with her tale of accidental death. Elise threatened to tell the sheriff it was premeditated murder if Dollie didn't do as bidden. Of course by then Elise hated Dollie for having that affair with Hal all those years ago. That was the basis for the church squawbles and all the competition. Elise was out to prove she was better than Dollie in every possible area. In the meantime, Dollie obeyed.

"Poisoning me went against the grain, which meant her attempts, though sickening, to me, were so half-hearted I never quite died. And, yes, she grew the poisonous plants out in that overgrown area beyond the villas. She'd used Donny's books from his studies of botany. And no, Donny never did know anything about any of this. He's a head-in-the-clouds kind of guy.

"As for Dr. Wallaberra's bones buried in Dollie's patio, that came as a complete surprise. That's why she fainted in front of Juan and me when Hugo dug them up. She realized at last there was no end to how far Elise would go. Still, she didn't confess even one small part of her role 'til Donny was arrested."

Mom and Hernandez spoke at once. He wondered who'd siphoned my cycle's gas and blown up the RV. Mom demanded more info on the bones.

"I'm betting Fess was responsible for the former," said Juan. "As for the bones, we've been talking about that. Makes no sense why the pastor's arm would be buried in Dollie's patio. His arm but not the rest of him. His arm bones, I should say, with no flesh."

"That's where the tale gets bizarre. If the Goodmans were going to use Dr. Wallaberra's grave to cache drugs until the buyers showed, what were they to do with the pastor's body? Into the garden plot, of course, alongside Hal Goodman. Except that Fess was pretty stoned when he set about digging up the parson's coffin. Too much work, so he used some of the explosive materiel he had left from blowing the RV. It was the dead of night, with Elise and Dollie standing by—Dollie reluctantly forced into all this. Boom! The explosion loud enough to wake the dead. Out popped the coffin, minus the lid and one of Dr. Dubya's arms. Fess races off with the corpse to the church garden before the sun comes up and people are up and about. Dollie too excuses herself.

"That's the end of Dollie's first-hand account. Even then, at the very end, Dollie was still willing to make excuses for her once beloved cousin. 'She had to eat, didn't she? Besides,' Dollie went on. 'Elise gets easily irritated. She's diabetic, you know.' Unbelievable."

"People will do just about anything to make sure they get loved," Vanna said, referring to Dollie and Elise but staring meaningfully into my eyes. I smiled and squeezed her hand, the one atop my leg. Then I returned to the tale.

"It was only after Dr. Wallabarra's bones had been identified as his that she confronted Elise. Apparently the day after transferring the parson's body, Elise discovered that those arm bones were blown off. She had to get rid of those, too. Since she was forever dreaming up schemes to implicate Dollie in something—the stolen golf clubs, tennis rackets, and fur coat, remember—here was another chance. Besides, if the authorities ever did recover those bones from Dollie's patio, they would be confused enough, probably, to garble the rest of the known facts."

Vanna patted my leg beneath the tablecloth. "What happened to those bones, to get rid of the flesh?"

"Fess boiled them."

Mom shrieked and Merry Derry squealed. Megan's hands flew to cover her face and, beside me, Vanna groaned.

#######

"We're selling out!" Matt exclaimed the next day, after a night's rest.

After Vanna and I disappeared, back to her place, and mom and Luis to Brother John's. After the sheriff had been by, not to say *Thank you*, just to jaw; get more accolades, we figured.

"You can't mean it," I hollered, amazed. "Why?"

"Too dangerous in these parts," Matt added, completing his thought.

"Where will you go?"

"Up to Wyoming with you, Oliver," said Mike, grinning.

"We want to see your yacht," said Megan, nudging Derek, who nodded.

Everybody laughed.

The baby cooed.

Hugo yapped. Having finished gnawing on another bone, he'd hunkered down atop my zippered jacket.

My conclusion: this whole episode was like a farcical game. Score: Devil, zero; God wins.

Printed in the United States
1173700002B/37-255